Ishmael on the Border

A volume in the SUNY series in
Judaica: Hermeneutics, Mysticism, and Religion
Michael Fishbane, Robert Goldenberg, and Elliot Wolfson, editors

Ishmael on the Border

Rabbinic Portrayals of the First Arab

Carol Bakhos

State University of New York Press

The author and the publisher are grateful to the Koret Foundation's Jewish Studies Publication Program for their generous support.

Cover image: Dreamstime.com

Published by
State University of New York Press, Albany

Printed in the United States of America

For information, contact State University of New York Press, Albany, NY
www.sunypress.edu

Production by Judith Block
Marketing by Susan M. Petrie

Library of Congress Cataloging-in-Publication Data

Bakhos, Carol.
Ishmael on the border : rabbinic portrayals of the first Arab / Carol Bakhos.
p. cm.
Includes bibliographical references and index.
ISBN 978-0-7914-6759-6 (hardcover : alk. paper)
ISBN 978-0-7914-6760-2 (paperback : alk. paper)

1. Arabs in the Bible. 2. Bible. O.T. Genesis—Criticism, interpretation, etc. 3. Ishmael (Biblical figure) 4. Esau (Biblical figure) 5. Ishmael (Biblical figure) in rabbinical literature. 6. Esau (Biblical figure) in rabbinical literature. I. Title.

BS1199. A66B35 2006
296.1'2083058927—dc22 2005018667

10 9 8 7 6 5 4 3 2 1

Contents

Acknowledgments

Ishmael on the Border: Rabbinic Portrayals of the First Arab builds on and develops the ideas explored in my doctoral dissertation, Rabbinic Portrayals of Ishmael. Although this work for the most part retains the overarching framework of the former, and reaches some of the same conclusions, the study of rabbinic texts here is significantly more detailed and nuanced, and thus leads me to draw different conclusions with respect to why the rabbinic treatment of Ishmael changes in the early medieval literature. There has been a marked resurgence of interest in the intertwined relationship of rabbinic Judaism and early Christianity over the past several years. Taking into account and addressing the matters raised in recent works, I have considerably refined my earlier discussion on the degree to which rabbinic literature reflects an engagement with Christian and Muslim theological claims, and redressed related issues.

It would have been impossible to complete this work without the gracious support of family, friends, and colleagues whose warmth and well wishes sustained me during various stages of this project.

I am grateful to the faculty of the Jewish Theological Seminary, especially Richard Kalmin whose dedication, patience, wealth of knowledge and good judgment contributed greatly to my formation as a scholar. Stephen Garfinkel, Raymond Scheindlin, Stephen Geller, Benjamin Gampel and Eliezer Diamond each in his own way was and ever remains, a fount of knowledge and a source of encouragement.

This work has benefited enormously from the attention of Seth Schwartz, whose erudition never ceases to amaze me. I am grateful for the many enlightening and engaging conversations we have had over the years, for his critical reading of this work, and above all for his friendship.

I also wish to thank my former colleagues in the Department of Religion at Middlebury College, O. Larry Yarbrough and Katherine

Sonderegger, a most inspiring interlocutor who helped me sharpen the conceptual framework of my thesis.

I am indebted to William Schniedewind and Michael Cooperson, my colleagues at UCLA, who commented on earlier versions of some of the chapters. Reuven Firestone, Robert Goldenberg and Joel Kaminsky read a first draft of the manuscript. Their keen reading of the manuscript improved it immeasurably. And finally, I am thankful to Dana Foote, Maccabee Avishur, and Candice Levy for their editorial assistance. Of course it goes without saying (but I will state it anyway) that no one other than I should be held accountable for shortcomings one may find in the work.

This study was made possible in part by funds granted by the Charles H. Revson Foundation, the Memorial Foundation for Jewish Culture, and most recently by the Koret Foundation. The statements made and views expressed, however, are solely the responsibility of the author.

I wish to thank my mentors Jon Levenson, who introduced me to the playful, yet reverent world of midrash, and Brother Jerome O'Connell, who passed away in 1998. Brother Jerome fostered my love of literature and often reminded me of Ireneaus's words, "God's glory is man fully alive."

In *A Driven Leaf*, Milton Steinberg writes: "No matter what other doubts we entertain, we cannot question the reality of friendship. And in a world where so little is certain, that is a good deal." Indeed it is so. I thank Barbara Butterworth, Paul Dry, Vivienne Kneider, Alexa Midthassel, and Walid Saleh for their constant support and friendship, which is a very good deal.

This book is dedicated to the memory of my father, Mehsen Bakhos (1932–1998), who believed me when I said, "soon." The world of academia, let alone the world of the rabbis, was alien to him. Yet, in his own way he delighted and took pride in my pursuit. This book is also dedicated to Dr. Arthur Carr, Professor Emeritus of Columbia University, who despite the near fifty years between us, is a steadfast friend and confidant. Arthur's zest for life—that is, his deep appreciation of the ordinary—his intellectual curiosity, and his passion for the Arts inspire me endlessly. I thank him for encouraging me, for often chiding me (there is nothing like a good tongue-lashing to whip one into shape), but more than anything else, I thank him for the laughter. For this and more I am grateful.

Introduction

More than any other figure in the Hebrew Bible, Ishmael evokes a variety of associations from nomads to *Moby Dick*. A recent question put to me by a rabbi highlights the unusual place Ishmael has in Jewish thought: "So, your work is not about Rabbi Ishmael, but the Ishmael of Islam?" Though Ishmael is a prominent figure in Islam's theological history, and in Arab genealogy, the rabbi's question reveals a widely held assumption about the figure of Ishmael; namely, that he plays no role in the Jewish tradition. Today more than ever, this assumption plays itself out in references to the putatively antagonistic brothers "Isaac and Ishmael," who have come to represent Judaism and Islam. The rabbi's question implicitly relegates Ishmael to a status that inaccurately reflects Ishmael's position vis-à-vis Judaism. Indeed, since the medieval period, Ishmael has often, but not exclusively, symbolized Islam. Ishmael's place nonetheless is marginal, but is it marginal *within* the Jewish tradition. As Abraham's rejected son, he cannot play a consequential role in Judaism. At the same time, as a figure who was part of early Israelite history, he cannot be excluded—set fully apart—from that history. Because rabbinic literature implicitly recognizes his marginalized status, it can neither embrace nor disavow him unequivocally.

To answer the rabbi's question, this work is not about R. Ishmael or Islam's Ishmael. Rather, it focuses narrowly on the figure of Ishmael in classical rabbinic literature from the tannaitic period (ca. first through third centuries CE) through the early Middle Ages and traces the nuances and shifts in rabbinic portrayals of Ishmael over a period of a thousand years. Compilations such as the Tosefta, Sifre Deuteromony, Genesis

Rabbah, and the Tanḥuma literature provide a basis for distinguishing trends in the ways in which the rabbis grappled with the elusive nature of Ishmael's character. This work also examines rabbinic depictions of Esau, the Ishmaelites, and the children of Keturah to the extent that an understanding of their portrayal sheds light on the rabbinic treatment of Ishmael.

A study of rabbinic sources dealing with Ishmael leads to the following conclusions: The portrayal of Ishmael before the rise of Islam can be neutral, positive, or negative; after the emergence of Islam, however, he is consistently portrayed more negatively. Despite the connection made between Ishmael and Arabs in early Jewish writings such as Jubilees and the works of Josephus, as well as in tannaitic texts, Ishmael rarely symbolizes the Arab people but rather, like the Ishmaelites and the children of Keturah, he often represents the rabbinic Other. By and large, the literature on these biblical figures reflects the rabbinic self-legitimizing emphasis on Israel's election over and against other peoples in general, and not a full-blown engagement with Christianity.

In the course of examining tannaitic depictions of these biblical figures, we discover that very little is said about them. While they are referred to more often in amoraic compilations (ca. third through fifth centuries CE) such as Genesis Rabbah, Leviticus Rabbah, and Lamentations Rabbah, as well as in the Palestinian and Babylonian Talmuds, the increase is not substantial, and may in large measure be attributed to other factors such as the type of literature produced in this period. In pre-Islamic midrashim (here I am referring to rabbinic interpretations prior to the mid-seventh century), the rabbis create a dichotomy between the unfit issue of Abraham and Isaac and the righteous children of Jacob; the rabbis conceive of Israel as the righteous nation chosen by God to fulfill a unique role as God's people. After the rise of Islam, this rabbinic self-identification vis-à-vis an invented Other, by means of the midrashic process, plays a less pronounced role.

In midrashic corpora redacted after the seventh century, however, we find not only midrashim that separate Israel from Ishmael in terms of fit and unfit status, but also midrashim that depict him in a more derogatory manner. In these later texts, the referent is no longer a fabricated antipode, but rather a real entity, that is, Islam. Vituperative references to Ishmael are in large measure an internal rabbinic response to Islam's political hegemony and have less to do with its religious claim to Abraham through Ishmael, although that, too, eventually becomes a contributing factor.

Indeed, the changing ethnic, religious, and political landscape of the Near East in the seventh century affected later rabbinic depictions of Ishmael, whereby he becomes the eponymous prototype of Islam. The emergence of Islam's political power fostered dismissive, vitriolic rabbinic depictions of Ishmael. Even though not all depictions after the Islamic conquest are invidious, there is a greater rabbinic tendency to portray Ishmael critically than is found in pre-Islamic rabbinic sources.

This phenomenon of note has its antecedent in rabbinic representations of Esau/Edom as Roman rule. In other words, in the instances whereby Esau and Ishmael represent specific others, we have examples of the ways in which the rabbis dealt with their minority status under foreign rule—the ways in which they reacted to political power and domination in light of their status as God's chosen people. A characteristic of these references is the prophecy of the destruction of Israel's enemies, vanquished by the hand of God. In fact, in some cases Ishmael himself represents the Arabs who are regarded as those who will liberate the Jews from Christian rule.

Contrary to regnant views among scholars, in pre-Islamic midrashim the depiction of certain biblical figures—Ishmael, Esau, the children of Keturah, and the children of Ishmael—as "unfit" does not allude to a specific religious or ethnic group such as Christians, Samaritans, or Arabs. Rather, the rabbis use these figures to define themselves vis-à-vis an imagined Other; that is, it is an aspect of a conceptualization of Israel as the righteous heir of the Abrahamic covenant. Moreover, when the rabbis metonymically refer to Esau in the tannaitic sources, it is usually to Rome and not to Christianity, although this changes over time and we find later sources dealing with competing theologies.

Furthermore, despite recent studies on the nascent relationship between rabbinic Judaism and early Christianity that emphasize the intertwined, complex world of cultural and spiritual discourse in which both partook, rabbinic biblical interpretation of the classical period seems not to have been as preoccupied with vying Christian theological claims as one would imagine. Of course there are polemical midrashim, as well as midrashim that simply attest to the very interfacing of both groups. Surprisingly, however, the Christian supersessionist understanding of itself as the true Israel probably was not an immediate factor inducing rabbis to distinguish between Israel and marginalized biblical figures, although over the centuries it, like Islam, certainly played other roles in the development of Jewish systems of thought, beliefs, and practices.

To begin with, there is no appreciable difference between depictions of Other in tannaitic and amoraic sources that would lead one to suspect Christian claims affected rabbinic self-understanding in the amoraic period. That is, the content of these midrashim does not attest to a rabbinic reaction to Christianity. To reiterate, this of course is not to say Christianity had no bearing on rabbinic biblical interpretation, for scholars have compellingly demonstrated that rabbis were indeed aware of Christian biblical interpretation, as well as theological and christological assertions. Christianity nonetheless made relatively little impact—the use of Esau at times to represent Christian Rome notwithstanding—on the rabbinic portrayal of marginalized biblical figures.

In detecting the various factors that contributed to depictions of Ishmael, this work illustrates the way in which extratextual factors, that is, religious, sociopolitical, and cultural concerns, are inextricably part of the hermeneutical process. To be sure, every act of exegesis is affected by factors that have as much to do with the interpreter as with the text itself. Although it is difficult to locate precisely the extratextual factors that help generate a particular interpretation, we will attempt to show that at times they can be brought to the surface.

This examination of rabbinic portrayals of Ishmael, furthermore, provides a framework for studying midrashic sources as literary artifacts for purposes of historical inquiry. In attempting to show that tannaitic and amoraic midrashim on Ishmael are reworked in later corpora to the extent that they reflect greater contempt for Ishmael, I will argue that this analysis contributes to our historical understanding of rabbinic literature. That is, it shows that one can use historically derived information as a hermeneutical tool to understand interpretive texts, even redacted, multilayered compilations of earlier works and oral traditions. It must therefore address the extent to which rabbinic literature reflects social reality, that is, the extent to which midrashim as literary texts are not only embedded in history but also reflect and convey history.

We are therefore concerned with two integrated issues in the past often dealt with separately by scholars: the utility of midrashim as historical sources and the use of history as a hermeneutical tool to explain difficulties and surprising patterns or shifts in literary texts.

The study of midrash thus allows us not only to delight in the wealth and expansive imagination of rabbinic hermeneutics, but it also opens a portal through which we can observe aspects of late antique Judaism.

Methodology

The philosophical underpinning of this inquiry into rabbinic exegesis as reflective of the rabbis' historical situatedness is Heidegger's notion that interpretation need be understood in ontological terms, and as such is rooted in the historicality of the very notion of being-in-the-world. "And interpretation," writes Heidegger, "is never a presuppositionless apprehending of something presented to us. If, when one is engaged in a particular kind of interpretation, in the sense of exact textual interpretation, one likes to appeal [*beruft*] to what 'stands there,' [but] then one finds that what 'stands there' in the first instance is nothing other than the obvious undiscussed assumption [*Vormeignung*] of the person who does the interpreting."[1] What "stands there" is twofold in that one must attempt to grasp what *stands there* for the rabbis who interpreted Scripture and also come to recognize what *stands there* for us as interpreters of rabbinic texts. As G. Bruns observes, the process of interpretation is never purely philological, that is the hermeneutical circle "is not simply an exegetical movement between the parts and the whole of a text that is present before us as an object. Instead, it is an ontological movement between the text and our situation as interpreters of it."[2] In attending to our own presuppositions—from which we are never free, but an awareness of which and through which we better understand and elucidate the past and present—we are better attuned to the very movement, as Bruns notes, "between the text and our situation as interpreters of it."[3] This, I believe, allows us to appreciate the ways in which rabbinic literature itself is the very expression of the experience of the historically situated interpreter and the text.

With this in mind, our investigation of midrashim adduces the importance of understanding basic characteristics of midrash that give voice to a multivocal, yet unified notion of Scripture, for as we learn in the Babylonian Talmud, Ḥagigah 3b, "The words of Torah are fruitful and multiply." It also demonstrates the need to understand how contemporary social, theological, and political issues precipitated by historical events such as the rise of both Christianity and Islam played a role, significant or otherwise, in the development of midrashim. Furthermore, both extratextual and textual factors such as the rabbinic image of Abraham, the notion of a righteous and untainted Israel, and the belief in Israel as God's chosen people also conform to the development of as well as shape the midrashim.

Whereas authors such as Y. Heinemann[4] and J. Kugel[5] have emphasized the exegetical and hermeneutical presuppositions of the rabbis as they dealt with the biblical texts, Joseph Heinemann has focused on the cultural and ideological aspects of midrash, aspects deemed secondary by other scholars. About the rabbis, Heinemann writes:

> [They] looked back into Scripture to uncover the full latent meaning of the Bible and its wording, at the same time, they looked forward

> into the present and the future. They sought to give direction to their own generation, to resolve their own religious problems, to answer their theological questions.[6]

In developing a process of "creative exegesis," the rabbis were able to make Scripture relevant to contemporary needs. They "were able to find in Scripture," Heinemann contends, ". . . the new answers and values which made it possible to grapple with the shifts and changes of reality."[7]

All midrashim are characterized by this second meaning and, depending on the way in which one uses midrashic sources, one can gain insight into what for lack of a better term is deemed rabbinic Judaism. At the same time, however, one must tread cautiously, for reading midrashim, be they smaller units of interpretation or larger compilations, as historical documents that reflect rabbinic realia is a hazardous enterprise.

The questions of whether and how to provide historical contexts for midrash have been discussed in the past, most explicitly by Steven Fraade in *From Tradition to Commentary: Torah and Its Interpretation in the Midrash Sifre to Deuteronomy*, where he examines the "inextricable interconnection" between the hermeneutics and historicity of scriptural interpretation. Fraade writes:

> These two tendencies, even as they face, and view commentary as facing, opposite directions, are really two sides of the same coin. That is the coin that presumes that the hermeneutics and historicity of scriptural commentary can conveniently and neatly be detached from one another, in the first case by viewing the hermeneutics of commentary's *interpretations* apart from the socio-historical grounding of its performance and in the second by viewing the historicity of commentary's *representations* apart from the hermeneutical grounding of its performance. . . . I wish to deny neither of these facings or groundings, but to assert their inextricable interconnection.[8]

Following Fraade, I argue that any discussion of midrash must take its dual nature into account. At times the biblical verse is explicitly the focal point of rabbinic exegesis; in other cases it is the vehicle through which the rabbis express their theological, social, and political concerns. Even when the focal point is exegesis, one must keep in mind that several factors come into play. Although lately midrashic scholars have emphasized the exegetical aspect, no one denies the interplay between the verse and extratextual factors that give rise to a certain interpretation. Whether or not one aspect overshadows the other in certain cases, as we shall see in chapter 2 of this work, we must remember that they are intrinsically interrelated. The issue therefore is not whether extratextual factors are part of exegesis but, rather, *how* and *when* we can use such texts as historical sources.

In his most recent book, *The Sage in Jewish Society of Late Antiquity*, Kalmin highlights the historical significance of midrashic texts by comparing texts produced more or less at the same time but in different locations. He shows how the differences between Babylonian and Palestinian rabbinic social structures help explain distinctions between their depictions of biblical heroes. He compares, for example, the treatment of Ezra by Palestinian and Babylonian Amoraim, demonstrating that their different approaches to Ezra reflect each locality's attitude toward the other, and cautions that while it would be a mistake to exaggerate the differences between Babylonian and Palestinian rabbis, they nonetheless exhibit opposing tendencies. That is to say, Palestinian Amoraim lessen the importance of Ezra, a Babylonian leader, who assumes the genealogical superiority of the returning Israelite community. Babylonian Amoraim, in contrast, are "consistently enthusiastic about a biblical hero who is 'their own,' " as also is the case with Esther.[9] This tendency is explicable when one reads the Babylonian and Palestinian Talmuds with an eye to the extratextual.[10]

In her aim to provide a methodological model for understanding the halakhic discrepancies between the Palestinian and Babylonian Talmuds, Christine Hayes provides an elaborate series of case studies of particular passages from tractate ʿAbodah Zarah. According to Hayes, these passages illustrate the need to examine internal reasons for differences before attributing those differences to external factors. Her work brings to light the shortcomings of reductive historicism, an approach that "often stems from a reading of talmudic sources that ignores the textual, hermeneutical, and dialectical characteristics of the sources in question, resulting in the production of tendentious historiographical claims."[11] In her endeavor to correct a tendency in talmudic studies that privileges external data over internal exegetical factors in determining halakhic discrepancies between the two Talmuds, she, too, contends that rabbinic texts can and do yield cultural-historical information, provided "one attends to the special characteristics of rabbinic texts that condition their historical use, such as the rhetorical and dialectical strategies."[12]

In *Carnal Israel*, Boyarin argues that the body in rabbinic Judaism had the same degree of significance that the soul had in other formations of Judaism and Greek-speaking Christianity. In fleshing out his methodology, Boyarin asserts that both halakhic and aggadic texts, texts of different genres, "share the same cultural problematics as their underlying (sometimes implicit) themes." He continues: "I assume that both the halakha and the aggada represent attempts to work out the same cultural, political, social, ideological, and religious problems."[13]

The focus of this discussion has been to point out the importance of acknowledging that there are several valid approaches to the study of rabbinic literature. With regard to the study of midrash in particular, Kugel has focused on discrete, smaller units of interpretation in order to understand their literary significance as rabbinic interpretation, and in doing so has made a weighty contribution both to our understanding of midrash qua rabbinic exegesis, and to our knowledge of the reception history and textual transmission of biblical interpretation in the ancient period.[14] Heinemann, on the other hand, has paid closer attention to the historical and cultural aspects of rabbinic exegesis, yet his masterful work has also left an indelible mark on the field of midrashic studies.[15]

The approach taken in this study is an integrative approach, sharing many of the suppositions of, and drawing on the work of, several of the aforementioned. Moreover, according to Boyarin, cultural poetics is "a practice that respects the literariness of literary texts . . . , while attempting at the same time to understand how they function within a larger socio-cultural system of practices."[16] This notion of cultural poetics as expressed by Boyarin undergirds my understanding of the synergistic relationship between the historical and exegetical aspects of rabbinic literature. In his recent book, *Talmudic Stories: Narrative Art, Composition, and Culture*, Jeffrey Rubenstein also draws on Boyarin's notion of "cultural poetics," but for different reasons.[17] In *Talmudic Stories* he insightfully reads six well-known rabbinic stories. In addition to a literary and source-critical analysis of these texts, Rubenstein endeavors to investigate "the cultural world of the redactors," that is, the world of the stammaim, to whom he attributes the redaction of the Bavli.[18] This work will also attempt to go beyond a literary analysis, in this case of midrashim, but it will not venture deeply into the familiar, yet distinctively distant and complex cultural world of the rabbis.

An analysis of discrete midrashim as literary texts and of the historical context provided by the putative dating of the compilations in which the midrashim are found makes possible a gainful study of how midrashim are reworked in later compilations. Our study of how depictions of biblical characters differ from one period to the next thus yields insight into the historical situation of the rabbis. The concern here is not whether or not the stories are themselves historical, but rather how their literariness reveals rabbinic attitudes toward Other, and therefore how this in turn contributes to a historical understanding of rabbinic Judaism.

Because the dating of rabbinic texts is a nettlesome—and according to some, insoluble—problem to resolve, a few remarks are in order. The scholarly wrangling over the question of how to define a rabbinic text as "early" or "late" and the issue of the ways in which textual transmission calls into question the very value of rabbinic texts as historical sources is far from over.[19] I can only state the position that informs this work. I am well aware that transmitters of texts are in their own right authors of texts, that medieval copyists emend texts, that reconstruction of a so-called urtext is a new text, and that words such as text, recension, urtext, version, redaction, and final redaction are thorny terms that need constant clarification and qualification. In the sense that rabbinic writings were transmitted gradually in a cumulative manner they are impervious to fixed dating. Yet, wide acceptance of a basic chronology based on comparative philological and literary analyses makes it possible to use these rabbinic works for historical purposes. As S. Stern rightly notes:

> It is fair to assume that at some point, redacted works began to emerge and to be treated, if only by name, as single identifiable entities. Thus the *Talmud* itself treats the *Mishna*, if not as a finished product, at least as an identifiable work around which its argumentation can revolve. In this respect it may be possible to assign approximate dates to these redacted works, even if the continuous process of multilayer redaction did not entirely cease thereafter, and even if we find that variations between different manuscript traditions and early printed editions can be quite considerable.[20]

While I avoid the conflation of tannaitic and amoraic texts and thus pay attention to appreciable differences from corpus to corpus and from period to period, for the purposes of this study I nonetheless also regard them broadly as early or pre-Islamic, whereas texts that came into being in the later medieval period are deemed later or referred to as post-mid-seventh-century (post-rise of Islam) texts. I also take into account manuscript variations, and the conclusions of this work in turn corroborate the dating of these texts that is accepted by most scholars of rabbinics.[21]

As stated above, the study of rabbinic portrayals of Ishmael provides an occasion to address the question of the extent to which rabbinic texts are useful for historical purposes. I hope to demonstrate that the historical background of the early medieval period, in particular the emergence of Islamic hegemony explains a shift in the midrashim pertaining to Ishmael.

With this desideratum in mind, we would be presumptuous to assume our study will explain with mathematical certainty why there are more negative portrayals of Ishmael in later midrashim, or prove definitively that Islam's formidable political rise in the Near East, for example, resulted in changes in the portrayal of Ishmael. But a critical and thorough analysis of the texts, characterized by attentiveness to rhetorical similarities and shifts in midrashim found in more than one redacted compilation, reveals a significant shift in the rabbinic attitude toward Ishmael. Moreover, observing the frequency and, more importantly, the intensity of the negative portrayals of certain types of midrashim in various corpora, such as the midrashim of the unrighteousness of Abraham's marginalized descendants, or for that matter the infrequency of such midrashim, coupled with a knowledge of the complexity of the historical, cultural, and theological development of Islam, can yield a well-grounded understanding of the synergistic relationship between rabbinic texts and their historical embeddedness. This approach to midrashic texts, both synchronic and diachronic, if applied properly, can enhance our understanding of the rabbis of late antiquity and the early Middle Ages.

Overview

To set the stage for an analysis of rabbinic portrayals of Ishmael, I detail the biblical story of Ishmael in chapter 1 and compare the biblical depiction of Ishmael to that of Esau. While the stories demonstrate significant differences, they parallel each other, and in fact intersect when Esau marries Ishmael's daughter in Genesis 28:9. The similarities, such as their displacement as primogenitors, lead to their postbiblical rabbinic affiliation. At the same time, as we shall have occasion to see in chapter 2, they are treated differently by the rabbis in large part because of their differing biblical portrayals.

Chapter 2 is a comprehensive analysis of the figure of Ishmael in tannaitic and amoraic midrashim, and chapter 3 examines the Ishmael-Esau pairing. It is often taken for granted that both Ishmael and Esau are portrayed negatively in rabbinic literature. For historical and exegetical reasons, however, the rabbis treat Ishmael and Esau differently, even though they often pair them together. Whereas Esau, the sibling rival, is displaced in rabbinic literature and oftentimes symbolizes Rome, Ishmael, the marginalized son, retains his complex biblical character in rabbinic literature of this period. In an attempt to give greater definition to the ambiguous nature of Ishmael's character, however, the rabbis sometimes use Esau to vilify Ishmael. That is, the need to clarify Ishmael's character for exegetical and theological purposes induced the rabbis to affiliate him with Esau. Thus, when he is affiliated with Esau, he is depicted negatively by the rabbis in all but one midrash. This negative rabbinic portrayal of Ishmael and Esau contrasts the pre-Islamic rabbinic portrayal of Ishmael without Esau, which on the whole is less negative. Furthermore, this pairing becomes prevalent in the Middle Ages when the rabbis interpret both figures typologically. Like Esau, who served to represent Rome in the amoraic period, Ishmael is used to represent Islam in the Middle Ages.

Chapter 3 also examines the depiction of the Ishmaelites and the children of Keturah who, like Esau and Ishmael, represent Other. As Alon Goshen-Gottstein remarks, "Rabbinic stories express collective concerns that reflect a collective mentality."[22] Indeed, paying attention to the literariness of rabbinic texts will reveal aspects of rabbinic attitudes toward Other.

As noted earlier, I will suggest that Christian supersessionist claims do not seem to have contributed greatly to the prominence of the rabbinic theme of distinguishing the righteous descendants of Abraham from his unfit progeny in amoraic sources. While there are more amoraic than tannaitic midrashim dealing with the notion of Israel's election, the quantitative difference is inconsequential.

In recent decades, research in such fields as anthropology, sociology, psychology, religion, and postcolonial studies, recognizes a phenomenon whereby group-identity formation is to a greater extent marked by internal, that is, by self-conceived, multileveled notions of "us and them," rather than by objective boundaries.[23] In reviewing rabbinic literature on the chosenness of Israel vis-à-vis the unrighteous offspring of Abraham and Isaac, a discernible pattern based on theoretical formulations of identity emerges. The extent to which we can read these texts as descriptions of rabbinic attitudes toward the non-Jewish population whom they encountered in daily life is exceedingly limited, if at all possible. And yet, they are useful in understanding—again for want of a better term—rabbinic Judaism.

Chapter 4 analyses midrashim dealing with Ishmael in Midrash Tanḥuma, Numbers Rabbah, and Exodus Rabbah. In the later midrashic compilations, Ishmael is depicted as opprobrious. Abraham rejects him, for example, because of his wicked ways. Not only is he described as wicked, but he is also pitted against Isaac in a more explicit rivalry. Often we find comments that Ishmael hated Isaac. Such comments, however, are not found in earlier midrashim.

In order to understand more fully the subtle yet significant shifts in rabbinic portrayals of Ishmael of the early Medieval period and what contributed to them, part of chapter 4 is devoted to the depiction of Ishmael and the Ishmaelites in Pirke de Rabbi Eliezer.[24] In PRE we have a strikingly complex depiction of Ishmael whereby Ishmael's portrayal is ambiguous, but the Ishmaelites who undoubtedly symbolize Islam are portrayed negatively.

A large portion of the chapter is also devoted to the Jewish and Muslim versions of Abraham's visits to Ishmael. Taking into consideration the work of B. Heller, J. Heinemann, A. Schussman, and R. Firestone, I compare the story of Abraham's visit to Ishmael in chapter 30 of PRE to Islamic renditions of the same story found in the works of al-Azraqī, al-Bukhārī, al-Ṭabarī, al-Thaʿlabī, al-Ṭabarsī, and Ibn Kathīr. Are the passages that describe Abraham's visit to Ishmael found in PRE a response to Islamic renderings of the same story, or was the midrash adapted and altered by Muslims for their own exegetical purposes? Is it in either case a form of apologetic? What, for example, is the relationship between Islamic legends and rabbinic midrashim of the early Middle Ages? An analysis of the story of Abraham's visits to Ishmael provides us with greater appreciation for the complexity of the social and intellectual interaction between these religious communities.

The presence of the story in both traditions reflects cross-cultural diffusion, a phenomenon that illustrates how external sources influence faith traditions in shaping literary expression and theological development. It seems advantageous, therefore, to look at how the story works within each faith tradition and to explore the varying degrees to which intercommunal relations affect the internal development of a tradition. In this chapter, I will therefore study the narrative of Abraham's visit to Ishmael in light of the larger narrative of PRE, which portrays Ishmael as the supplanted yet beloved firstborn of Abraham. I will also study the narrative in light of Islam's theological history, which focuses on the prophet Abraham and his righteous son, Ishmael.

Unlike other studies of Abraham's visits to Ishmael, this work examines the story within the larger context of PRE and within the context of Islamic theological history. Previous studies, for example, ignore other references to Ishmael in PRE. This shortsightedness leads to misguided assumptions about the role of Ishmael in the story.

The final chapter briefly recapitulates the conclusions of the previous chapters.

1

Ishmael and Esau: Marginalized Men of the Bible

> As for Ishmael, I have heeded you. I hereby bless him. I will make him fertile and exceedingly numerous. He shall be the father of twelve chieftains, and I will make of him a great nation.
>
> —Genesis 17:20

> And Esau said to his father, "Bless me too, Father!" And Esau wept aloud. And his father Isaac answered, saying to him, "See, your abode shall enjoy the fat of the earth. And the dew of heaven above. Yet by your sword you shall live and you shall serve your brother; but when you grow restive, you shall break his yoke from your neck."
>
> —Genesis 27:38–40

The displacement of the firstborn by the younger sibling is a recurring motif found throughout the book of Genesis.[1] Indeed, the central theme of Genesis, as Sarna states, is "the fortunes of those who are heirs to God's covenant"[2] and as Robert Alter asserts, the entire book of Genesis "is about the reversal of the iron law of primogeniture, about the election through some devious twist of destiny of a younger son to carry on the line," thus "the firstborn very often seem to be losers in Genesis by the very condition of their birth."[3] First encountered in the narration of primordial history, that is, in the story of Cain and Abel, this motif comes to the fore in the Patriarchal narratives. Indeed, Ishmael and Isaac, Esau and Jacob, Leah and Rachel, Ephraim and Manasseh are part and parcel of this motif.[4] At the same time, however, the extent to which a sibling is marginalized, the motive for, and the effects of marginalization differ from story to story. A literary analysis of the biblical texts pertaining to Ishmael and Esau demonstrates that while there are significant differences, their narratives consist of particular parallel features that, in turn, contribute to a postbiblical Ishmael-Esau pairing found in rabbinic literature.

An analysis of the biblical narrative of Ishmael in light of the story of Esau[5] will set the stage for our ensuing examination of the rabbinic use of both biblical figures. Both men, deliberately placed "outside" the family not by the will of the father, but rather the mother, who carries out the providential plan (in Sarah's case unbeknownst to her), resemble one another, yet have distinct features. The narratives parallel and eventually intersect.

Ishmael in the Bible

The biblical narrative dealing with the figure of Ishmael is a story of marginalization par excellence. He is Abraham's firstborn, circumcised with Abraham, yet he is not the son of the covenant. He is part of the family, yet he is excluded. His presence is felt, yet his actions are few. He is spoken about, yet never speaks. God hears his voice, but the reader hears silence. He will be a great nation, but "his hand will be against everyone, and everyone's hand against him." He is loved, and although expelled from Abraham's house, he is not rejected. As we shall see, the difficulty in discerning the meaning of several biblical references to Ishmael contributes to his ambiguous role in the patriarchal narrative. What, for example, does it mean that he will be a *pere' 'ādām*, a "wild ass of a man," that his hand will be against all, that he will live *'al pĕnê*, "in the face of" his kinsmen? Before we look at how the rabbis interpreted these phrases and how they portrayed Ishmael, let us examine the biblical story.

The figure of Ishmael is introduced in Genesis 16[6] when the messenger of God appears to Hagar. He informs her that God will multiply her seed exceedingly, that she is with child, and that she shall call him Ishmael, which means "God hears," because the Lord has heard her affliction. Moreover, in Gen. 16:12, one learns that he will be a wild ass of a man whose "hand shall be against everyone, and everyone's hand against him; and he shall dwell alongside[7] all his kinsmen."

"Part of the announcement of the birth of a son," Westermann points out, "is a preview of his later destiny, as for example: he will be one of renown, a king, a savior. The son in these cases (as Judg. 16; Lk. 1) will be of significance for the people."[8] The birth announcement of the ill-fated first-born is no exception:

> The fierce, aggressive way of life of the sons of Ishmael . . . is other than the peaceful nomadic life-style of the patriarchs. It presupposes the sedentary and bedouin desert tribes living in Canaan side by side and in confrontation in the period after the settlement.[9]

Wenham offers a different understanding of the verse: "This verse describes Ishmael's future destiny, to enjoy a free-roaming, bedouinlike existence. The freedom his mother sought will be his one day. The *pere'*, 'wild ass,' lives in the desert, looks more like a horse than a donkey, and is used in the OT as a figure of an individualistic lifestyle untrammeled by social convention" (Jer. 2:24; Hos. 8:9).[10] In a similar vein, Sarna writes:

> Like the wild ass among the beasts, so are the Ishmaelites among men. In their nature and destiny they call to mind the sturdy, fearless, and fleet-footed Syrian onager (Heb. *pere'*), who inhabits the wilderness and is almost impossible to domesticate . . . Hagar, the abused slave woman subjected to the harsh discipline of her mistress, will produce a people free and undisciplined.[11]

Syren also considers Gen. 16:7–14 as expressing a favorable, or at least neutral position toward Ishmael:

> Elsewhere in the Bible the wild ass is the typical unfettered wild animal, alone and free to go its own way (Hos. 8:9; Job 39:5). . . . In Hos. 8:9 and Jer. 2:24, the animal serves as an illustration of Israel's apostasy; as the wild ass in her heat exposes herself to her mates, Israel lustfully submits itself to foreign gods. Apart from this, nothing pejorative is associated with the wild ass—and in this instance it symbolized Israel and not her seducers. Like the wild ass, Ishmael is predestined to a solitary, wandering life. In this respect he can be compared to Cain, although unlike Cain, the biblical narrator does not impute any crime or guilt to Ishmael. Yet . . . Ishmael's life . . . is not unlike Cain's: both are sent away from their own family and community.[12]

Von Rad proposes an even more positive understanding of the verse: "He will be a real Bedouin, a 'wild ass of a man' . . . free and wild (Cf. Job 39:5–8) . . . eagerly spending his life in a war of all against all—a worthy son of his rebellious and proud mother! In this description of Ishmael there is undoubtedly undisguised sympathy and admiration for the roving Bedouin who bends his neck to no yoke. The man here pictured is highly qualified in the opinion of Near Easterners."[13]

Finally, Speiser makes a connection between the Hebrew *pere'* and the Akkadian phrase *lullu-awelu*, approximately translated "savage of a man," a phrase used to describe not only Enkidu but also the first human created by gods.[14] The similarity drawn between Enkidu and Ishmael, as will be shown later, is also drawn between Esau and Enkidu.

What then did the messenger of the Lord mean when he told Hagar that her son shall be a *pere' 'ādām*, "a wild ass of a man; his hand against everyone, and everyone's hand against him; he shall dwell alongside all his kinsmen"? Given the various ways of interpreting *pere'* and *'al pĕnê*, the connotation is ambiguous and thus ripe for interpretation. The description, however ambiguous, is clearly of the "natural" person who is unrestrained, uninhibited by agrarian life. And, while *'al pĕnê* may express hostility, it more likely describes the close proximity of the nomadic Ishmaelites to other tribes.

Whether or not the description of Ishmael as a "wild ass of a man" is deemed negative seems more to depend upon one's own bias than on the context. That is to say, for some, the free-roaming bedouin existence is uncouth and unconventional, whereas for others, an unshackled lifestyle unencumbered by social convention and unrestricted by geography is desirable. The characterization of Ishmael is neither inherently negative nor pejorative. It presents the antithesis of the "civilized" sedentary Israelites. It is thus not surprising to learn in Gen. 21:21 that when Ishmael grew, he dwelt in the wilderness.[15] The notion that "his hand will be against everyone and everyone's hand against his" does depict tension between sedentary and nomadic tribes in the Near East,[16] but this tension need not be understood as negative. In fact, upon revisiting Westermann's understanding of Gen. 16:2, we find that he says, "It presupposes the sedentary and bedouin desert tribes living side by side," however, taking it a step further by claiming, "and in confrontation in the period after the settlement." Again, there is nothing inherently negative in the text to warrant this particular reading.

Moreover, in Genesis 17[17] God makes his covenant with Abraham and his seed.[18] God tells Abraham that Sarah is to give birth and that God will establish his covenant with Isaac, not Ishmael. Abraham responds, "Oh that Ishmael might live by Your favor!"[19] God responds, "Nevertheless, Sarah your wife shall bear you a son, and you shall name him Isaac; and I will maintain My covenant with him as an everlasting covenant for his offspring to come. As for Ishmael, I have heeded you; I hereby bless him, I will make him fruitful, and exceedingly numerous. He shall be the father of twelve chieftains,[20] and I will make him a great nation" (Gen. 17:19–20). Like Isaac through whom twelve tribes are established, Ishmael will be a great nation and father of twelve chieftains. Ishmael and Isaac, as will be explored later in greater detail, are not presented as paired opposites, but rather as siblings who rarely interact, yet live parallel lives.[21]

The theological implications of the promise in Genesis 17, however, are far-reaching. As Westermann writes:

> The promise concerning Ishmael means that the effect of God's blessing extends beyond Israel to other nations as well. That universal trait which appeared in Gen. 1 and 10 continues here. Even though the covenant is carried on only in Isaac, that does not mean that God no longer acts in regard to nations outside Israel; he blesses, increases, and grants greatness to them too. Abraham then is father, not only the father of the people of Israel, but father in a broader sense, so that Ishmael, the tribal ancestor of the Ishmaelite people, remains Abraham's son with not the least diminution. We have here a truly wide-sweeping historical outlook: the God of Israel has to do not only with Israel, but also with other nations; God's blessing is not confined to the borders of Israel.[22]

That said, in discussing God's four-pronged response to Abraham in Gen. 17:19–21, Westermann claims, "The division of the response shows that the emphasis lies on the promise destined for Isaac, which is distinguished clearly from Ishmael."[23] Westermann's understanding of the covenant takes into account the difference between the distinct futures of Ishmael and Isaac, no doubt a providential difference, but his attempt to locate the universal trait in Genesis 17 attenuates the distinction made between them. Like his father and like his brother, Ishmael will be a father of a great nation, but God will maintain his covenant with Isaac.[24]

To be sure, there is an inherent paradox in Genesis 17. On the one hand, Ishmael is excluded: "But my covenant I will maintain with Isaac" (v. 21), yet on the other, he is included: "Then Abraham took his son Ishmael . . . and he circumcised the flesh of their foreskins on that very day" (v. 23).[25] Ishmael is not only placed under the auspices of the God of Israel, but he is also a member of Abraham's family, indeed, his firstborn. Therein lies the rub. According to the narrative motif of Genesis, as firstborn he is de facto placed on the periphery. Ishmael and his descendants are relegated to the margin, a most tenuous position that, as we will see in ensuing chapters, generates ambiguous portrayals at best and engenders hostile and negative depictions of them in postbiblical literature at worst.

In Genesis 17 God "hears." He heard Hagar and now God hears Abraham. In Genesis 21,[26] an expansion of the aetiology of Genesis 16, in which God hears Hagar, he hears Ishmael, and as in Genesis 17, God promises to make Ishmael a great nation. The expulsion of Hagar and Ishmael in Genesis 21, however, is in many respects unprecedented:[27] "Sarah saw the son whom Hagar the Egyptian had borne to Abraham playing (*mĕṣaḥēq*).[28] She said to Abraham, "Cast out that slave-woman and her son, for the son of that slave shall not share in the inheritance with my son Isaac" (Gen. 21:9–10). Commentators, ancient and modern alike, have grappled with this verse: Why did Sarah, who provided Abraham with Hagar, now want her and her son "cast out"? What does *mĕṣaḥēq*, "playing," mean? In what horrendous act was Ishmael engaged?

Mĕṣaḥēq, derived from the same root as Isaac's name, "to laugh" (*ṣḥq*), can mean either "playing"[29] or "laughing." As J. Schwartz points out, the piel form of the verb has many meanings that connote positive activities such as laughing, playing, and rejoicing, as well as negative, abusive behavior such as mocking and deriding.[30] Since the negative meanings are usually dependent upon the addition of the preposition *be-*, missing in Gen. 21:9, Schwartz notes, "most modern commentators translate 'playing' or 'laughing,' although these activities need not be the same or mutually inclusive."[31] Indeed, as Westermann states: "Even from the purely grammatical point of view (*mezaheq*) without a preposition cannot mean 'to mock' or the like."[32] And, as many scholars have pointed out, the word has sexual connotations.

In the book of Jubilees, a retelling of Genesis 1 through Exodus 12 usually dated to the second century BCE,[33] there is no hint of "foul" play on Ishmael's part. On the contrary, the image presented is endearing, warm, and touching:[34]

> In the first year of the fifth week, in this jubilee, Isaac was weaned. Abraham gave a large banquet in the third month, on the day when his son Isaac was weaned. Now Ishmael, the son of Hagar the Egyptian, was in his place in front of his father Abraham. Abraham was very happy and blessed the Lord because he saw his own sons and had not died childless. . . . He was very happy because the Lord had given him descendants on the earth to possess the land. With his full voice he blessed the creator of everything. When Sarah saw Ishmael playing and dancing and Abraham being extremely happy, she became jealous of Ishmael. She said to Abraham: "Banish this girl and her son

> because this girl's son will not be an heir with my son Isaac." In Abraham's opinion the command regarding his servant girl and his son—that he should banish them from himself—was saddening. (17.1–6)[35]

The image is one of a celebration in which Abraham rejoiced. He was "very happy," not because Isaac was weaned but because "he saw his own *sons*," because "the Lord had given him descendant*s*." Furthermore, Abraham is portrayed as being very much involved in Ishmael, who is seated "in his place in front of his father," whose "playing and dancing" delights Abraham.

In Jubilees, as in Genesis, Ishmael's playing is not inherently negative. This is not to say, however, that his playing may not be perceived as offensive. As Schwartz comments:

> Bearing in mind that children often play at what they see among adults and that children's play also often includes "role-play" reflecting dreams and aspirations,[[36]] it is not unlikely that the author of Jubilees wished to suggest that Ishmael's play reflected in some way the role and position of his father. Perhaps indeed Jubilees hints that Ishmael "played" at celebrating such a feast and he played the role of his father. One can well imagine Sarah's terror at all of this.[37]

Although Schwartz is speculating, his comment points to a plausible cause of Sarah's unease and a motive for her behavior, namely Ishmael's status as Abraham's legitimate son.

Scholars claim that the original meaning of *mĕṣaḥēq* is impossible to determine, yet this conclusion does not preclude them from offering suggestions for interpreting the verse and understanding Sarah's behavior.[38] von Rad writes: "Whether the verb . . . [*zahaq*] here means simply 'playing' or 'behaving wantonly with someone' can no longer be decided. What Ishmael did need not be anything evil at all. The picture of the two boys playing with each other on an equal footing is quite sufficient to bring the jealous mother to a firm conclusion: Ishmael must go! Every year he, the older one, becomes a stronger rival for Isaac, and at last he will even divide the inheritance with him."[39] Speiser comments: "There is nothing in the text to suggest that he was abusing him, a motive deduced by many troubled readers in their effort to account for Sarah's anger."[40] As noted earlier, the "playing" itself is not necessarily negative;[41] rather, it is read negatively by some rabbis in order to vindicate Sarah. Ishmael must have done something, innocent or not, to provoke Sarah's response.

The story is either missing a piece that answers the question, or the text is complete as it is and therefore an understanding, perhaps justification, of Sarah's actions is sought by biblical interpreters, particularly by the rabbis. Unlike Westermann, who does not make the connection between Isaac's name and *mĕṣaḥēq* in the verse, Hackett argues that Ishmael may have been "Isaac-ing," which is a typical biblical pun, and therefore a likely explanation for Sarah's ire. Hackett contends, "And this is perhaps what Sarah is complaining about in the next verse, that she noticed he was doing something to indicate he was just like Isaac, that they were equals, and it is this that threatens her so."[42] If this were the case, then Ishmael's "Isaac-ing" is perceived as negative and his intentions are left ambiguous. Moreover, what Sarah perceives as ill-intentioned and threatening may have been an innocuous gesture on Ishmael's part.[43]

In trying to determine the meaning of *mĕṣaḥēq* in Genesis 21:9, Schwartz draws a connection between the weaning feast of Isaac and Ishmael's play and thus offers an interpretation similar to that of the author of Jubilees. Schwartz claims that whether or not Ishmael was seventeen (as found in the P version) or, as E would have it, still a child,[44] he was certainly old enough to be with his father and would not have been relegated to a section for toddlers. "As a child," Schwartz maintains, "his play at the feast would not have been considered inappropriate or out of place. On the contrary, it might have been considered amusing or entertaining."[45] Schwartz continues, "One can well imagine Sarah looking at her husband playing with his eldest son and the wave of panic that must have come over her. What will happen if Abraham should suddenly die? Who will inherit, in spite of the weaning feast? The public expression of intimacy, suggested by our reading and understanding of play in the text, must have been harrowing for Sarah."[46]

Schwartz argues further that children were reared either by their mothers or by some other female surrogate who played with them, and that contact with men of the family and fathers was limited to formal occasions and ceremonies. He writes: "Fathers rarely played with their children and such scenes that we do have regarding *father's* play with their offspring, albeit from periods later than the biblical period at present under discussion, are specifically meant to express touching scenes of fatherly love and devotion" (emphasis in the original).[47] Schwartz seems to have been strongly influenced by the book of Jubilees. His comments are highly appropriate if he were commenting on Jubilees 17:1–6. There is a possibility that Ishmael was with his father at the feast and perhaps he indeed was "playing" before him, but the notion that Abraham was delighting in his playfulness and that it was a touching scene (Schwartz refers to sources from the Greco-Roman period) is tenuous at best. Be that as it may, this attenuates neither Schwartz's insightful connection between the feast and Ishmael's play, nor his positive reading of Ishmael's *mĕṣaḥēq* that takes into account why Sarah would command Abraham to cast out Hagar and his elder son. Although the biblical account does not explicitly place Ishmael at the feast with his father, it is reasonable to infer this from the flow of the narrative: "And the child grew, and was weaned. And Abraham made a great feast on the day that Isaac was weaned. And Sarah saw the son of Hagar the Egyptian, whom she bore for Abraham, making sport" (Gen. 17:8–9).

Perhaps, Ishmael's presence alone alarms Sarah. His existence threatens Isaac's entitlement to full inheritance. Phyllis Trible's literary analysis explains Sarah's behavior as a response to a menacing situation:

> The presence of Ishmael in Canaan plagues the future of Isaac, whose inheritance is threatened. In her move to eliminate the danger, Sarah debases Hagar[48] and Ishmael while exalting herself and Isaac. The phrase, "her son," without the name Ishmael, counters "my son . . . Isaac." The description "this slave woman," rather than "my maid" (cf. 16:2), increases distance between Hagar and Sarah. Not only is the possessive adjective *my* missing, but also a change in nouns connotes a change in status. From being a maid (*shipha*) to Sarai in scene one, Hagar had become a slave (*'ama*).[49]

Trible, like Westermann, Hackett, and Schwartz, demonstrates the extent to which Ishmael's fate is predicated not on his own behavior but rather on Sarah's. Why is she threatened? Does Ishmael threaten Isaac's entitlement to full inheritance?

Hackett asserts that given the contradictory evidence in the Bible and evidence from legal materials of Ancient Near Eastern societies, it is difficult to know what Ishmael's inheritance rights would have been. She maintains, nevertheless, that Sarah thinks that if Ishmael were to remain in the house, he would have had inheritance rights.[50] Sarna, Speiser, and Thompson, on the other hand, examine the Near Eastern texts and demonstrate that indeed Ishmael had inheritance rights as a member of the household, but his expulsion abrogates these rights.[51]

The Code of Hammurapi (pars. 170 and 171) states that if the father of children of a slave-wife legitimates the children by claiming them as his own, then they have an equal share in the inheritance. If he does not claim them as his children, they have no share in the inheritance. Furthermore, both the slave and her children are given their freedom.[52] As Sarna suggests, although we do not know whether or not legitimization would be required if the wife supplied the slave to provide a son, as in the case of Sarah and Hagar, the heir would doubtless not have been inferior to the children of an ordinary slave. And, in the case of Ishmael, Abraham explicitly recognized him not only as a member of his household, but also as his son.[53]

Sarna also brings the Code of Lipit-Ishtar to bear on the issue: "The laws of Lipit-Ishtar, about one hundred and fifty years earlier than Hammurapi, stipulate that the offspring of a slave-wife relinquish their inheritance rights in return for their freedom."[54] He therefore concludes that Ishmael, as Abraham's legitimate son, was entitled to a share of the inheritance and that because of this, Sarah demanded Hagar and her son be given their freedom. In this way, they would forfeit their stake in the inheritance. "This being the case," writes Sarna, "the entire episode can be seen as having taken place according to the social custom and legal procedure of the times. Abraham's distress would then not be over the legality of the act, which was not in question, but because of both fatherly love and moral considerations."[55] For Sarna and others, it is clear that the issue at hand is one of inheritance.[56]

The question, however, still remains whether, and to what degree, the Bronze Age Mesopotamian laws were applied in the (proto) Israelite legal system. Greenspahn, in fact, contends that primogeniture "may not be as ancient or as universal a human practice as is commonly supposed."[57] He states:

> Biblical accounts of Israelite inheritance and succession confirm the impression that holders of both property and hereditary office were free to grant preferential treatment to whichever offspring they wished. . . . This system of fraternal sharing and paternal autonomy is confirmed by every incidental reference to inheritance in the Bible.[58]

Given the legal codes of Near Eastern societies and the narrative structure of the Genesis story, it is reasonable to believe that Ishmael, as Abraham's legitimate son, would inherit along with Isaac. Even if Greenspahn is correct that there are no rigid laws of inheritance in the Bible that obliged the father to treat the firstborn preferentially (a dubious idea), in the case of Ishmael it seems likely that inheritance was an issue for Sarah. Legitimate or not, Ishmael, she assumed, would inherit with her son—if not by law, then by Abraham's choice. Fearing that Abraham's affection for Ishmael would lead to his inheriting with her son and certainly unwilling to have him share in the family fortune, Sarah sought Ishmael's expulsion. It is Sarah who sets the siblings in opposition. As a result of the strife between her and Hagar, Sarah creates an implicit atmosphere of competition, of fraternal conflict between Ishmael and Isaac. That an explicit rivalry existed between Ishmael and Isaac is textually unsubstantiated.

Rivalry existed in as much as the brothers participate in the larger narrative structure of Genesis that sets one line of Abraham's descendants apart from others. The promise made to both Hagar and Abraham as to Ishmael's fate, however, does not put him in direct conflict with Isaac, nor is there anything in the story that would lead one to believe that the brothers engaged in interpersonal conflict. To be sure, the prophecy depicts Ishmael's fate as riddled with strife, but it is not strife exclusively with Isaac: the statement that "His hand will be against everyone and everyone's hand against him" (Gen. 16:12) reflects the general tensions between sedentary and nomadic populations in the Near East.[59] There is no mention of competition or warfare between the brothers.

Sibling rivalry between Ishmael and Isaac is neither divinely ordained nor explicit in the narrative. In fact, they appear together only once in the narrative when they bury their father: "And Isaac and Ishmael his sons buried him in the cave of Machpelah" (Gen. 25:9). The text reverses the birth order by mentioning Isaac before Ishmael. As we soon shall have occasion to see, this reversal figures prominently when comparing this narrative to that of Esau and Jacob.

ESAU IN THE BIBLE

The following section looks at particular features of the Esau narrative and describes similarities and distinctions between Ishmael and Esau in order to establish a basis for understanding their depiction in rabbinic literature. It will become apparent that while the biblical character of Esau is more fully developed than that of Ishmael, the converse is true in rabbinic literature in which Ishmael is more multidimensional.

Jacob's twin brother, Esau, is red[60] (Gen. 25:25), which is connected to Edom, *'adāmâh*, "the red land, the land of the red clay," and his "hairiness" is related to Seir, the region in Edom[61] that Esau makes his home (Gen. 32:4). In both cases, Esau's identity is, as Vawter observes, "accorded by geography, but physical characteristics draw attention to it."[62]

Esau's hairiness calls to mind the story of Enkidu in the Epic of Gilgamesh. Both are covered with hair, "a condition that was popularly taken to be a sign of boorish uncouthness."[63] As Speiser indicates: "Yet J is . . . able to depict Esau as a sort of Enkidu figure: the child emerges 'like a hairy mantle all over,' which is almost the same as 'shaggy with hair was his whole body,' applied to Enkidu in Gilg., Tablet I, column ii, line 36 (where the phrase *su'ur sarta* is cognate with Heb. *seʿar*); and Esau, like Enkidu, is a man of the open spaces."[64] Similarly, Ishmael is depicted as an Enkidu-type figure. Not only is he a "wild ass of a man," which as we saw earlier, recalls the Akkadian phrase, *lullu-awelu*, used to describe Enkidu, but in Genensis 21:20, Ishmael is a "skilled bowman"[65] whose home is the "wilderness of Paran." "Skilled bowman," *rōbe qaššāt*, resonates with "hunter-man," a familiar term from the Epic of Gilgamesh.[66] Both Ishmael and Esau, connected with the outdoors, the former a bowman, the later a hunter, call to mind the image of Enkidu. Both biblical figures have Enkidu-like features and the association between Esau and Enkidu may be deliberate.

At the outset, Esau and Jacob are pitted against each other. Rebekah is given an oracle about the struggling children in her womb: "Two nations are in your womb, two separate peoples shall issue from your body; one people shall be mightier than the other, and the older shall serve the younger" (Gen. 25:23). At the outset, competition and conflict plague the twins. "The theme of hostile twins whose mutual opposition manifests itself already while they are still in their mother's womb," explains Vawter, "is a frequent enough detail of myth and folklore. Biblical tradition has adapted it to the careers of Edom and Israel, two peoples closely bound to each other by ties of blood and history who were destined to live in constant enmity and border warfare."[67] Esau, the archenemy, is Edom and the prenatal struggles of Esau and Jacob prefigure the eventual struggles between Edom and Israel. The strife between the fathers of two nations, one greater than the other, begins in Genesis, but the bitter rivalry continues throughout Israelite history.

The Edomites, whose land is traditionally located southeast of the Dead Sea, do not permit the Israelites to pass through their territory on their way from Kadesh to the promised land, thus forcing the Israelites to circumnavigate Edom (Num. 20:14–21).[68] Moreover, there is conflict between Edom and Israel throughout the period of the monarchy. Several texts from the exilic period recollect Edom's disdainful role in the fall of Jerusalem (e.g., Ezek. 25:12–14; Obad. 10–14; Ps. 137:7). As an ally of the Babylonians, Edom assists in preventing Judeans from escaping their enemy. The prophetic literature portends the destruction of Edom and its incorporation into the kingdom of Israel, thus fulfilling the prophecy, "the older will be slave of the younger."

It is important to note, however, that the depiction of Edom and Esau is not consistent throughout the biblical text. In Genesis 25 and 27 Esau is the "rude natural man," who shuns his birthright, lives by his sword, and holds a grudge against his brother. On the other hand, in Genesis 33 the reader is presented with a noble chieftain in charge of a clan who is both gracious and sympathetic to his brother. Esau, the brother who hates his sibling and seeks revenge, is the same brother who in Genesis 33:4 runs to meet Jacob, who falls on his neck and kisses him.[69] But perhaps rather than inconsistency, what we find is the development of his character.

In the case of Edom, its representation in the Bible may be categorized as mostly negative, but in some cases we find neutral and positive depictions.[70] A positive attitude toward Edom, for example, is found in Deuteronomy 2, and several neutral passages are found elsewhere.[71] Edom evidently plays a greater role in Israelite history than the Ishmaelites, the nomads who live in the desert of northern Arabia.[72] Psalm 83:7 notwithstanding, like their eponymous ancestor Ishmael, they are not generally depicted as an enemy but rather simply as one of the neighboring peoples. Tension between the Ishmaelites and the Israelites does not exist to the same extent as it does between the Edomites and the Israelites. It is therefore no surprise that the relationship between this second set of brothers, Esau and Jacob, differs to a large extent from that of Ishmael and Isaac.

The brothers are depicted as polar opposites: "When the boys grew up, Esau became a skillful hunter, a man of the outdoors; but Jacob was a mild man who stayed in camp. Isaac favored Esau because he had a taste for game; but Rebekah favored Jacob" (Gen. 25:27–28). Esau is hairy, "The first one emerged red, like a hairy mantle all over" (Gen. 25:25), and Jacob is "smooth-skinned" (Gen. 27:11). In Genesis 27:22 we read: "So Jacob drew close to his father Isaac, who felt him and wondered: 'The voice is the voice of Jacob, yet the hands are the hands of Esau.'" The twin brothers complement each other.[73] Ishmael and Isaac, rather than binary opposites, parallel each other. A close reading of Genesis 21 and 22 illustrates the point. In both cases Abraham confronts the loss of a son.[74] Even the compositional strategy of Genesis 21:3, 8–14, and 22:2 draws attention to the symmetry between the brothers. L. Lyke also makes this point. By analyzing the broad narrative structures and compositional strategies of Genesis 21 and 22, Lyke convincingly argues that the stories told in Genesis 21:8–21 and 22:1–14 are parallel.[75]

Not only is the pairing of siblings different, the nature of their interaction also differs. Esau and Jacob engage in dialogue, whereas Ishmael and Isaac exchange no words. One may, however, argue that the biblical account implicitly refers to Ishmael and Isaac's positive interpersonal relationship. As will be discussed in the next chapter, the rabbis, attuned to scriptural subtleties, take notice of Genesis 24:62, "Isaac had just come back from the vicinity of Beer-lahai-roi, for he was settled in the region of the Negeb," and recall Hagar. But Hagar is not the only person with whom this area is associated. As the site of God's promise of a son to Hagar, it is arguably associated with Ishmael. In fact, in his commentary on Genesis 25:11, "and Isaac settled near Beer-lahai-roi," Sarna suggests that Isaac's settling in this area "may be a symbolic assertion of hegemony over his brother."[76] The idea of hegemony over Ishmael is unwarranted. Given the preceding analysis of Genesis 16 and 17, there is no indication in the promises to Hagar and Abraham that augurs a fate riddled with fraternal strife for Ishmael. If anything, it is plausible that they dwelt "alongside" one another under relatively peaceful conditions. And certainly, unlike the other siblings and relations in the Genesis genealogies, Ammon, Moab, Edom, and for that matter, Aram and Midian, the Ishmaelites do not figure as significant enemies of the Israelites.

Furthermore, according to Genesis 25:9, "Isaac and Ishmael buried him [Abraham] in the cave of Machpelah." Unlike the burial notice of Isaac (Gen. 35:29) where Esau and Jacob bury their father, in this notice the younger son is mentioned first. Commenting on 35:29, Alter states: "At this end point, they [Esau and Jacob] act in unison and despite the reversal of birthright and blessing the firstborn is mentioned first."[77] By the same token, if Genesis 25:9 and 35:29 are contrasted, it becomes clear that the reversal, "Isaac and Ishmael" portrays the brothers acting not only in unison but also in accordance with God's preordained plan.

In the story of Esau and Jacob we have a prenatal struggle that sets the tone for the story, whereas in the story of Ishmael and Isaac the rivalry is not so much between brothers as between rival wives. There is no prenatal struggle. Not only is there no explicit sibling rivalry, there is no notion that one nation would serve the other. Since there is no portent of domination in the case of Ishmael and Isaac, the reversal of names may be symbolic of acceptance of the divine plan. That is, Isaac is the son of the covenant yet Ishmael is recognized as a great nation that will live "alongside" its kinsmen. Where? Perhaps in Beer-lahai-roi, where Isaac settles, where Ishmael was born.

The images of the two sons burying their father and living in proximity evoke reunion, reconciliation, and renewal. To be sure, there is no mention of Ishmael in the text, however, we know that Ishmael dwelt in the wilderness of Paran (Gen. 21:21), which is located in the Negeb, in the same vicinity as Beer-lahai-roi, that is, near Kadesh.[78] There is no internal nor archaeological evidence that they are the same place, nonetheless, they both clearly refer to the southern region. Furthermore, the verse ordering of Genesis 25:11–12 indicates a connection between not only the two areas, but also between these siblings. In Genesis 25:11 we learn that Isaac dwells in Beer-lahai-roi and the very next verse begins listing the generations of Ishmael who, we are informed in Genesis 25:18, "dwell from Havilah unto Shur that is before Egypt." They, too, dwell nearby, or at least in the same vicinity. A careful reading of the texts supports the notion that they may have settled in the same area, unlike Esau and Jacob who part ways.

The fact that "Esau and Jacob bury their father," on the other hand, is symbolic of future conflict and tribal clashes. Indeed the biblical text explicitly states that they separate.[79] Genesis 33:12 reads as follows:

> And [Esau] said, "Let us start on our journey, and I will proceed at your pace." But he said to him, "My lord knows that the children are frail and that the flocks and herds, which are nursing, are a care to me; if they are driven hard a single day, all the flocks will die. Let my lord go on ahead of his servant, while I travel slowly, at the pace of the cattle before me and at the pace of the children, until I come to my lord in Seir." . . . So Esau started back that day on his way to Seir. But Jacob journeyed on to Succoth. (Gen. 33:12–16)

After Esau and Jacob bury Isaac, we learn that Esau took his entire family and all his belongings and "went to a land away from his brother Jacob" (Gen. 36:6). In contrast to Isaac and Ishmael, the later set of siblings separate and their future descendants will be in conflict with each other.

It is worth mentioning that the annunciation of Ishmael's birth more closely resembles the annunciation of the birth of Samuel, Solomon, Josiah, and Emmanuel than that of Esau.[80] To give an example, in 2 Kings 13:2, Josiah's birth is announced: "Thus said the LORD: A son shall be born to the House of David, Josiah by name; and he shall slaughter upon you the priests of the shrines who bring offerings upon you." And also in I Chronicles 22:9 we read of Solomon's birth: "But you will have a son who will be a man at rest, for I will give him rest from all his enemies on all sides; Solomon will be his name and I shall confer peace and quiet on Israel in his time." The annunciation of Ishmael's birth follows a similar pattern: "Behold, you are with child and shall bear a son; You shall call him Ishmael, for the LORD has paid heed to your suffering. He shall be a wild ass of a man" (Gen. 16:11–12). As in the examples given, especially in the case of

Josiah's birth announcement, here too one learns of a child's birth, his name, and his destiny. Esau's birth announcement, in contrast, does not include the child's name, nor does it deal specifically with one child: "Two nations are in your womb" (Gen. 25:23).

Other differences between the narratives include the more active role Esau takes in his fate. Though he is acted upon, unlike Ishmael he acts and speaks. In both instances, however, mothers effect the marginalization. Both mediate God's preordained plan. Rebekah's behavior, albeit surreptitious, is not only known to the reader, it is justifiable given the oracle Rebekah received as well as the threat Esau posed to her favored son, Jacob. Even though Sarah's command to Abraham, "Cast out that slave-woman and her son, for the son of that slave shall not share in the inheritance with my son" (Gen. 21:10), fulfills no previously announced predestined program (Isaac's destiny as bearer of the covenant is another matter), nor is it obvious why Sarah is determined to remove Ishmael from her household, God approves of Sarah's request. Ishmael's destiny is to be a great nation. God says to Abraham, "I will make him fertile and exceedingly numerous" (Gen. 17:20), but Esau, however, a victim of ill-fortune, receives a negative blessing from Isaac.[81]

In contrast with Ishmael, Esau is a fully developed character whose destiny is to serve his brother. He is the father of a nation that plays a greater role in Israelite history than the Ishmaelites. Associated with outdoor activities, both characters are dispossessed and forced to live outside the family circle, in the desert where their lives intersect.

Thus in Genesis 28:6–9 we read:

> When Esau saw that Isaac had blessed Jacob and sent him off to Paddan-aram to take a wife from there, charging him, as he blessed him, "You shall not take a wife from among the Canaanite women," and that Jacob had obeyed his father and mother . . . Esau realized that the Canaanite women displeased his father Isaac. So Esau went to Ishmael and took to wife, in addition to the wives he had, Mahalath the daughter of Ishmael, sister of Nebaioth.

Esau goes to Ishmael and marries his daughter, Mahalath. This may be understood as Esau's attempt to appease his father after having married the Hittite women. Bringing them together creates a relationship between the two ostracized elder brothers and confirms their shared marginalization.

As Jacob's rival, Esau's future in rabbinic literature is less ambiguous than Ishmael's. Ishmael, who is present, yet for the most part passive in the biblical narrative, presents the rabbis with greater difficulty, which in turn provides them with more space for the imagination to fill. After all, he is Abraham's circumcised son, a son whom Abraham found difficult to cast out. In trying to vindicate Sarah, the rabbis are forced to vilify Ishmael. At the same time, they must accept his place as Abraham's legitimate son. In the following chapters, we will examine how these ostracized figures, along with the Ishmaelites and the children of Keturah, come to represent Other, for purposes related to group-identity formation, boundary maintenance, and rabbinic notions of Jewish self-identity.

2

Ishmael in Tannaitic and Amoraic Literature

Sarah saw the son whom Hagar the Egyptian had borne to Abraham playing. She said to Abraham, "Cast out that slave-woman and her son, for the son of that slave shall not share in the inheritance with my son Isaac."

—Gen. 21:9

Four were named before they were born. They are: Isaac, Ishmael, Josiah and Solomon. *Isaac*: "And you shall call his name *Isaac*" (Gen. 17:19). *Ishmael*: "And you shall call his name *Ishmael*" (Gen. 16:11). *Josiah*: "Behold a son is to be born to the House of David. *Josiah* is his name" (I Kings 13:2). *Solomon*: "*Solomon* shall be his name" (1 Chron. 22:9). This is the case regarding the righteous people.

—PT. Berakot 1:6

In the course of examining rabbinic texts on Ishmael, Esau, the Ishmaelites, and the children of Keturah, themes such as their unfit status and the election of Israel figure prominently. In the sources of the tannaitic and amoraic periods, these marginalized figures come to represent the Other rather than specific others, despite some instances where they are associated with Arabs, as in the case of Ishmael and his sons, and the more frequent association of Esau with Rome. We must, however, resist reading anti-Christian polemic into every reference to Esau, or readily equating Ishmael with Arabs unless the text demands it. By the same token, we must not lose sight of how historical events such as the rise of Islam effect changes in midrashim. Thus, in order to understand rabbinic interpretation, we must look at both textual and extratextual factors that are inextricably connected in the midrashic process.

Take, for example, the midrash found in Gen. Rab. 48:13 which interprets the verse: "And Abraham ran toward the herd and took a calf, tender and good, and gave it to a servant-boy, who hastened to prepare it" (Gen. 18:7).[1] The midrash is as follows: " 'And gave it to a servant-boy [who hastened to prepare it]' refers to Ishmael, in order to train him to be quick, ready in performing commandments." Contrary to some historically minded interpretations of Ishmael's role in Genesis Rabbah,[2] Ishmael is portrayed as Abraham's son, not Rome, not an Arab, not Other. In this case, reading midrash through a historical lens is extraordinarily difficult and thus the usefulness of the text to us as a historical source is not readily apparent.

And yet, there are innumerable people with whom the servant could have been plausibly identified. So we must ask: Why does the midrash identify Ishmael in particular and what made it possible for the rabbis to use him in this context? We can posit the possibility that there was no theological, social, or political motive for them not to. In other words, the rabbis were reading the story not as a cipher, but on its own terms. We simply do not know. The very absence of such a motive, the very fact that the rabbis make this identification, however, is a historical observation. At the same time, we can offer the following conjecture: Perhaps the desire to portray Abraham as a loving father and to emphasize that this involves training sons to do *mitzvot* factored into this midrash.

In analyzing midrashim on the aforementioned biblical characters, we will look at the various extratextual factors contributing to specific interpretations. These factors are sometimes more recognizable than not, and because several factors, some probably unknowable, may contribute to the development of a midrash, we must be cautious in attributing a midrash to any single factor.

The Tannaitic Sources

The earliest extant midrashim about Ishmael attempt to resolve the ambiguity of *mĕṣaḥēq* in Genesis 21:9, "But Sarah saw the son of Hagar the Egyptian whom she had borne to Abraham making sport," and thus illustrate a variety of readings of *mĕṣaḥēq*. That is to say, the tannaitic texts that have survived are primarily concerned with the exegesis of *mĕṣaḥēq* and to some extent with its implications for the portrayal of Ishmael, Abraham, and Sarah.

A tannaitic source of Palestinian provenance probably codified in the middle of the third century, Tosefta Soṭah gives an explanation for Sarah's harsh request in Genesis 21:10, " 'Cast out this maidservant and her son':

This teaches that our mother Sarah saw Ishmael building altars, hunting locusts, making offerings, and burning incense for idol worship. She said, 'Perhaps Isaac, my son, will learn to do thus and will go and worship thus and the Name of Heaven will be profaned by this' " (T. Soṭah 5:12). In legitimizing Sarah's demand, the rabbis implicitly refer to Genesis 21:9 and interpret *mĕṣaḥēq*, playing, as idol worship; the exegetical basis for this interpretation is *lĕṣaḥēq*, "to make sport," in Exodus 32:6.

T. Soṭah 6:6 presents a more elaborate exposition of Genesis 21:9. By means of midrashic exegesis three interpretations of *mĕṣaḥēq* are given: idol worship, engagement in forbidden sexual acts, and the shedding of blood. R. Shimon, however, disagrees with the aforementioned readings and proffers his own interpretation:

> R. Shimon b. Yohai said, "There are four things which R. Aqiba used to expound and my words are more fitting than his. R. Aqiba expounded, 'Sarah saw the son of Hagar the Egyptian, whom she had borne to Abraham, making sport.' 'Making sport' (*mĕṣaḥēq*) here means nothing other than idol worship, as it is said, 'Early next day, the people offered up burnt offerings and brought sacrifices of well-being; they sat down to eat and drink, and then they rose to revel (*lĕṣaḥēq*)' (Exod. 32:6). This teaches that our mother Sarah saw Ishmael building altars, hunting locusts, and making offerings for idol worship." R. Eleazar b. R. Yosi the Galilean said, "Here 'making sport' means nothing other than forbidden sexual acts, as it is said, '. . . the Hebrew servant, whom you have brought among us, came to dally with me (*lĕṣaḥēq*)' (Gen. 39:17). This teaches that our mother Sarah saw Ishmael having homosexual intercourse and raping women." R. Ishmael said, " 'Making sport' is nothing other than the shedding of blood, as it is said, 'Abner said to Yoab, Let the young men, I pray you, arise and play before us (*viśaḥaqu*). . . . Each one grasped his opponent's head and thrust his dagger into his opponent's side; thus they fell together' (2 Sam. 2:14–16). This teaches that our mother Sarah saw Ishmael take a bow and arrows and shoot at Isaac, as it is said, 'As a madman who casts deadly firebrands and arrows, so is the man who deceives his neighbor and says, I was only making sport. (*mĕṣaḥēq*)' " (Prov. 26:19).[3]

R. Shimon, however, is troubled by the notion that the son of Abraham, a righteous person, behaved immorally:

> But I (R. Shimon) say, "Heaven forbid that such [behavior] should take place in the house of a righteous person. Can this be said of

> Abraham, of whom it is written, 'For I have singled him out, that he may instruct his children and his posterity [to keep the way of the LORD by doing what is right, in order that the LORD may bring about for Abraham what He has promised him]' (Gen. 18:19)? In his house is it possible there would be idol worship, forbidden sexual acts and the shedding of blood? Rather, the word 'making sport' (*mĕṣaḥēq*) here refers only to inheritance. For when our father Isaac was born to Abraham our father, everyone was happy. They said, 'A son has been born to Abraham! A son has been born to Abraham! He will inherit the world and take two shares.' Ishmael played (*mĕṣaḥēq*) with the idea in his mind and said, 'Don't be fools. I am the firstborn, and I shall take the double portion.' From the answer to the matter, you learn . . .' for the son of this slave woman shall not inherit with my son, with Isaac'" (Gen. 21:10).

The various renderings of *mĕṣaḥēq* as well as the explanations of the verse seem to form a single unit in T. Soṭah 6:6 and Gen. Rab. 53:11, whereas in T. Soṭah 5:12, we read only of Ishmael as an idol worshiper and in Sifre Deuteronomy 31,[4] we have a shorter version of T. Soṭah 6:6:

> From Abraham came out Ishmael who worshipped idols; [these are] the words of R. Aqiba, as it is said . . . R. Shimon b. Yohai said, "There are four things which R. Aqiba used to expound and I expounded them and my words are more fitting than his. He said, '"And Sarah saw the son of Hagar the Egyptian" means idol worship,' and I say that they were only contending about fields and vineyards. For when they (Ishmael and Isaac) went to divide (up the inheritance), Ishmael said to him (Isaac), 'I am taking two shares because I am the firstborn.' And thus Sarah said to Abraham, 'Cast out this servant and her son' (Gen. 21:10) and I prefer my words to his words."

In Sifre Deuteronomy 31, R. Shimon does not discuss the four examples where he and R. Aqiba differ, nor are R. Eleazar and R. Ishmael's interpretations of *mĕṣaḥēq* included. The interpretation of Genesis 21:9 in Tosefta Soṭah 5:12, that Sarah saw Ishmael building altars, hunting locusts, and offering them for idol worship, has no attribution. Moreover, in Gen. Rab. 53:11, as in T. Soṭah 6:6, all four renderings of *mĕṣaḥēq* are found in one place as part of R. Shimon's discussion of the four interpretations of his that differ from those of R. Aqiba. In Gen. Rab. 53:11, however, R. Aqiba expounds: "'Making sport' is none other than forbidden sexual acts" and it is R. Ishmael who teaches on tannaitic authority that "making sport" in this case is idol worship.

Furthermore, in T. Soṭah 6:6, Ishmael "plays" with the idea of double inheritance in his mind, whereas in Sifre Deuteronomy 31, while he and Isaac are dividing the inheritance, he claims his right to a double share. And, as in T. Soṭah 6:6, in Gen. Rab. 53:11 Ishmael addresses everyone who delighted in Isaac's birth: "Ishmael said to them, 'You are fools. I am the firstborn, and I shall take a double portion.' "[5]

The sources indicate that *mĕṣaḥēq* had several interpretations that were by and large negative assessments of Ishmael's behavior. And yet, the midrash attributed to R. Shimon—that the issue was one of inheritance—is as persistent as the notion that Ishmael was an idol worshiper or fornicator. In fact, Shimon is even allowed the final word in some contexts. What is significant about R. Shimon's opinion is the question that motivates it: How could the son of Abraham the righteous who is to keep the way of the LORD, engage in sinful activities? The earlier opinions are based on the use of a scriptural verse to illuminate the meaning of *mĕṣaḥēq*, and are very likely to justify Sarah and to contrast Ishmael unfavorably with Isaac, thereby justifying God's choice of the latter. R. Shimon, on the other hand, does not quote Scripture[6] but rather creates a dialogue between Ishmael and himself in Tosefta Soṭah 6:6, with Isaac in Sifre Deuteronomy 31, and with others in Gen. Rab. 53:11. He explains *mĕṣaḥēq* contextually, in light of Sarah's dictate ("for the son of that slave shall not inherit with my son Isaac," Gen. 21:10), rather than associatively (that is, elsewhere *mĕṣaḥēq* means "idol worship," inter alia).

R. Shimon's interpretation is an explicit example of how extratextual concerns factor into rabbinic hermeneutics. Genesis 21:9 is read with an eye toward its implications for the rabbinic characterization of Abraham. While the other interpretations adhere to the rules of rabbinic exegesis (although they, too, are probably not motivated by exegesis alone), they implicitly impute to Abraham guilt—like father, like son. That is unacceptable to R. Shimon. In a sense, his interpretation serves as a corrective. By the same token, it could be that Genesis 18:19, "For I have singled him out, that he may instruct his children," motivates his response. However, this verse is found only in one version. It seems likely that both Genesis 18:19 and a concern for Abraham's character play a role in R. Shimon's response.

As we can see, the earliest midrashim on Genesis 21:9 are not all negative. On the contrary, for R. Shimon, Ishmael is actually right in following halakha properly. This is consistent with other tannaitic and amoraic portrayals of Ishmael. In Tosefta Qiddušin 5:17–19, for example, we read:

> 17. Thus you find with Abraham our father on whom in his old age than in his youth the LORD bestowed more blessings, as it is written, "Abraham was old, advanced in years, and the LORD blessed Abraham in all things" (Gen. 24:1). R. Meir said, "In that he had no daughter." R. Shimon in the name of R. Yehudah said, "In that he had a daughter." R. Lazar the Modite said, "This refers to Abraham's astrological powers such that everyone came to him." R. Shimon b. Yohai said, "This was a precious stone which hung around Abraham's neck that all who saw were cured immediately. When Abraham our father died, the LORD took it and hung it around the orb of the sun." 18. A second reward: That Esau did not rebel during Abraham's lifetime. 19. A third reward: That Ishmael repented during Abraham's lifetime. Others say Abraham had a daughter and her name was *Bakol*, "in all things" [a play on the last words of the verse—"And the LORD blessed Abraham in all things"].[7]

The primary issue at hand is not Ishmael's character, but rather the ways in which Abraham was blessed in his old age. In their explication of Gen. 24:1, the rabbis nonetheless make assumptions about Ishmael. It is implied that Ishmael went astray, that he needed to reform. At the same time the midrash assumes that his repentance would be a blessing to Abraham. In other words, Abraham has not completely shunned his son to the extent that he is no longer of any significance. On the contrary, not only is Ishmael reformed, but this is a blessing to Abraham.

A midrash recorded in the Mekilta, the Palestinian Talmud, and in Genesis Rabbah portrays Ishmael in a positive light.[8] In PT. Berakot 1:6 Ishmael is included among those who were named before they were born:

> Four were named before they were born. They are: Isaac, Ishmael, Josiah and Solomon. *Isaac*: "And you shall call his name *Isaac*" (Gen. 17:19). *Ishmael*: "And you shall call his name *Ishmael*" (Gen. 16:11). *Josiah*: "Behold a son is to be born to the House of David. *Josiah* is his name" (I Kings 13:2). *Solomon*: "*Solomon* shall be his name" (1 Chron. 22:9). This is the case regarding the righteous people. But regarding the wicked, "The wicked are strangers from the womb" (Ps. 58:4) [emphasis mine].

In a tannaitic source, Mekilta de-Rabbi Ishmael, Pisha 16, and in Gen. Rab. 45:8, only three were named by God before they were born. These sources, however, also mention Ishmael: "There are some who say that also Ishmael among the Gentiles." The Mekilta goes on to say, "We learn the names of the righteous and their deeds are revealed before the Omnipresent."[9]

In all three instances, that is, in PT. Berakoth 1:6, Mekilta de-Rabbi Ishmael, Pisha 16, and Gen. Rab. 45:8, Ishmael is mentioned; in PT. Berakot 1:6 and in the Mekilta he is named among the righteous.[10] The fact that PT. Berakot 1:6 includes him with Isaac, Josiah, and Solomon, and the other two sources with the Gentiles, exemplifies the complexity of determining the concerns of the rabbis in these sources. On an exegetical level, it is possible to include Ishmael among the others. To include him, however, would make his status tantamount to that of Isaac, Josiah, and Solomon. Even though they are not equal, all of them are deemed righteous. While including him was not an issue for the Palestinian Talmud, it seems to have been for the Mekilta and for Genesis Rabbah. If the concern were more than explicating the verse, then why does the Palestinian Talmud include Ishmael with the others? If the concern were only this, then why is a distinction made in the Mekilta and in Genesis Rabbah? The Mekilta and Genesis Rabbah include him for a philological reason, but exclude him in order to make a theological statement about Israel's divine election, a theme found in both tannaitic and amoraic texts.

By and large very little is said about Ishmael in tannaitic sources. His depiction, as well as that of the other marginalized figures, varies and has as much to do with exegetical concerns as it does with extratextual issues, such as the rabbinic expression of Israel's divine election to the exclusion of others. And as illustrated in the discussion of T. Qiddušin 5:17, and in the examination of several amoraic sources later, neutral depictions are often the result of exegetical maneuvers in which the raison d'etre is to resolve textual irregularities or ambiguities.

The Amoraic Sources

The figure of Ishmael in Genesis Rabbah is as multivalent as it is in tannaitic sources. As in the sources we examined earlier, the rabbis treat Ishmael according to their interpretive needs or concerns. Whereas Esau is often, though not exclusively, the archetypal character representing Rome or Edom,[11] Ishmael is portrayed more fluidly, to the extent that while some sages regard him as opprobrious, others regard him favorably. Indeed, the following example, Gen. Rab. 47:4, reflects Abraham's satisfaction with Ishmael:

> "And Abraham said to God, O that Ishmael might live in your sight!" (Gen. 17:18). R. Yudah in the name of R. Yudan said, "The matter may be compared to a king who wished to increase his friend's stipend. He said to his friend, 'I wish to double your stipend.'[12] He answered the king, 'Do not fill me with false hopes. If only you would give me what you have given me in the past.' So, too, Abraham said, 'O, that Ishmael might live in your sight!' "[13]

In this *mashal*,[14] the notion of having another son appeals to Abraham, but not wanting to get his hopes high, he expresses satisfaction with the son he has, with Ishmael. The midrash does not portray Abraham as a disgruntled father who wants another child. The friend does not complain about his stipend; rather he requests his income be maintained. That is, double would be nice, but not necessary. The *nimshal*, the explanation of the *mashal*, is that two sons mean more descendants but one son, Ishmael, suffices. To the extent that Abraham is content with Ishmael, the midrash conveys a neutral, if not favorable, attitude toward him.

As discussed earlier, Gen. Rab. 48:13 interprets the verse, "And Abraham ran toward the herd and took a calf, tender and good, and gave it to the servant, who hastened to prepare it" (Gen. 18:7) as follows: " 'And gave it to the servant who hastened to prepare it' refers to Ishmael in order to make him quick, ready in performing commandments." Here is a good example of the midrashic propensity to use characters close by to fill in missing names. The more likely identity, Eliezer, is not given. Doubtless Ishmael is portrayed as Abraham's son and does not represent a specific historical personality or nation. Abraham is not lazy, but wants to involve others in the *mitzvot*. The implication is that Abraham is concerned that his son will perform the commandments, that he will follow the Torah, which the slave need not follow. The implication is that Abraham loves his son.

If we make too sharp a distinction between exegetical and extratextual concerns, we lose sight of the questions informing the midrash. If the identity of the servant is the only question the midrash addresses then one could argue that the midrash is indeed motivated only by exegetical concerns. This, however, is not the case. The midrash answers another question: Why did Abraham give the calf to someone else and not prepare it himself? While interested in elaborating on the verse, the rabbis, in giving the generic servant a name, are consciously or unconsciously concerned with reconciling their conception of Abraham with the implications of the verse as it is found in Genesis.

Gen. Rab. 48:16 is another example of this impartial treatment of Ishmael:

> The LORD said, "I will surely return to you in due season, and Sarah your wife will have a son." Sarah was listening at the tent door which was behind him (Gen. 18:10). Literally, "He was behind him"[15] refers to Ishmael. "He was behind him" on account of the principle of *yiḥûd*.[16] "He was behind Him"—Sarah realized the guest had arrived.[17]

In explaining Genesis 18:10, the rabbis take the opportunity to promote the rabbinic principle that a woman is not to be left alone with a man other than her husband. Again, one could argue Eliezer is a more likely choice than Ishmael, but this assumes that using Ishmael has significant implications. In other words, in the late antique period before Ishmael becomes synonymous with Islam, there is no compelling reason for the rabbis to refrain from using Ishmael. Because the rabbis do not attribute any significant meaning to Ishmael's character, they are able to depict him in multiple ways.

Gen. Rab. 53:14[18] illustrates God's abounding mercy not only for Ishmael but also for humanity at large. Ishmael is depicted as one who is suffering, and in the moment of his suffering, he is righteous. The midrash uses Ishmael in order to exemplify God's compassion for all who repent, even for those whose children in the future will inflict harm on Israel. As previously stated, because no significant meaning is attached to Ishmael's character, the rabbis can use him in this impartial manner.

Several midrashim in Genesis Rabbah interpret verses in Genesis 21, the chapter relating the expulsion of Ishmael and Hagar. For example, Gen. Rab. 53:13 deals with Genesis 21:14, "So Abraham rose early in the morning, and took bread and a skin of water, and gave it to Hagar, putting it on her shoulder, along with the child, and sent her away. And she departed, and wandered in the wilderness of Beer-sheba." This verse troubles the rabbis for various reasons. Why did Abraham send them away with only bread and water?[19] Gen. Rab. 53:13 states that Abraham's household was generous, thus, on the contrary, Abraham was unstinting when he put bread and a skin of water on her shoulder. According to the midrash, "This is the way of passers-by,[20] to carry water in their pitcher."

Furthermore, how could Abraham possibly have put both the pitcher of water on her shoulder "along with the child" if Ishmael was, as the midrash claims, twenty-seven years old?[21] The midrash asks, "How is this so? This teaches that she [Sarah] cast an evil eye on him and he became feverish. Know that this is so, for it is written, 'And the water from the bottle was spent': A sick person drinks water every hour." In this midrash the rabbis show no regard for the portrayal of Sarah, who behaves maliciously. Making sense of the biblical verse seems to take precedence over Sarah's reputation.

Gen. Rab. 53:15 deals with the end of Genesis 21:20:

> "And God was with the lad and he grew up. He lived in the wilderness and became an expert with the bow" (Gen. 21:20). R. Ishmael asked R. Aqiba, [saying to him], "Because you served Nahum of Gimzu for twenty-two years, who contends that the words 'only' (*raq*) and 'but' (*akh*) are used to exclude, whereas the use of *'et*, [the accusative particle, or "with"] and 'also' (*gam*) serve to include, what is the meaning of *'et* [the accusative particle] in this verse, 'And God was (*'et*) the lad'?" He [R. Aqiba] replied, "If the verse excluded the accusative particle, *'et*, the verse would be difficult [it would state literally, 'And God was the young lad'],[22] therefore it says, '*'et* the lad,' 'for it is not a trifling thing for you' (Deut. 32:47), that is, if it seems meaningless, it is because you do not know how to interpret it. 'God was (*'et*) the lad,' meaning he was with him, his ass-drivers, his camel-drivers and his household."

The issue here is also exegetical. What does the accusative particle mean? R. Aqiba, who interprets it as a *ribbui*—that which includes something in addition to the thing itself—claims that God was not only with Ishmael but also with his household. The unusual syntax of the verse demands interpretation, or at least provides a challenge for R. Aqiba to derive meaning from the *'et*. Be that as it may, the interpretation shows God's concern for Ishmael. Although the midrash does not seem to set out to say anything positive or negative about Ishmael, but rather simply to resolve a syntactic problem in the verse, it nevertheless conveys a favorable attitude toward him. As in the previous example, extratextual factors play a role in how a verse is interpreted; however, they are not as apparent as the textual factors.

Gen. Rab. 47:8 is prima facie also an example of a midrash concerned primarily with syntactic exegesis:

> "And Abraham was ninety-nine years old when he was circumcised in the flesh of his foreskin. And Ishmael was thirteen years old when he was circumcised in the flesh of his foreskin" (Gen. 17:24). Here it is

> written, "the flesh of his foreskin," and further [when referring to Ishmael] it says, "*'et*" [the accusative particle] the flesh of his foreskin." In the case of Abraham, [his foreskin] was rubbed off through a woman, but in the case of Ishmael, [whose foreskin] was not rubbed off through a woman, "*'et*" is written.

In this midrash the rabbis resolve the syntactical inconsistency of the verse by determining why the accusative participle is missing in the first part of the verse which refers to Abraham. The missing "*'et*," according to the rabbis, distinguishes Abraham, who had intercourse with a woman, from Ishmael, who was still a lad. This is clearly an example of rabbinic exegesis that is first and foremost concerned with resolving a difficulty in the text. At the same time, it is important to note how the rabbis treat Ishmael. While Genesis 17:24, and probably any verse, provides a possible occasion for the rabbis to malign Ishmael, they choose rather merely to distinguish Abraham from Ishmael in terms of sexual experience.

But Gen. Rab. 53:15 continues: "He became an expert with the bow—As he grew, so did his cruelty. As he grew, he taught himself how to use the bow. Also, he was master of all who shot the bow." The first interpretation of Genesis 21:20 is a negative comment on Ishmael's character; the second, however, is more ambiguous, depending on how the rabbis viewed archery. Be that as it may, the perplexing phrase gives rise to a negative interpretation.

The midrash ends with an interpretation of Genesis 21:21:

> "And he lived in the wilderness of Paran; and his mother took for him a wife from the land of Egypt." R. Isaac said, "Throw a stick in the air and it lands on its original spot. According to what is written, 'An Egyptian handmaiden, named Hagar' (Gen. 15:1), thus, 'And his mother took for him a wife from the land of Egypt.' "

R. Isaac makes a connection between Hagar's Egyptian heritage and the fact that she sought an Egyptian woman for her son. The reference may have been an attempt to cast a negative light on Ishmael, that is, to associate him with Egypt. Alternatively, it may be an interpretation based on another biblical verse. In other words, the textual factor here is the Egyptian identity of Hagar in Genesis 15:1. In this example, both factors may have played an equally prominent role.

The rabbinic portrayal of Ishmael in Genesis Rabbah, however, is not always neutral. In the following midrash, Gen. Rab. 62:5, Ishmael is referred to as "that wicked man," the only time he is described as such in amoraic literature. To be sure, even though he is not called *raša'*, wicked, elsewhere, some of the actions imputed to him are those of a wicked person. Yet, it is important to note that this depiction in amoraic literature is not prevalent. The fact that he is not called "wicked" is significant, particularly when we take into consideration the different treatment of Ishmael in sources of the period after the rise of Islam.

Expounding Genesis 25:12, "Now these are the generations of Ishmael, Abraham's son . . . ," the midrash reads:

> R. Hama bar 'Uqba and the rabbis once were sitting and discussing a difficulty: What is the reason Scripture records the generations of that wicked man here? When they saw R. Levi pass by, they said, "He is a master of traditions. Let us ask him." R. Levi in the name of R. Hama b. R. Hanina said, "It is to let you know how old your ancestor [Jacob] was when he was blessed by Isaac." Why does Scripture say, "And these are the years of the life of Ishmael" (Gen. 25:17)? Because he came from far away in the desert to bury (to honor) his father.

What then are we to make of this reference? Ishmael is called "that wicked man" but his behavior is praiseworthy. If we examine sources in the Babylonian Talmud, we find a similar phenomenon where a sage or biblical figure is described one way, while his actions are of a contrary nature.

BT. Qiddušin 81b tells a story of R. Hiyya b. Ashi, whose behavior was far from righteous. To begin with, he neglected his conjugal obligations and lusted after another woman, whom we soon discover is actually his wife in disguise. When she discloses the truth, he nonetheless feels that he has done wrong and thus fasts his entire life, an act frowned upon by rabbis who deemed such behavior extreme.[23]

It could be that the comment was added later to the text in order to counteract R. Hiyya's questionable actions. In the case of Gen. Rab. 62:5, the reference to Ishmael as "that wicked man" similarly seems to have been added to the text. Moreover, if we look at BT. Megillah 16b–17a and BT. Yebamot 64a, sources that also ask why Ishmael's years are counted, we discover no mention of "that wicked man." It is therefore reasonable to conclude that the comment was probably added at a later stage.[24]

Indeed, the reference to Ishmael as "that wicked man" is problematic, for not only does "that wicked man" return to bury his father after he has been banished, but Scripture refers to him as *"ben Abraham"* (son of Abraham). Moreover, the midrash itself gives us another impression. Here he is a loyal son who traveled from afar in order to honor his father. Once again, the relationship between Ishmael and Abraham is implicitly affirmed. Be that as it may, the continuation of Gen. Rab. 62:5 gives us another impression of Ishmael, one that characterizes Ishmael as wicked:

> "They dwelt from Havilah to Shur, which is opposite Egypt in the direction of Assyria; he settled [*nāpal*, 'fell'] over against all his people" (Gen. 25:18). Here the verb "fell" is used, whereas later on "dwelt"(*yiškon*) is used. Rather, during Abraham's lifetime, Ishmael "dwelt" but when our father Abraham died, he "fell." Before he stretched out his hand against the Temple, he "dwelt," but when he stretched out his hand against the Temple, he "fell." In this world, he "dwells," but in the world to come, "he falls."[25]

Whether Ishmael, the Ishmaelites, and Nebuchadnezzar are interchangeable in this midrash is debatable. In Gen. Rab. 45:9, however, on Genesis 16:12, "He shall be a wild ass of a man, his hand against everyone and everyone's hand against him; and he shall dwell opposite his kinsmen," Ishmael is more explicitly associated with Nebuchadnezzar:

> R. Yohanan and Resh Laqish: R. Yohanan said, "While most people grow up in a settled community, he grew up in the wilderness." Resh Laqish said, "A wild ass of a man literally means that while everyone plunders property, Ishmael plunders lives. '. . . his hand against everyone and everyone against him' (*kol bo*) means his hand and the hand of his dog (*kalbo*) are alike. Just as his dog ate carrion, so he ate carrion." R. Eleazar said, "When is it the case that 'his hand is against everyone and everyone's hand is against him'? When he comes concerning whom it is written, 'And into whose hand he has given, wherever you dwell, the sons of men, the beasts of the field, and the birds of the air, making you rule over them . . .' (Dan. 2:38). This is what is written, 'Of Kedar and of the kingdoms of Hazor, which Nebuchadnezzar [*n-ṣ-r*] conquered' (Jer. 49:28). His name is written Nebuchadrezzar (*reṣar*) because he gathered them up (*'āṣar*) in the desert and killed them. '. . . He shall dwell opposite his kinsmen'—here it is written 'dwell' and later it is 'fell'[The merit of his father is no longer Ishmael's safeguard] (Gen. 25:18). Rather, while Abraham was alive, Ishmael 'shall dwell' but when Abraham died, Ishmael 'fell.' Before he laid hands on the Temple, he 'shall dwell,' but when he laid his hand on the Temple, he 'fell.' In this world, 'he shall dwell,' in the world to come, 'he fell.' "[26]

This midrash exemplifies rabbinic punning. To begin with, the rabbis play with "everyone against him," *kol bo*, and his dog, *kalbo*. Furthermore, the rabbis make the association between "his hand against everyone's hand," *yado bakol ve-yad kol bo*, and the phrase "and into whose hand"—"*uvkol di*" of Daniel 2:38, which connects Nebuchadnezzar and Ishmael. The rabbis also play with Nebuchadnezzar's name in order to derive the verb *'āṣar*, "to gather," or "lock up."

In contrast to Resh Laqish's interpretation, which accuses Ishmael of murder, R. Yohanan's interpretation seems neutral. The discussion on Nebuchadnezzar seems to associate Ishmael, but not necessarily identify him, with Nebuchadnezzar, the destroyer of the first temple. This midrash is most unusual for we do not find this affiliation made between these figures anywhere else in rabbinic literature of this period, with the exception of PT. Taʿanit 4:5 (4:69b), which associates the Ishmaelites with Nebuchadnezzar. Since in this period of rabbinic literature Ishmael is not identified with a particular person, it seems unlikely to me that he is identified with Nebuchadnezzar. In both cases this reference to Nebuchadnezzar may be an analogue, exemplifying the contrast between "fell" and "dwelt."

According to Neusner, who analyses Gen. Rab. 45:9 as an extended metaphor of Israel as family, Ishmael, Esau, and Edom represent Rome, but both Nebuchadnezzar and Rome (Ishmael) will destroy the Temple. The ending of the midrash nevertheless gives Israel hope, for in the world to come the enemy will perish. He contends, "So the passage is read as both a literal statement and also as an effort to prefigure the history of Israel's suffering and redemption. Ishmael, standing now for Christian Rome, claims God's blessing, but Isaac gets it, as Jacob will take it from Esau."[27] To be sure, there is a great deal of merit in Neusner's notion that the analogy of family delineates the social entity of Israel, which therefore creates boundary markers setting others apart, in this instance Christian Rome from Jewish Israel, but as we will have occasion to see, this is not always the case in rabbinic sources. Gen. Rab. 45:9 is an exception. Prior to the rise of Islam, Ishmael is not discussed in midrashim with a future orientation, that is, in midrashim that envisage future events in light of a new world order. There are numerous examples of amoraic midrashim, apocalyptic in character, that treat Esau in such terms, but not Ishmael. It seems to me that Neusner's reading of this midrash is clever and correct, but this is a unique instance of the rabbinic use of Ishmael to refer to a specific Other.

Biblical figures at times represent real entities or concepts and other times do not. In Gen Rab. 45:9, a rare but plausible instance, Ishmael represents Rome—not necessarily Christian Rome. Each interpretation therefore must be examined first and foremost in light of scriptural textual irritants or narrative lacunae which afford the rabbis an opportunity to solve syntactic issues through wordplay, and also an opportunity to address theological, social, and political issues.

The preceding midrash highlights both the literary and historical aspects of rabbinic interpretation. Firstly, it is indicative of the tannaitic and amoraic resistance to stabilizing the meaning of words according to a system of symbolization, and is a reminder of the rabbinic penchant for multiple meanings and verbal maneuverings. Secondly, Gen. Rab. 45:9 exemplifies the ways in which the rabbis addressed, as Heinemann notes, "the burning issues of the day," and the ways in which their writings reflect a real engagement with historical events such as the destruction of the Temple, and Roman rule.

Amoraic and tannaitic compilations contain midrashim that degrade and disparage Ishmael, as well as those that evince an impartial attitude toward him. In general, the negative depictions, however, are not particularly vituperative. These depictions, in turn, vary according to the interpretive needs or extratextual concerns of the rabbis.

3

The Rabbis and Their Others

> And it is probably safe to say that among the groupings of people in every society are always some that distinguish people who are my people, or are more my people, from people who are not so much my people. The We-They difference, in some form, arranges the human elements on the universal stage.
>
> —Robert Redfield, *The Primitive World and Its Tranformations*

The idea that the Other is a creation of the subjective self and not a discrete, objectively existing entity has been the topic of several works in various fields and disciplines.[1] Indubitably, the study of the conception of Other in its myriad manifestations has contributed inordinately to our understanding of literature, society, culture, politics, and religion. And, here, too, as a conceptual framework, the Other offers insight into modes of rabbinic thought.

For the most part images of Ishmael, the children of Keturah, and Esau (when coupled with Ishmael) are neither violent nor vicious. This is not to say that all representations of non-Jews in early rabbinic literature are evenhanded.[2] But even these are mild compared to what one encounters in early medieval Jewish texts. In addition, what our observation offers, then, is an understanding of the ways in which the rabbis expressed the election of Israel. With the exception of their treatment of Esau, who signified Rome and then Christianity,[3] and whom they depict in harshly negative terms even in the earlier literature, the rabbis do not point to the inherent evil of a real other, but rather address the unique status of the Jewish people. That is, the focus is not on maligning the other nations, but on separating Israel from them. Differentiation, not denigration, defines the character of these rabbinic texts.

More to the point, the Other is used as the antipode of the self-conceived rabbinic notion of Israel. In these instances the Other is a means by which the rabbis establish self-identity. It would be misleading to approach these sources as if they were descriptive of real entities. Rather, by creating a contrast between Israel and the Other, the rabbis use such marginalized figures as Ishmael and the children of Keturah in order to make statements about Jewish identity in antiquity. As S. Stern rightly states: "The compression of the non-Jewish nations into a single, monolithic entity, the 'nations', serves the purpose of opposing a coherent—and equivalent—'other' to the single entity of 'Israel'. This results in a balanced contrast between self and other, upon which Jewish identity can be predicated."[4] He writes elsewhere, "It should . . . be noted that the 'nations' in rabbinic writings do not represent an observable reality 'out there', but rather a logical opposite to the identity of Israel, thus defined in rabbinic writings in purely self-referential terms."[5]

Indeed, Stern's detection of the interplay between Jacob and Esau as reflective of the dialectical conceptual contrast between Israel and the nations is highly appropriate in describing many midrashic texts, but while G. Cohen reads the historical background into the foreground, Stern ignores nuances that indeed indicate the extent to which the rabbis were aware of "the vicissitudes of historical change."[6]

> Furthermore, as R. Goldenberg observes: This notion that the name of an ethnic group can be specific and generic at the same time, indirectly reflects the ambiguity in the covenant . . . Israel as a nation could recognize the distinctive character of each of its neighbors, while Israel as cult community saw all other peoples as alike in their worship of false gods. In its turn this double meaning gave rise to a corresponding duality in later rabbinic thought: when it served their needs rabbis could distinguish very carefully between one foreign nation and another, but at other times the whole non-Jewish world was homogenized into "the gentiles," *ʾummot ha-ʿolam*, the *goyim*.[7]

Goldenberg is abundantly correct in arguing that the rabbis could think typologically and realistically equally well; among everyone, "everyone" has multiple Others.

To be sure, we cannot afford to make blanket statements that blind us to the rabbis' awareness of the world around them, and to the ways in which they dealt with real peoples and places. Therefore in order to understand how they lived in and made sense of the world in practical terms, we must delineate historical, social, ideological, and theological contexts and take into account real and imagined notions of self vis-à-vis real peoples and antipodal Others.

In what follows, we will look at how Ishmael is set apart from Isaac, the chosen son, and how the literary context, as well as theological and ideational considerations, illumines these midrashic sources; but looking ahead, let us keep in mind that later rabbinic compilations reflect a shift in the attitude toward Ishmael such that the Other is a real, distinct other.

One of the most prevalent ways in which the notion of Israel's election manifests itself is in the distinction, not rivalry, between Ishmael and Isaac. Only two midrashim pit the two against each other as rivals. As noted in the previous chapter, the issue of inheritance is one of the reasons given for Ishmael's expulsion in tannaitic sources. This is also found in Gen. Rab. 56:4, an amoraic source, but here, as a response to demonic prodding, the rivalry is explicit, at least from Isaac's point of view:

> "And Isaac said to Abraham his father, 'Father' " (Gen. 22:7). Samael[8] came to our father, Abraham, and said to him, "What is the reason your heart is despairing? Are you really going to slaughter the son given to you at the age of a hundred?" He said to him, "Indeed so." He [Samael] said to him, "If he tests you even more, will you be able to stand it?" "If a thing be put to you as a trial, will you be wearied?" (Job 4:2). He [Abraham] said to him, "Even more so." He [Samael] said to him, "Tomorrow he will say to you that you are a murderer and that you are culpable." He [Abraham] said to him, "Indeed so." When Samael saw that his efforts were of no avail, he went to Isaac. He said to him, "Oh son of an ill-fated mother, he is going to slaughter you." Isaac replied, "This is so." He said to him, "If so, all those lovely cloaks that your mother made will be the inheritance of Ishmael, the hated one of her house." If a word is not entirely effective, it enters in part, as it is written, "And Isaac said to his father Abraham, 'My father' " (Gen. 22:7). . . . It was so that Abraham should be filled with mercy for him.[9]

In an attempt to explain Isaac's response, "My father," the rabbis weave an elaborate narrative involving Samael, Abraham, and Isaac. After Samael unsuccessfully tries to dissuade Abraham from obeying God's command, he goes to Isaac who accepts his fate. When Samael, however, tells him that his inheritance will go to Ishmael, his resolve flags. Thus, he says, "My father" so that Abraham would reconsider and not carry through as planned.

It is not death that threatens Isaac, but rather the thought that Ishmael will inherit what is his. The midrash is not pejorative toward Ishmael, but it does tell us something about how Sarah felt about him. If the midrash wanted to disparage Ishmael, it would have said, "the hated one of your *father's* house."

Promoting the notion of sibling rivalry between Isaac and Ishmael, Gen. Rab. 55:4 is another midrash that relates the well-known debate between them:

> Isaac and Ishmael were arguing with one another. One said, "I am more beloved than you because I was circumcised when I was thirteen years old." The other said, "I am more beloved than you because I was circumcised on the eighth day." Ishmael said to him, "I am more beloved than you because I could have refused but did not." At that moment Isaac said, "Would that the Holy One, Blessed be He appear to me and tell me that He will cut off one of my limbs, I would not tarry!" The Holy One, Blessed be He said to him, "On account of your willingness to sacrifice yourself and not tarry"—Thus, "After these things, God put Abraham to the test" (Genesis 22:1).[10]

With the exception of Gen. Rab. 56:4 and Gen. Rab. 55:4, this rivalry is not found in tannaitic and amoraic literature. It is, however, found more frequently and emphatically in later midrashim where Ishmael is characterized as one who hates his brother.

The midrashim of the amoraic period instead contrast these siblings. For example, Gen. Rab. 46:2 explains why Abraham did not circumcise himself sooner, when for example, God spoke to him in Genesis 15: "Rather it was so Isaac would come out of a holy drop [of semen]. Let him be circumcised at the age of eighty-six when Ishmael was born." To this objection, R. Shimon b. Laqish offers a resolution: " '[God said] I will plant a cinnamon tree in the world.' Just as this cinnamon tree produces so long as you manure and hoe it, so too in the case of Abraham when his blood coagulates and his desires and passion wane.' " That is, Abraham bears fruit when he is "hoed"; when he is circumcised, he becomes potent.

In these midrashim, there is no indication whatsoever that Ishmael refers to a particular Other but rather to non-Jews in general. Gen. Rab. 47:5 also distinguishes between Ishmael and Isaac in terms of the covenant:

> God said, "No, but Sarah your wife shall bear you a son, and you shall call his name Isaac. I will establish my covenant with him as an everlasting covenant for his descendants after him. As for Ishmael, I have

heard you; behold, I will bless him and make him fruitful and multiply him exceedingly; he shall be the father of twelve princes, and I will make him a great nation" (Gen. 17:19–20). R. Yohanan said in the name of R. Yoshua b. Haninah, "This means that what applies to the son of the servant applies to the son of the mistress: Behold I will bless him refers to Isaac. I will make him fruitful refers to Isaac. Behold I will multiply him refers to Isaac. As for Ishmael, I have informed you of your blessing through an angel." R. Abba bar Kahana in the name of R. Birai said, "This means that what applies to the son of the mistress also applies to the son of the servant: I will bless him refers to Ishmael. I will make him fruitful refers to Ishmael. I will multiply him refers to Ishmael. All the more, I will establish my covenant with Isaac." R. Isaac said, "It is written, 'All these are from the twelve tribes of Israel' (Gen. 48:28). These are from the mistress of the household. But Ishmael established twelve tribes, did he not? They, however, are like 'vapors' (*neśî'îm*), (Prov. 25:14). [This is a play on the word for princes, *neśî'îm*. In other words, their power would be fleeting, meaningless]. But as to these tribes [of Isaac], it is written, 'Sworn are the staffs (tribes, *maṭōt*) of the word, selah'" (Hab 3:9). [*Šhebeṭ* and *maṭeh* (sing.) are synonyms that mean staff and tribe, thus compared to the tribes of Ishmael, these tribes would endure like a planted rod or staff.]

All three interpretations of Genesis 17:19–20 are an attempt to distinguish between Ishmael and Isaac. In the first case, everything that applies to Ishmael also applies to Isaac, vice versa in the second case. A *kol va-homer*, an a fortiori argument, drives the second instance. That is, if God will bless both sons, will make both of them fruitful, and will multiply both, then surely God will establish His covenant with Isaac, the son of Sarah and Abraham. In other words, the midrash assumes no parity between Isaac and Ishmael. On the contrary, if God treats them equally, that is, blessing them, making them fruitful, and multiplying them, when in fact they do not have the same status, then no doubt God, who will establish only one covenant, will establish it with Isaac.

Moreover, R. Isaac's comment qualitatively distinguishes between them. The word "princes" also means "vapors," as in the prooftext (Prov. 25:14), thus he describes the ephemeral nature of the rule of Ishmael's princes as opposed to the tribes of Isaac that are enduring, like planted rods. By treating Ishmael and Isaac differently, the aforementioned interpretations of Genesis 17:19–20 indicate that Israel's covenantal relationship sets it apart from the nations of the world.[11]

The following midrash, Gen. Rab.53:12, unequivocally states that Abraham's seed will be through Isaac:

> "And the matter was very displeasing to Abraham on account of his son. But God said to Abraham, Let it not be grievous in your sight. . . . For through Isaac shall your descendants be named," as it is written, "And he shut his eyes from looking upon evil" (Isa. 33:15). R. Yudan b. Shillum said, "Isaac is not written but rather '*through Isaac.*'" R. Azariah said in the name of Bar Hutah, "The *bet* denotes two, that is, one who admits the existence of two worlds will inherit both." R. Yudan b. Shalum[12] said, " 'It is written, Remember his marvelous works that he has done, the signs and judgments of his mouth' (Ps. 105:5). I have given a sign to one who proclaims [God's judgment]: therefore, whoever believes in the two worlds shall be called 'your seed,' and the one who rejects belief in the two worlds will not be called 'your seed' " [emphasis added].

The first part of this midrash is somewhat ambiguous. What was displeasing to Abraham? Assuming Ishmael was an idol worshiper, a fornicator, or shedder of blood, does the verse in Isaiah refer to Ishmael's treacherous behavior? Was the notion that Ishmael will inherit with Isaac displeasing? Another possible interpretation is that Isaiah 33:15, "And he shut his eyes from looking upon evil" refers to the expulsion of Ishmael, in which case the midrash does not condemn Ishmael, but rather reflects Abraham's anxiety in having to comply with Sarah's request.

The remainder of the section deals with the phrase "through Isaac." R. Yudan b. Shillum points out that the seed is not Isaac but *through* Isaac.[13] Using the numerical value of *bet* (two), R. Azariah derives that anyone admitting to the existence of this world and the world to come will inherit both, "therefore, whoever believes in the two worlds shall be called 'your seed,' and the one who rejects belief in the two worlds will not be called 'your seed.' "

Judah bar Shillum's comment serves as a buttress to R. Azariah's interpretation, which not only reads the people of Israel into "through Isaac," but specifies what constitutes Israel, namely believers in this world and the world to come. The explication of "through Isaac" gives rise to the occasion of expressing proper Jewish belief vis-à-vis sectarians, or it is simply an affirmation of rabbinc belief in the world to come. In other words, "through Isaac" metaphorically maintains the notion that Israel constitutes those who believe in the world to come; those who deny the world to come, Jewish or not, are simply excluded from "Israel." Neither R. Azariah nor R. Yudan b. Shillum explicitly distinguishes between the biblical Isaac and Ishmael, or even between the concept of Israel and Gentiles, although clearly an opposition is assumed—believers and unbelievers. That is to say, Ishmael alludes to anyone who does not believe in the world to come. Thus, while on the one hand the midrash adduces the covenantal primacy of Isaac, the second part of the midrash qualifies Isaac such that Isaac and Ishmael are metaphors for orthodox and unorthodox theological tenets.

Be that as it may, the sages juxtapose Ishmael, the unfit firstborn on the one hand, with Isaac, the chosen younger sibling on the other, yet elsewhere in the same compilation they present an alternative view of their relationship. Expounding Genesis 25:9, "And Isaac and Ishmael his sons buried him," the midrash reads: "It is now that the son of the bondmaid showed honor to the son of the mistress" (Gen. Rab. 62:3). Ishmael gives Isaac honor by giving him precedence, by accepting the relationship dictated by Sarah's wishes. As we noticed in the previous chapter, the statement "Esau and Jacob his sons buried him [Isaac]," in contrast, does not reverse the birth order. Perhaps this is a harbinger of the strife to follow between the two nations. After all, the Bible is explicit, "Esau hated Jacob" (Gen. 27:41), but nowhere do we learn of Ishmael's feelings toward Isaac and vice versa.[14]

Again, as noted in chapter 1, the two verses mentioning Isaac in connection with Beer-lahai-roi implicitly refer to the relationship between Ishmael and Isaac. Genesis 24:62 states, "Isaac came back from the vicinity of Beer-lahai-roi, for he was settled in the region of the Negev" and Genesis 25:11 states, "After the death of Abraham, God blessed his son Isaac. And Isaac settled near Beer-lahai-roi." Beer-lahai-roi, located in southern Palestine, is associated with the birth of Ishmael. So, in Genesis 24:62 why was Isaac coming from Beer-lahai-roi? The rabbis respond, "To fetch Hagar" (Gen. Rab. 60:14). Keturah, whom Abraham marries five verses later in 25:1, according to some rabbis is Hagar.[15] So, in other words, Isaac sought Hagar for his father. That the rabbis avoid explicitly associating Isaac with Ishmael in this instance is not surprising. To do so would undermine the larger enterprise of differentiating between Israel and non-Jews. Their reading of the biblical story, however, allows us to appreciate the nuances in the biblical text, but more importantly, for our purposes, it illustrates how both textual and extratextual factors are integrally related in the hermeneutical process. The biblical text lends itself to the interpretation that Isaac was in Beer-lahai-roi to fetch Hagar, but there is no indication in the text that Hagar and Keturah are the same person. Rather, the rabbinic importance placed on portraying Abraham as righteous, in that he brings

Hagar back from the desert and makes her his wife, may have given rise to this identification.

In our examination of these amoraic texts, we find the theme of distinguishing Isaac from Ishmael, the unfit firstborn. With the exception of Gen. Rab. 55:4 and 56:4 where Ishmael and Isaac argue, there is no active rivalry between them, nor is there uniformity in the rabbis' treatment of Ishmael. Thus, different textual and extratextual concerns yield various portrayals, such that in the case of Gen. Rab. 53:12, Ishmael represents unorthodox belief. While an irregularity in a biblical verse or a discrepancy between verses gives rise to an interpretation, the midrashic process is always made up of factors that exceed the bounds of the biblical text. How an irregularity or discrepancy is resolved has as much to do with the verse or verses as it does with the rabbis' weltanschauung, with their predilections and presuppositions. Extratextual factors are more discernible in some cases than in others and play a more significant role in the interpretation.

The diversity of ways in which the rabbis treat Ishmael leads us to conclude that they did not systematically set out to use Ishmael for one purpose. In many instances he, like Esau, and as we shall see, the children of Keturah, represents non-Jews in general. But he is also treated as a member of Abraham's household in a way that results in a positive or neutral depiction. Not until the emergence of Islam is he portrayed with greater consistency. We also found evidence that Ishmael is sometimes portrayed as a conceptualized Other in Amoraic literature, not specifically as an Arab. This is also the case with the children of Ishmael and the children of Keturah, but before examining the rabbinic treatment of these figures, let us look at the way in which the rabbis use Ishmael as an Other by pairing him with Esau.

The Pairing of Ishmael and Esau in Rabbinic Literature

By and large, Esau is referred to as "the wicked Esau" in Genesis Rabbah and throughout rabbinic literature. Interestingly, Ishmael is referred to as "wicked" only once in Genesis Rabbah, but as noted, even this one reference is problematic. As we will have occasion to see, negative depictions increase in the early medieval period. In Midrash Tanḥuma, for example, tentatively dated to the ninth century,[16] and in Exodus Rabbah,[17] dated to the tenth, Ishmael's behavior is referred to as "wicked" and his descendants are maligned.

It also bears mentioning that the use of Ishmael as a Jewish name was common in the tannaitic and amoraic periods, but fell into disuse some time after the rise of Islam. This is not the case with Esau, whose name became for the most part synonymous with Rome[18] and, according to rabbinic sources, was never used as a Jewish proper name.[19]

Nevertheless, the biblical narratives dealing with Ishmael and Esau have parallel features. Both are firstborn sons loved by their fathers, yet both are ostracized. Both belong to the family, yet do not partake fully in the covenant. Both are cast out. Their paths intersect and their irredeemable fates meet when Esau marries Ishmael's daughter Mahalath.

Yet, the differences in the biblical narratives make it difficult for the rabbis to treat Esau and Ishmael in an unvaried manner. In the Bible, Esau was destined before his birth, as the progenitor of a separate people, to serve his younger brother—to struggle with his kindred. Ishmael, although a less colorful biblical character, had a less defined destiny vis-à-vis his brother. This being the case, the rabbis used Esau to give more definition to Ishmael, the ambiguous Other. As a result, in amoraic midrashim both are often paired. This rabbinic technique served a number of different purposes, namely, to depict the Other as unrighteous, to assert Israel's chosen status, and to maintain the marginalization of Ishmael and Esau and, in turn, other peoples.

The rabbis are keenly aware of Ishmael's and Esau's position as the rejected firstborn. And because they are the sons of two of the Patriarchs, Abraham and Isaac, they are of special concern to the rabbis. The figure of Esau, as the preponderance of rabbinic evidence demonstrates, became the symbol of Rome.[20] In his work on the development of the identification of Rome with Edom, Gershon Cohen writes: "By such midrashic equation, Rome was identified with the Biblical Edom, and every name connected in Scripture with Esau was applied to the city of Romulus and the empire of the Caesars."[21] As amply documented earlier, however, Ishmael in early rabbinic literature is neither a prototype nor an entirely negative character. Moreover, while the figure of Esau throughout rabbinic literature, with the exception of some tannaitic and amoraic material,[22] symbolizes Rome or is portrayed as Jacob's nemesis, the elusive figure of Ishmael is multivalent.

Several tannaitic midrashim are based on the biblical notion that Israel is the chosen people, and therefore both Esau and Ishmael are depicted as unworthy issue. In the following examples, Ishmael and Esau are depicted as the unfit issue of Abraham and Isaac and their descendants are the peoples who initially reject the Torah before God offers it to the Israelites.[23] In Sifre Deuteronomy on Deut. 32:9, Ha'azinu 312[24] we read:

> "For the LORD's portion is his people, [Jacob is the lot of his inheritance]" (Deut. 32:9). It may be compared to a king who had a field

> and gave it to tenants.[25] The tenants began to rob it [of the produce of the field][26] so he took it from them and gave it to their children and they became wickeder than the previous. He gave it to their children's children but they became wickeder than the previous. A son was born to him and he said to them, "Get out of what is mine. It is impossible for you to be in it. Give me my portion so I will recognize it." So when Abraham our father came into the world something unfit[27] came from him—Ishmael and all the children of Keturah. Isaac came into the world and something unfit came from him—Esau and all the chieftains of Edom. They became wickeder than the previous ones. When Jacob came into the world nothing unfit came from him, rather all his children were proper when they were born, as it is said, "And Jacob was a perfect man dwelling in tents" (Gen. 25:27). When will the LORD recognize his share? From Jacob, as it is said, "For the LORD's portion is his people, Jacob his own allotment" (Deut. 32:9).[28]

The midrash asks, why does scripture say "Speak to the children of Israel" and not the children of Abraham or Isaac? Only Jacob's children deserve unprecedented recognition; they merit God's direct commandments because of their own merits and because of their father's merits:[29] "Jacob was fearful all his days and said, 'Woe is me, perhaps something unfit will come out from me as it came out from my fathers. . . . From Abraham came Ishmael. From Isaac came Esau but from me nothing unfit will come forth as came forth from my fathers and thus it is said, 'And Jacob vowed a vow, saying . . . ' " This notion that both Abraham and Isaac produced blemished offspring is fairly common in rabbinic literature of the amoraic period.

So, too, in another tannaitic source, Sifre Deuteronomy 343 on Deuteronomy 33:2, "The LORD came from Sinai," we read:

> When the Holy One, Blessed be He is about to exact punishment from Seir, he will shake the entire world with its inhabitants just as he shook it with the giving of the Torah. . . . The matter may be compared to a king who wanted to give a gift to one of his children but the king was afraid on account of his brothers, his friends and his relatives. What did the son do? He stood and dolled himself up and cut his hair. The king said to him, "To you, I am giving you a gift." Thus, when Abraham our father came into the world, something unfit came from him, Ishmael and the sons of Keturah. They became more evil than the previous ones. And when Isaac came, something unfit came from him, Esau and all the chieftains of Edom. They became more

> evil than the previous ones. When Jacob came, nothing unfit came from him, but rather all the children born to him were perfect, as it is said, "And Jacob was a perfect man dwelling in tents" (Gen. 25:26). The Holy One, Blessed be He said to him, "I am giving the Torah to you," as it is said, "The LORD came from Sinai; he rose upon them from Seir."

Israel is set apart from all the unfit, unworthy issue of Abraham and Isaac because *it* chose to set itself apart. The king wanted to give something special to one son, but did not until the son set himself apart. So, too, God gave the Torah to Israel when it set itself apart through righteous behavior.

The distinction between Jacob's sons and Ishmael and Esau is also found in a baraita in BT. Taʿanit 10b:

> Our rabbis taught: Whoever has fasted over distress and it passed, or for a sick person, and the person recovered, one should still complete the fast. If one goes from a place where they do not fast, to a place where they fast, one should fast with them; from a place where they fast to a place where they do not fast, one should complete the fast. If one forgot and ate and drank, let the person not show himself in public nor should he indulge in delicacies, as it is written, "And Jacob said to his sons, 'Why do you show yourselves?'" (Gen. 42:1). Jacob said to his sons, "When you are sated, do not show yourselves in front of Esau and in front of Ishmael so that they will not envy you."

Esau and Ishmael, who represent non-Israel,[30] are set apart from the children of Jacob who are sated, literally and metaphorically. Jacob reprimands his sons for their haughtiness, and prescribes humility, or at least an attitude that does not call attention to "Israel's" good fortune, whether in material or spiritual terms.

Below are more examples found in the Babylonian Talmud, namely in BT. Šabbat 145b and BT. Pesaḥim 56a and 119b, of setting Israel apart from the other nations. In BT. Šabbat 145b we read the following:

> Rav Yosef repeated (a tannaitic statement): "Why do idol worshippers stink? Because they did not stand on Mount Sinai. For when the serpent came to Eve, he put a foul smell into her. Israel, who stood at Mount Sinai, their stench ceased, but the idol worshippers who did not stand on Mount Sinai, their stench did not cease." R. Aha son of Raba asked R. Ashi, "What about converts?" He said to him, "Though they were not present, their stars were present, as it is written, '[Neither with you only do I make this covenant and this oath],

> but with him who stands here with us this day before the Lord our God, and also with him who is not here with us this day'" (Deut. 29:14). He differs with R. Abba b. Kahana, for R. Abba b. Kahana said, "Until three generations a foul odor did not cease from our Fathers: Abraham produced Ishmael, Isaac produced Esau and Jacob produced twelve tribes in whom there was no taint."

R. Abba says the stench ceased after Jacob. The others say it was only after Sinai.

A similar notion is found in BT. Pesaḥim 56a:

> R. Shimon b. Laqish said: "And Jacob called to his sons and said, 'Come together that I may tell you [what is to befall you in days to come]' (Gen. 49:1). Jacob wanted to reveal to his sons the end of days, when the Shekhina left him. He said, 'Perhaps, God forbid, there is among my children one unfit like Abraham from whom came out Ishmael and my father Isaac from whom came out Esau.' His children said to him, 'Hear O Israel, the LORD our God is one.' They said, 'Just as there is only one in your heart, so there is in our heart only One.' At that moment, our father Jacob opened his mouth and said, 'Blessed be the name of His glorious kingdom forever and ever.'"[31]

As in Sifre Deuteronomy, Ha'azinu 312, and Sifre Deuteronomy 343, this midrash deals with the unfit status of Ishmael and Esau, that is, the illegitimacy of all except Israel. BT. Pesaḥim 119b reiterates this notion:

> R. ʿAvira expounded, sometimes stating it in R. Ammi's name, sometimes in the name of R. Assi: "What is the meaning of the scriptural verse, 'And the child grew and was weaned?' In the future the Holy One, Blessed be He will make a banquet for the righteous on the day He manifests His love to the seed of Isaac. After they have eaten and drunk, they will give the cup of Blessing [the cup of wine used for grace after meals] to Abraham our father and he will say to them, 'I cannot say Grace because Ishmael came from me.' He will say to Isaac, 'Take [the cup] and say Grace.' He will say to them, I cannot say Grace because Esau came from me.' He will say to Jacob, 'Take [the cup] and say Grace.' He will say to them, 'I cannot say Grace because I married two sisters in their lifetimes and the Torah was destined to forbid me to do so.' . . . He (Joshua) will say to David, 'Take [the cup] and say Grace.' He will say to them, 'It is fitting for me to say Grace, as it is written, I will lift up the cup of salvation and call upon the name of the LORD'" (Ps. 116:13).[32]

In this midrash, even Jacob is not worthy to say Grace, for he transgressed Torah by marrying both Leah and Rachel; unlike Jacob, Abraham and Isaac are disqualified because of their progeny, not because of transgressing Torah. Furthermore, Jacob's disqualification does not affect his children. That is to say, even though in this midrash Jacob himself is declared ineligible, his children, who are mentioned later in the midrash, are nonetheless untainted. It is worth noting that the category of "unfit" is vague, ripe for a polemic that we do not find in these texts. Since, however, we want to avoid *argumenta ex silentio*, we must pay attention to the ways in which Other is described, and here it seems that the depiction of non-Israel is nothing short of an attempt to define abstractly the concept of Israel as ritually proper, ideal.

By forging a close connection with Esau, the rabbis justified condemnation of Ishmael in order to distinguish him from Isaac. Gen. Rab. 67:13 reads as follows:

> "And Esau saw that the daughters of Canaan pleased not Isaac his father, so Esau went unto Ishmael and took Mahalath" (Gen. 28:9). R. Yoshua b. Levi said: "He [Esau] made up his mind to become converted [possibly to reform]. She is called Mahalath because the Holy One, blessed be He forgave (*māḥal*) him his transgressions. [She is also called] Basemath—[the name she is called in Gen. 36:3] [meaning] that his character grew better [*nitbaśâh*, to grow better, improve]." [This is a play on her name *bāśmat*.] R. Eleazar said to him: "Had he divorced his first wives, you would have spoken well, however Scripture says, 'Unto the wives he had,' that is, adding grief to grief [derived from a play on her name, Mahalath; *māḥalâh* means sickness], adding to a house already full." R. Yudan quoted in R. Aibu's name: "'In the transgression of the lips is a snare to the evil man, but the righteous comes out of trouble' (Prov. 12:13). Through the revolt of Esau and Ishmael against the Holy One blessed be He, there came a stumbling-block to them. 'But the righteous come out of trouble' refers to Jacob, as Scripture says, 'And Jacob went out from Beer-sheba'" (Gen. 28:10).

In its biblical context, Genesis 28:8 is Esau's attempt to make amends for the past. It is also his attempt to propitiate his father. Since Jacob obeyed his parents and went to Paddan-Aram to seek a wife, Esau went to his father's kindred. Genesis 28:9 illustrates Esau's desire to gain his parents' favor, or at least his father's, but of course by marrying Ishmael's daughter he marries out.

Gen. Rab. 67:13 casts aspersions on his character, notwithstanding R. Yehoshua ben Levi's positive play on the name Mahalath. His reading explicity recognizes Esau's action as well-intentioned. Other rabbis offer an alternative view. R. Eleazar also puns but at the cost of Esau's character: "'Unto the wives he had,' that is, adding grief to grief, adding to a house already full." The implication may be that a house full of women is undesirable; it is a life of grief. Or, simply, the more people one must support, the more misery one must endure. In either case, R. Eleazar interprets Esau's action negatively. Finally, the midrash ends with a depiction not only of Esau but of Ishmael revolting. R. Yudan in R. Aibu's name states: "Through the revolt of Esau and Ishmael against the Holy One blessed be He, there came a stumbling-block to them. 'But the righteous come out (*vayyēṣē*ʾ) of trouble' refers to Jacob, as Scripture says, 'And Jacob went out (*vayyēṣē*ʾ) from Beer-sheba.'" [*Vayyēṣē*ʾ, went out, is the philological lynchpin of this intertextual interpretation and Beer-sheba may be associated with Ishmael (Genesis 21:14)]. Esau and Ishmael are deemed unrighteous in relation to Jacob.

Genesis 28:9 establishes a palpable connection between Ishmael and Esau, thus facilitating the rabbis' juxtaposition of Ishmael and Esau—the unrighteous, the marginalized—and Jacob—the righteous, the chosen. The reference to Ishmael in the midrash is not surprising since he is mentioned in the verse. The manner of reference, however, is striking. Esau adds grief to grief because he did not divorce his first wives. Had he done so, the midrash maintains, he would have received God's forgiveness. In other words, he adds grief for taking another wife but not for going to Ishmael. Esau's character is not diminished because he went to Ishmael. Moreover, the verse, providing the rabbis with ample fodder, is not only used to take a major swipe at Esau's character, but it also gives the rabbis an occasion to indict Ishmael and to associate him with Esau. That is to say, the end of the midrash that decries Esau as well as Ishmael is one illustration of how both together are used in setting Israel apart from the Other.

In BT. Baba Qamma 92b, where Esau and Ishmael are explicitly paired, Ishmael and Esau are equally "men of low character":

> Rava said to Rabbah b. Mari: "From where can the popular saying, 'A bad palm will usually make its way to a grove of barren trees' be derived?" He said: "This matter was written in the Torah, repeated in the Prophets, a third time in the Writings and also learned in the Mishnah and taught in a Baraitha. It is written in the Torah, 'And Esau went to Ishmael' (Gen. 28:9), repeated in the Prophets, as it is

> written, 'Men of low character gathered about Jephthah and went out raiding with him' (Jud. 11:3), and a third time in the Writings, as it is written, 'Every bird dwells near its kind and people near their equal' " (Ecclesiasticus 13:15).[33]

This is also the case in Gen. Rab. 71:3:

> "And Leah conceived and bore a son and she named him Reuben" (Gen. 29:32). Said R. Yose b. Haninah, "There are four categories for names: First, there are those who have pleasant names but their deeds are repulsive. Second, there are those who have ugly names and their deeds are nice. Third, there are those who have nasty names and their deeds are also nasty. Fourth, there are those whose names are nice and their deeds are nice. Esau is an example of the first, that is, of those who have nice names but whose deeds are nasty. His name means 'he does' [*ʿośeh*] but he does not do. Ishmael is also an example of the first category. His name implies 'he obeys' [*yišmaʿ*] but he did not."[34]

In both examples, they are grouped together because they are evil men. They belong together because their deeds are nasty, despite the positive connotations of their names.

As we have seen, there are several midrashim like Gen. Rab. 66:4 that pair Ishmael and Esau in order to depict the chosen line of Jacob. Yet at the same time it should be noted that contrasts are made. In Gen. Rab. 67:8, Esau wants to use his status as Ishmael's son-in-law in order to have Ishmael kill Jacob:

> "Let the days of mourning for my father be at hand [and I will kill my brother]" (Gen. 27:41). . . . The rabbis said, He [Esau] said, "If I kill him [Jacob] Shem and Eber will sit in judgment of me and say, 'Why did you kill your brother?' Rather, I will go and become Ishmael's son-in-law and he [Ishmael] will come and dispute the birthright [for his daughter's sake] and kill him. And, I will stand against him as a *go'el ha-dam* [a blood kinsman, one who is legally entitled to take vengeance for the life of a relative], and kill him and inherit two families," as it is written, "Because you have said, 'These two nations and these two countries shall be mine, and we shall possess it' " (Ezek. 35:10).[35]

To begin with, the midrash offers no indication that Ishmael wanted to cooperate with Esau. Furthermore, in this midrash, Esau schemes to gain the inheritance not only of Jacob but also of Ishmael. He plans to kill Jacob by creating familial ties with Ishmael that would give Ishmael the right to kill Jacob. Not satisfied with Jacob's inheritance, Esau seeks Ishmael's. Like Jacob, Ishmael is the target of Esau's greed.

Another example of this distinction is found in BT. Baba Batra 16b, which discusses Genesis 24:1, "And the LORD blessed Abraham in all things":

> Another interpretation: Ishmael repented while he was still alive. R. Yohanan said: "That wicked one [Esau] committed five sins on that day. He had sex with an engaged woman, he committed a murder, he denied God, he denied the resurrection of the dead and he spurned his birthright.' "[36] . . . How do we know that Ishmael repented while Abraham was still alive? It is like the time when Rabina and R. Hama b. Buzi were sitting in the presence of Rava who was dozing. Rabina said to R. Hama b. Buzi, "Is it true that they say all deaths that are described with the term *geviʿah* [expired] are deaths of the righteous?" He said to him: "Yes." "But what about the generation of the flood?" He said to him, "I said both *geviʿah* and *ʾasefah* [gathered]." "But what about Ishmael, about whom it is written both *geviʿah* and *ʾasefah*?" [The two words are used in Gen. 25:17: "Then he breathed his last (*vayyigvaʿ*) and died, and was gathered (*vayyēʾasep*) to his kin."] Rava woke up and said to them, "Children, thus said R. Yohanan: 'Ishmael repented during his father's lifetime,' as it is written, 'And Isaac and Ishmael his sons buried him' (Gen. 25:9). Why does it say that? Ishmael was older than Isaac. Why does it mention Isaac before him?[37] Perhaps it is arranged according to their wisdom. If that were so, then why is "And Esau and Jacob his sons buried him" (Gen. 35:29) not arranged according to their wisdom? Rather, since it, namely Scripture, places him [Isaac] first, he let Isaac precede him. Derive from this that he repented in Abraham's lifetime."[38]

Whereas R. Yohanan refutes the interpretation that Esau did not rebel in Abraham's lifetime by enumerating five egregious acts he committed in one day, he, however, supports the interpretation that Ishmael repented while Abraham was still alive by referring to Genesis 25:9.

In regard to the question as to how Abraham was blessed, Tosefta Qiddušin 5:17, a tannaitic source, gives the much disputed interpretation that Esau did not rebel, whereas Gen. Rab. 59:7 makes no mention of this claim, and perhaps deliberately omits it. Why does Gen. Rab. 59:7 not include this interpretation? Moreover, why does the Bavli not only endorse the idea of Esau's rebellion but also indicts Esau of sacrilegious behavior? Very likely, the rabbinic identification of Esau as Rome was not prevalent during the time the Tosefta was compiled or when the particular statement was authored.[39]

Esau as Real Other

> Bare Your holy arm
> and draw near the time of salvation.
> Avenge the blood of Your servants
> from the wicked nation.
> For the time of Salvation is far from us,
> and there is no end to the days of wickedness.
> Repel the Red One in the nethermost shadow
> and establish for us the seven shepherds.
>
> Sixth Stanza of "Maoz Tzur"
> ("O Mighty Stronghold")

In refuting assertions that the identification of Rome with Esau and Edom was made in the latter part of the first or early part of the second century in the book of IV Ezra, an apocalyptic work composed around the end of the first century, G. Cohen remarks:

> Actually, it is only from the middle of the second century that we can discern the conversion of what may have been but one midrash among many—in any event, of a restricted apocalyptic circle—into a popular and explicit symbolism.
>
> As far as I can determine, the first Rabbi to have clearly identified Rome with Esau and Edom was none other than Rabbi Akiba ben Joseph. He, it would appear, was the one who explained that the verse, "The voice is the voice of Jacob, but the hands are the hands of Esau" (Gen. 27:22) was illustrated by the *anguished cry* of Jacob because of what the hands of Esau had done to him. The meaning of Esau is here clear and unequivocal.[40]

Cohen continues: "Once this identification had been made and accepted, all the classical associations, biblical as well as rabbinic, connected with the name Esau and his descendants could come into play in connection with Rome." Notwithstanding a few ad hoc concessions expressing appreciation of imperial Rome, "no possible hint in Scripture with reference to the contemporary situation was left uninterpreted."[41]

To be sure, Cohen's argument is convincing. The evidence, however, suggests that the identification of Rome with Esau and Edom did not play itself out everywhere,[42] particularly in tannaitic literature. What, for example, does one make of PT. Bikkurim 3:3 where one interpretation of Esau's betrothal to Mahalath is that his sins were forgiven? Indeed one is hard pressed to find Rome in this example:

> R. Zeʿeira . . . just as in the case of a convert, they forgive him all his sins, so too in the case of a sage who is appointed [a public official], they forgive him all his sins. A groom: Esau went to Ishmael and took Mahalath, the daughter of Ishmael (Gen. 28:9). Is her name Mahalath? Was not her name Basemath? (Gen. 36:3). Rather, all his sins were forgiven (*nimḥalû*).

In this context, the Palestinian Talmud, unlike Gen. Rab. 67:13 where R. Eleazar and R. Yudan offer differing opinions, is untroubled by the possibility that Esau was forgiven.

In any case, the typological development of Esau in the amoraic period may therefore shed light on R. Yohanan's comment on the five offenses committed by "that wicked one," Esau. If Cohen is correct about R. Aqiba being the first to identify Esau with Rome, then the association may have originated in the middle of the second century but it may not have become widespread until the amoraic period. At the same time, it should be noted that Cohen was either unaware of or unconcerned with the problem of attributions.[43] Thus, it may very well have been a latter statement attributed to R. Aqiba in order to invest it with greater authority. Furthermore, even the amoraic sources are replete with midrashim that adduce the varied ways in which Esau figures into rabbinic literature.

Some observations: Many sages were acutely aware of the differences between Ishmael and Esau and therefore, while they sometimes pair these marginalized men, in other contexts they highlighted differences. Whereas Esau was relegated to the role of "the wicked one," Ishmael was not envisaged as such. Yet at the same time, attuned to the parallels in the narratives of Ishmael and Esau, the rabbis often associate them as a means of representing the Other. In an effort to maintain the Jewish people's exclusive status as God's chosen, rabbinic literature of the tannaitic and, to a greater degree, of the amoraic period reiterates the marginalized status of Ishmael and Esau. This marginalization is extended to the Ishmaelites and the children of Keturah.

Ishmael, the Ishmaelites, and the Children of Keturah

As we now begin our examination of texts pertaining to Abraham's other marginalized descendants—the Ishmaelites and the children of Keturah—we will have occasion to see that the literature of the amoraic period, in works such as Genesis Rabbah, Leviticus Rabbah, Lamentations Rabbah, and the Palestinian and Babylonian Talmuds,[44] there are more references to Ishmael, the children of Ishmael, and the children of Keturah. Nothing in the text, however, indicates that these figures represent Christians or any other contemporary group. As I will show in my detailed discussion of the midrashim that follow, they almost always refer to the Other generally rather than specifically to peoples or groups.

That there are more statements in amoraic literature about these figures than in tannaitic corpora may be attributed to the mere fact that there is more amoraic material, or that these midrashim are aggadic and are likely to be found in aggadic compilations. It could be argued that the nature of tannaitic sources, with their emphasis on halakha, on expounding rabbinic law, may have made it impossible for the rabbis to deal with issues that manifest themselves in amoraic texts. This line of thinking is based on a fallacious assumption that the type of discrete units contained in tannaitic and amoraic literature do not overlap. On the contrary, tannaitic sources contain a great deal of aggadah and amoraic sources contain halakha.[45] Furthermore, despite literary differences they share similar themes and concepts such as the notion that Israel, as God's chosen people, is set apart from the other nations.

Even if we were to concede that tannaitic and amoraic corpora are characteristically different, that each ostensibly deals with different subjects, and when on occasion they deal with the same issues they do so differently, we must ask ourselves, what, if anything, can we learn from the difference? Claiming status as the chosen people, for example, seems at first glance to loom larger in the amoraic period,[46] at a time when Christianity made a similar claim.[47] Is this quantitative comparison significant? In this case, I argue in the negative, but this is not necessarily so in all instances.

As I will discuss later in the chapter, Christian self-understanding as *Verus* Israel, as well as similar claims of other religious splinter groups, most likely made less of an impact on the development of rabbinic portrayals of marginalized biblical characters than otherwise assumed. These biblical figures do not represent Christians, Samaritans, and gnostics per se.[48] In other words, the need to identify Judaism apart from other groups is found in tannaitic literature, in fact in nearly all Jewish literature, and does not seem to have arisen from specific theological or philosophical claims made by nonrabbinic groups such as the Samaritans or gnostics.[49]

Indeed, the only qualitative difference is the use of Esau in amoraic texts to represent Rome, and when and how to differentiate between when Esau alludes to Rome, Christianity, or Christian Rome is highly problematic.[50] It is therefore misguided to read a historical referent behind such figures as Ishmael, the Ishmaelites, and the children of Keturah. The rabbis, for example, recognize the status of Keturah's children as the children of Abraham, but by the same token, they treat Isaac preferentially, for to treat them equally would attenuate Israel's chosenness, and thus challenge the fundamental thrust not only of the biblical narrative at hand, but also the metanarrative of the Jewish people. This does not mean that they represent a specific Other. In order to understand the rabbinic hermeneutical process of addressing current events and circumstances through biblical verses, themes, and narratives, we therefore must keep in mind that their use of biblical figures to define Israel vis-à-vis a conceptualized Other is not the same as using these figures to represent reality, although of course the conceptualization is based on real or desired perceptions of self.

As in the case of Ishmael and Esau, various exegetical and theological concerns, such as the need to emphasize Israel's exclusive relationship to God, generate the midrashim in Genesis Rabbah on the Ishmaelites and the children of Keturah who are juxtaposed with the righteous children of Israel. We, however, find few examples in which Ishmael and the Ishmaelites, terms often used interchangeably, are explicitly identified as Arabs. In other words, although there are examples where they have been identified as Arabs, the identification is not widespread.

That this association with a specific group of people was not pervasive is indeed striking. When Ishmael is identified as an Arab, it is always in neutral contexts, whereas the association of Ishmaelites as Arabs is at times negative. Nonetheless, like Ishmael, for the most part the Ishmaelites and the children of Keturah also serve to represent non-Jews. We will therefore look at the factors contributing to this portrayal and we will examine the extent to which rabbinic literature identifies Ishmael and the Ishmaelites as Arabs. Most often, they are depicted as marginalized people who have a connection to Abraham but nevertheless are excluded from Israel. In such instances, particularly in amoraic literature, the rabbis use these figures not to represent Arabs but rather to define themselves over and against an imagined Other.[51]

The Arab Descendants of Ishmael

Let us begin by examining portrayals of Ishmaelites as a distinct group—Arabs. According to the scholarly consensus, the earliest datable occurrence of the term "Arab" is an Assyrian inscription of the ninth century, BCE, and although, as Retsö warns, the designation is eventually associated with Ishmaelites in the Hellenistic period, we should avoid attributing "*ohne weiteres* . . . the ideas of later centuries to ethnic conditions in Assyrian, Chaldean and Achaemenid times."[52]

Biblical references to Arabs seem to imply a collectivity much like "Israel." Moreover the designation adduces a sense of peoplehood and not a geographic entity,[53] although there is no biblical genealogy for Arabs. They are nonetheless referred to in the Bible, as in Isaiah 13:20 and Jeremiah 3:2, which admonishes the promiscuous Judahites for their ravenous harlotry: "Look up to the bare heights, and see: Where have they not lain with you? You waited for them on the roadside, like an Arab[54] in the wilderness." We also know of an individual Arab, Geshem (Neh. 2:19; 4:7), Nehemiah's longstanding enemy; there is also mention of several Arabian regions (Jer. 25:24ff), such as Dedan, Tema, Buz, Sheba, and Midian. According to Montgomery, the genealogical list of Abraham's descendants with Keturah in Genesis 25 is "closely affiliated with Arabian groups."[55]

The Ishmael-Arab identity, however, is not mentioned in extrabiblical sources of the biblical period, nor does the Bible itself offer information concerning the relationship between the Arabs and Ishmaelites. In I. Eph'al's seminal article, "'Ishmael' and 'Arab(s)': A Transformation of Ethnological Terms," he demonstrates that the Ishmaelite-Arab identity has no historical basis, but rather is based on the ethnological midrash in Genesis 25 that links the sons of Ishmael with tribes known as "Arabs" in Assyrian sources. "But since it existed in the Bible," Eph'al writes, "the idea of such an association became established in Jewish tradition and consequently, among those in non-Jewish circles which in some way drew upon Jewish traditions."[56] Furthermore, F. Millar contends, it was not until the first century BCE that the Greco-Roman categorization and identification of Arabs as a distinct people took place.[57]

To be sure, in rabbinic literature, especially in both Talmuds,[58] we find instances where the Ishmaelites are depicted as a distinct people with particular attributes and customs. Their association with thievery, for example, is found in PT. Ta'anit 3:4 (15a):

> Said R. Yehosha b. Yair in the name of R. Pinchas b. Yair: "The Holy One, Blessed be He created three things which He regrets having created. And they are: Chaldeans, Ishmaelites and the evil inclination. . . . Ishmaelites [according to the following verse]: 'Robbers live untroubled in their tents, and those who provoke God are secure, those whom God's hands have produced' " (Job 12:6).[59]

This characterization of the Ishmaelites as robbers is found in an earlier source, Sifre, Zot Ha-Berakhah 343, and in fact in all versions of God's giving of the Torah to the nations. In all instances, the Ishmaelites refuse the Torah either because their father was a robber or because they are destined to steal.

In some instances, the Ishmaelites are specifically identified as Arabs. The ethnic identification of the Ishmaelites as Arabs is alluded to in Sifre, Zot Ha-Berakhah 343:

> When the Holy One, Blessed be He appeared in order to give Israel the Torah, he did not speak to them in one language but rather in four languages, as it is said, "And he said, The LORD came from Sinai"—this refers to the Hebrew language. "And he rose upon them from Seir" refers to the Roman language. "He appeared from Mount Paran" refers to the Arabic language. "And he came from holy multitudes" refers to the Aramaic language.

The mention of Mount Paran in this context is a telltale reference to Ishmael, who in Genesis 21:21 dwells in the wilderness of Paran, and the Arabic language is very significant, for this is possibly one of the earliest extant rabbinic references to Ishmael's Arab ethnicity.[60] Another early rabbinic source is Mekhilta Beshallah 5:

> R. Tarfon and the elders were sitting in the shade of a dove-house in Yabneh and they discussed the following verse: "[. . . behold, a caravan of Ishmaelites came from Gilead,] with their camels bearing spicery, balm and ladanum" (Gen. 37:25). This is to make known how very much the merit of the righteous is to help them. For if this beloved friend [referring to Joseph] had to go down with the Arabs, would they not have killed him with the smell of the camels and *ʿiṭrān* [tar residue; a sort of resin used for lighting, which whether extinguished or not gives off a foul odor]?[61] But God arranged it for him that there would be sacks full of spices and of good smelling balms so that he would not die from the smell of the camels and the smell of *ʿiṭrān*.[62]

The context of this midrash is the sale of Joseph by his brothers to the Ishmaelites. That the midrash indicates Arabs and not Ishmaelites leads one to conclude that the Ishmaelites were identified as Arabs.

Consider, too, Targum Onkelos, putatively dated to the third century CE.[63] This Aramaic translation of Genesis 37:25ff also does not mention Ishmaelites but rather Arabs.

The following is especially noteworthy for it is the earliest rabbinic mention of Ishmael as the progenitor of the Arabs. In Gen. Rab. 53:14, R. Shimon's interpretation of "where he is" (Gen. 21:17) alludes to the Ishmaelites who seem to represent Arabians. R. Simon said:

> The ministering angels jumped to prosecute him. They said before the Holy One, Blessed be He, "Master of the universe, will you provide a well for the man who is destined to destroy your children with thirst?" He said to them, "What is he now?" They replied, " A righteous man." He said to them, "I judge someone only where he is at the moment."[64]

The ministering angels find Ishmael's actions prosecutable even though nowhere does the Bible refer to an attempt by Ishmael to destroy the children of Israel with thirst.[65] R. Shimon's interpretation as in T. Soṭah 6:6 serves as an alternative,[66] a less accusatory interpretation of Ishmael's character.[67]

The reference, however, assumes knowledge of an idea recorded in a midrash found in PT. Taʿanit 4:5 that refers to the Ishmaelites. PT. Taʿanit 4:5 (4: 69b) reads as follows:

> R. Yohanan said: "Eighty thousand apprentice priests fled to the army of Nebuchadnezzar and they [went] to the Ishmaelites. They said to them, 'Give us something to drink for we are thirsty.' They brought them salty things and skins [bottles] that were blown up with air. They said to them, 'Eat and drink.' When one of them opened a skin and put it to his mouth, the air that was in it burst forth and choked him, as it is written, 'The oracle concerning Arabia. In the thickets in Arabia you will dwell, O caravans of Dedanites! Meet the thirsty with water, you who dwell in the house of Tema [i.e., Arabs],[68] greet the fugitive with bread' (Isa. 21:13–14). . . . Should cousins (*dodîm*) act in this way? For when Ishmael was thirsty was it not, 'to the thirsty bring water,' as it is said, 'Then God opened her eyes, and she saw a well of water' " (Gen. 21:19)?

The rabbis play on "Dedanites," inhabitants of an Arab region who are known in the Bible especially as traffickers of precious riding garments

(Ezek. 27:20, 38:13; Jer. 25:23), and *dodîm*, cousins, thus alluding to the Ishmaelites, from Arabia, as Israel's cousins. The kinship between Ishmaelites/Arabs and Israel in this midrash should be of no surprise since biblical genealogical schemes already establish this relationship.[69]

The previous sources indicate that even as early as the tannaitic period, the rabbis identified Ishmaelites as Arabs. This identification is also found in the Babylonian Talmud. Dealing with the interpretation of dreams, BT. Berakot 56b reads:

> A Baraita: The one who sees Ishmael in a dream his prayer will be heard [end of Baraita]. And only Ishmael the son of Abraham but an Arab[70] in general, no. The one who sees a camel in a dream, death has been decreed upon him from heaven and he has been saved from it.

BT. Moʿed Qaṭan 24a, for example, describes the Ishmaelite custom of wearing a covering up to the lip: Shemuel said, "Any rending [of clothes] not done at the moment of death is not a [proper mourner's] rending and any covering which is not like the covering of the Ishmaelites [up to the lip] is not a [proper mourner's] covering." While Arabs are not mentioned, we can maintain with some certainty that the reference is to Arabs. To begin with, it is clear that the reference is made to a specific group of people regarding a specific custom. Second, in other instances when the Ishmaelites have been associated with a group, it has been with Arabs.

BT. Baba Meṣiʿa 86b similarly identifies Ishmael as an Arab:

> "Let a little water be brought; wash your feet" (Gen. 18:4). R. Yannai son of R. Ishmael said, "They [the three traveling men] said to him, 'Do you suspect us of being Arabs who worship the dust on their feet? Ishmael has already come from you.'"[71]

In *Arabs in Antiquity: Their History from the Assyrians to the Umayyads*, Jan Retsö discusses, inter alia, the Arabs in talmudic literature. Although a thoroughly detailed, weighty work, Retsö hastily comes to the conclusion that there are "frequent expressions of a low opinion of them."[72] Similarly, in his essay "The Attitude of the Sage towards the Arabs," Aharon Oppenheimer states that "the image of the Arabs produced by the sages is generally negative,"[73] although he does note some favorable comments. While doubtless there are several statements that convey negative representations of Arabs, rabbinic comments must be read in context and measured against other references to Arabs. In addition, distinctions among the forms of talmudic narrative must be taken into account when assessing the extent to which such statements are either real, or realistic—that is, have verisimilitude but are not factually true—or the extent to which they are consciously fictional.

The Babylonian Talmud makes several references to Arabs, most often to *ṭayyāʿā*, an Arab tribe associated with caravans and Bedouin lifestyle, which later comes to refer to Arabs in general. Such references, often neutral and reflective of the group's nomadic practices and values, highlight real, as well as realistic, encounters rabbis had with certain members of the tribe. At the same time, the term *ʿArabîyyîm*, often, though not always, reflects a rabbinic type of Arabs, perhaps based like stereotypes on some distortion of observable reality. [Other less frequent references include Navatae, (Nabateans), Hagarae, (Hagarites), and Sarqayin, (Saracens).]

To support their assertion that Arabs were known for licentious behavior, both Oppenheimer and Retsö quote BT. Qiddušin 49b: "Ten kabs (a unit of measure) of sexual immorality descended to the world: nine were taken by Arabia, one by the rest of the world." The reference is part of a list that reflects stereotypical-like characteristics of a particular group.[74] Thus, we are told that ten kabs of wisdom descended to the world: nine were taken by Palestine and one by the rest of the world. Ten kabs of beauty descended to the world: nine were taken by Jerusalem and one by the rest of the world; ten kabs of strength descended to the world: nine were taken by the Persians. Ten kabs of vermin descended to the world: nine were taken by Media. Ten kabs of witchcraft descended to the world: nine were taken by Egypt, and ten kabs of gossip descended to the world: nine were taken by women. Ten kabs of drunkenness (or blackness according to textual variants) descended to the world: nine were taken by Ethiopians.

The Arabs in this list are typified fornicators. According to Aharon Oppenheimer, such immorality is also evidenced in BT. ʿAbodah Zarah 22b: "Rav Jeremiah of Difti said, "I saw an Arab who bought a side [of meat], made a hole in it for an indecent act, after which act, he roasted and ate it." But Oppenheimer ignores the remark immediately preceding the aforementioned: "Rab Judah said in the name of Samuel on behalf of R. Hanina: I saw a non-Jew ["idol worshippers" in printed additions] buy a goose in the market, use it immorally, and then strangle it, roast, and eat it." It seems likely here that the examples attempt to depict practices of non-Jews, neither necessarily the practices of Arabs, nor necessarily real practices. The narrative is realistic, but given the broader narrative context, it remains uncertain whether or not Rav Jeremiah actually saw an Arab behave in this manner.

BT. Ketubbot 72b is another example of Arab sexual immorality where we find the story of an Arab woman, weaving a rose-colored fabric, who when she saw a young man, dropped her spindle and asked the young man to pick it up for her. According to the rabbis, "R. ʿUkba spoke of her as one conversing with every man." This, however, is not a recurrent notion found in the Talmud regarding Arab women. Moreover, the statement is made as part of the talmudic discussion on the Mishnah pertaining to when a woman is to be divorced without receiving her Ketubah. The example of the non-Jewish woman's behavior is used to exemplify improper behavior in contrast with the ideal behavior of Jewish women. Here, too, it is difficult to know whether Rabbi ʿUkba indeed saw an Arab woman or if Arab here is used simply to denote non-Jew. The narrative is, to be sure, realistic, but we simply have no way of knowing if R. ʿUkba saw an Arab woman behaving in this manner. Even if we were to take these statements on face value, in light of the over thirty or so statements made about Arabs in the Talmud, these examples do not constitute a sufficient basis for Oppenheimer's assertion that "there are frequent expressions of a low opinion of them," or that the rabbinic image of Arabs is that of fornicators. That said, a prevailing stereotype of Arabs harking back to postbiblical interpretations of Ishmael and Ishmaelites is that of robbers, which dates well before the Babylonian Talmud. In addition to the tannaitic texts discussed above, Jerome also comments on their ill-repute as marauders.

While there are a few references to the sexual appetite of Arabs as well as to their thievery, such expressions need to be read in the context of generalizations that do not necessarily reflect the rabbinic attitude as a whole toward the group, for such depictions as these exist alongside other references to Arabs in the same manner that we find complimentary comments about women and Ethiopians in the Talmud. Statements in the Talmud to specific *ṭayyāʿā* or *ṭayyāʿê*, for example, belie real encounters. Many of the references to Arabs is specifically to *tayaʿae* who are depicted as desert wanderers who engage in nontraditional medicinal practices, are familiar with the land, and maintain values consonant with nomadic life such as fairness and propriety. We, for example, read that a certain *ṭayyāʿā*, Shaʿazrek, made a gift of a lamp to the synagogue of Rav Judah (BT. ʻArakin 6b). Furthermore, in BT. Yoma 84a, we read: "Abaye said: I tried everything without achieving a cure for myself, until an Arab recommended: 'Take the stones of olives which have not become ripe one third, burn them in fire upon a new rake, and stick them into the inside of the gums.'" So, too, in BT. ʿAbodah Zarah, 28a Abaye learns of the cure for scurvy from an Arab. Similarly, in BT. ʿAbodah Zarah 29a we learn of a cure for stomachache and in BT. Šabbat 110b a cure for jaundice.

Rabbinic sources tell us a great deal about Arabs: We know they were circumcised (BT. Yebamot 71a), their waterskins had special knots (BT. Menaḥot 5a), Arab women wore veils in public, and they had camels as well as cattle and horses.

"In general, most of the talmudic sources which mention the Arabs," avers Oppenheimer, "reflect the tensions between Arabs and Jews. However, it would appear that we can find differences between the sources from the land of Israel, and those from Babylonia; between the presentation of Arabs as nomads, and Arabs as a people; between theoretical debates and sources that reflect daily life. We may also be able to distinguish between the various names—such as Arabs, tayaʿae, Ishmaelites, etc."[75] Although I do not fully agree with Oppenheimer's assertion that generally most talmudic sources mentioning Arabs reflect a tension between Arabs and Jews, nor with some of his observations, passim, I nonetheless concur with the various significant distinctions he makes regarding differences between Babylonian and Palestinian sources, as well as depictions of real nomads and general comments about Arabs as a people.

Nuanced distinctions between terms used as types, and as references to real people and situations, and terms used as expressions of theological considerations must be taken into account when discussing the talmudic image of Arabs. The range of possible narrative discourse must not be overlooked and indeed sheds light on references to real Arabs and imagined Others.

Indeed, as mentioned above, the identification of Arabs as descendants of Ishmael was well established by the time of the redaction of the Talmud, in fact dating back to the Hellenistic period. In the book of Jubilees, Abraham exhorts his sons, including Ishmael and the children of Keturah, and their children to observe circumcision and to avoid fornication, uncleanness, and intermarriage with Canaanites. Then we read in Jubilees 20:11–13:

> And he [Abraham] gave to Ishmael and to his sons, and to the sons of Keturah, gifts, and he sent them away from Isaac, his son, and he gave everything to Isaac, his son. And Ishmael and his sons, and the sons of Keturah and their sons went together and they dwelt from Paran to the entrance to Babylon in all the land, which faces the east opposite the desert. And these mixed with each other, and they are called Arabs and Ishmaelites.[76]

We also find in Josephus several examples where Ishmaelites are identified as Arabs. Discussing the circumcision of Isaac, for example, Josephus writes: “Eight days later they promptly circumcise him; and from that time forward the Jewish practice has been to circumcise so many days after birth. The Arabs defer the ceremony to the thirteenth year, because Ishmael, the founder of their race, born of Abraham’s concubine, was circumcised at that age.”[77] Josephus also identifies the Ishmaelites as Arabs when he explicitly states: “But Judas, another of the sons of Jacob, having seen some Arab traders of the race of Ishmaelites conveying spices and Syrian merchandise from Galadene for the Egyptian market, after Rubel’s departure advised his brethren to draw up Joseph and sell him to these Arabs.”[78]

Josephus not only lists the descendants of Ishmael, but makes a significant editorial expansion: “These occupy the whole territory stretching from the Euphrates to the Red Sea, having given it the name ‘Nabatene.’ These are they who have named the people of the ‘Arabes’ and their tribes after themselves, because of their own distinction and the honour of Abraham.”[79] Curiously, the rabbis of the amoraic period do not, notwithstanding aforementioned examples, maintain this association found in Jubilees and Josephus. In the Babylonian Talmud, for example, the word *ʿArab* is used to refer to an Arab, a member of an ethnic group associated with a nomadic lifestyle, and *beney Yishmael* or *Yishmaelim* designate the Ishmaelites,[80] who at times refer to the descendants of Ishmael, and other times to Arabs. Thus, irrespective of the fact that the identification of Ishmaelites as Arabs was established as early as Jubilees, amoraic literature uses the Ishmaelites and the children of Keturah to represent also those excluded from the covenantal relationship God made with Israel and not exclusively to represent a specific ethnic group. The following examples illustrate how the rabbis use these marginalized descendants generically.

Abraham’s Descendants and Israel’s Divine Election

The notion of setting Israel apart from other peoples is illustrated in all renditions of the rejection of the Torah by all the nations of the world, except Israel, who accepts it.[81] Sifre Deuteronomy 343, for example, includes a midrash on the giving of the Torah to the Israelites:

> When the Holy One, Blessed be He appeared to give the Torah to Israel, he did not reveal himself only to Israel but to all the nations. At first he went to the people of Esau and said to them, “Do you accept the Torah?” They said to Him, “What is written in it?” He said to them, “You shall not murder.” They said to Him, “The very essence of those men and their father is a murderer,” as it is said, “And the

> hands are the hands of Esau" (Gen. 27:22), "By your sword you shall live" (Gen. 27:40). He went to the people of Ammon and Moab and said to them, "Do you accept the Torah?" They said to Him, "What is written in it?" He said to them, "You shall not commit adultery" (Exod. 20:13). They said to Him, "The very essence of fornication is theirs," as it is said, "Thus were both daughters of Lot with child by their father" (Gen. 19:36). So He went to the Ishmaelites and said to them, "Will you accept the Torah?" They said to Him, "What is written in it?" He said to them, "You shall not steal." They said to Him, "The very essence of their father is a robber," as it is said, "And he shall be a wild ass of a man" (Gen. 16:12).[82]

As noted previously, the theme of Israel's election as God's people is discussed throughout rabbinic literature (more so in the amoraic and later periods than in the tannaitic). By emphasizing the preference for the younger sibling over the older, by disqualifying Ishmael and Esau, as well as Abraham's children with Keturah, the rabbis reaffirm Israel's select role in history, but not necessarily at the expense of portraying God in exclusivist terms. Indeed, throughout rabbinic literature we find examples of the omnipresent, all-loving God showing concern for all humanity. Nonetheless, the biblical tradition itself provides the raw materials used to build a theological edifice of exclusivity, not at the cost of all humanity, but in light of the rabbinic understanding of the covenantal relationship between God and Israel.

Several midrashim illustrate Israel's election and maintain the marginalization of other peoples. As we saw in Sifre Deut. Ha'azinu 312, for example, the rabbis single out the children of Israel from the displaced sons, Ishmael and Esau, and their progeny. In Leviticus Rabbah 36:5 the children of Keturah are also included in the "unfit" category: "From Abraham came something unfit: Ishmael and the people of Keturah. From Isaac came forth Esau and all his chiefs. Jacob's bed was perfect in that only righteous ones were born to him."[83]

Providing another case in point, on a textual level, Gen. Rab. 68:11 is concerned with reconciling two verses, Genesis 28:11 and verse 18 of the same chapter. Genesis 28:11 reads, "Taking *one* of the stones of the place, he put it under his head and lay down in that place to sleep" (emphasis added), while Genesis 28:18 reads, "Early in the morning, Jacob took the stone." That is, in verse 11, reference is made to stones, but in verse 18 there is only one stone. According to the rabbis, the stones by miraculous means became one. In explaining the meaning of Genesis 28:11, the rabbis emphasize Israel's election. Jacob produced the twelve tribes. Abraham did not produce them because he fathered Ishmael and the children of Keturah. Isaac did not produce them because of Esau. Unlike his forefathers, all of Jacob's children will be righteous or at least will constitute Israel.

Similarly, in BT. Sanhedrin 59b we read:

> [Regarding circumcision] Abraham was the first to be warned by the Merciful One: "As for you, you and your offspring to come throughout the ages shall keep my covenant" (Gen. 17:9). "You and your offspring"—not others. Does this mean the children of Ishmael are obligated? "For in Isaac shall your seed be called" (Gen. 21:12). Are the children of Esau obligated? "In Isaac" but not all Isaac. R. Oshaia objects: then the children of Keturah are not obligated, but R. Yosi b. Avin or as others say, R. Yosi b. Hanina said: " '[And if any male who is uncircumcised fails to circumcise the flesh of his foreskin, that person shall be cut off from his kin;] he has broken my covenant' (Gen. 17:14). This includes the children of Keturah."[84]

If only part of Isaac is obligated to keep the commandments, then, R. Oshaia argues, the six sons Abraham had with his third wife, Keturah, are not obligated to keep the commandment of circumcision. R. Yosi b. Hanina disagrees. The children of Keturah are included, "And if *any male* . . . fails to circumcise the flesh of his foreskin . . ." (Gen. 17:14) (emphasis added). According to Rashi, R. Yosi b. Avin's response means that the sons of Keturah are included but not their offspring. Rashi is apparently bothered by the prospect that the mitzvah of circumcision could be incumbent upon anyone but Jacob's descendants. But to what extent were the descendants of Keturah a threat?[85] The children of Ishmael are marginalized here but not the children of Keturah. The rabbis acknowledge the Ishmaelites' claim to Abraham but, again, the Ishmaelites are marginalized in order to underscore Israel's chosen status.

Gen. Rab. 61:6, however, deals with the status of Abraham's descendants both through Keturah and through the line of Ishmael:

> "And everything Abraham had he gave to Isaac" (Gen. 25:5). R. Judah, R. Nehemiah and the sages. R. Judah said, "[He gave him] the birthright." R. Nehemiah said, "[He gave him] a blessing." The rabbis said, "[He gave him] burial and a gift [or document recording] on contemplation of death." R. Judah b. R. Shimon and R. Berekiah and R. Levi [said] in the name of R. Hama b. Hanina, "He did not bless him but rather he gave him gifts." [This may be compared] to a king who had an orchard which he handed over to a tenant. There were

> two intertwined trees in this orchard. One produced a life-bearing potion, the other a deadly poison. The tenant said, "If I water the life-bearing tree, then the death-bearing tree will live with it, and, if I do not water the death-bearing tree, how will the life-bearing tree live?" He said, "I will serve as tenant. Whatever the owner of the orchard wishes to do, let him do it." So too, said Abraham, "If I bless Isaac now, the children of Ishmael and Keturah are included, but if I do not bless the children of Ishmael and the children of Keturah, how can I bless Isaac?" He then said, "I am only human and will do my duty, and whatever the Holy One Blessed be He wishes to do in this world, He may do. When our father Abraham died, the Holy One Blessed be He appeared to Isaac and blessed him," as it is written, "And it came to pass after the death of Abraham that God blessed Isaac his son."[86]

Based on divine blessing, the midrash distinguishes between Ishmael's and Keturah's children and Isaac. Abraham, according to the rabbis, did not bless Isaac, for in blessing Isaac, Abraham would have to include the children of Ishmael and Keturah, who are compared to a tree that produced a deadly poison. Caught in a conundrum, Abraham submits to the will of God. When he dies, *God* blesses Isaac; preferential treatment of Isaac is providential.

Gen. Rab. 61:7 explicitly deals with the Ishmaelites' claim to the birthright:

> "But unto the sons of his concubines, Abraham gave gifts [and while he was still living, he sent them away from his son Isaac, eastward to the east country]" (Gen. 25:6). In the days of Alexander of Macedonia the Ishmaelites came to dispute with Israel about the birthright and with them came two wicked families, the Canaanites and the Egyptians. They said, "Who will go and dispute with them?" Gebiah, son of Qosem, said, "I will go and dispute them." They said to him, "Be careful lest you forfeit the land of Israel to them." He replied, "I will go and argue with them." . . . He went and disputed with them. Alexander of Macedonia said to them, "Who is laying claim against whom?" The Ishmaelites responded, "We are the claimants and we base our claim on their Torah," for it is written, "But he shall acknowledge the firstborn, the son of the hated . . ."(Deut. 21:17), and Ishmael was the firstborn." Gebiah, son of Qosem said, "My lord, the king, can not a man do as he likes with his sons?" "Yes," answered Alexander. Thus, it is written, "Abraham gave all that he had to Isaac" (Gen. 25:2). "But where is the deed of gift to the other sons?" He replied,

"But unto the sons of the concubines, that Abraham had, Abraham gave gifts." Shame-faced, they departed.[87]

As in midrashim previously discussed, the rabbis offer a justification for Israel's unique status. In this case, Abraham is a king who can do as he pleases and is therefore justified in giving all to Isaac. But one cannot, however, accuse him of inequity, for he bestows gifts to the children of his concubines.

There are other midrashim that depict the children of Esau, Ishmael, and Keturah as subordinate to the Israelites. We find this, for example, in BT. Sotah 13a in which the image of their children surrounding Jacob's coffin with crowns poignantly captures the esteemed position of Israel and the subservient status of the other nations.[88] This notion is also found in Gen. Rab. 66:4. Interpreting Genesis 27:29, "Let peoples serve thee, and nations bow down to thee: Be lord over your brother . . . ," by means of a clever wordplay, the rabbis depict the offspring of Ishmael and Keturah, along with Esau, as servants of Jacob:

> "Let peoples serve thee"—these are the seventy nations. "And nations (*Le'ummîm*) bow down to you" refers to the children of Ishmael and Keturah, as it is written, "And the sons of Dedan were Asshurim, and Letushim, and Le'ummim" (Gen. 25:3). "Be lord over your brethren" means Esau and his chiefs.

The word "nations," *Le'ummîm*, calls to mind the name of one of Abraham's descendants, Le'ummim, whom he fathered with Keturah. In order to explain the plural, "brethren," the rabbis add Esau's "chiefs." They would have been remiss had they overlooked the blatant word association between Abraham and Keturah's son, Le'ummim, and nations, "*le'ummîm.*" Yet here again, the rabbis use this opportunity to reiterate Israel's superiority over the children of Ishmael and of Keturah, and Esau, who represent no particular group of people but rather the concept of Other.

In these examples, the rabbis do not denigrate Ishmael, Ishmael's children, or the children of Keturah and Esau. These Others are not inherently evil. Rather, they are set aside in order to highlight Israel's unique status as inheritor of the covenant of Abraham.

This distinction may be based on a notion of ethnic supremacy or social superiority, but there is precious little evidence to support this notion. It may be based only on the theological belief that the God of Israel chose the Israelites, and the Israelites alone, from among all the nations to be His people, but this, too, is difficult to support. Appertaining to the complex of dyadic discourse, all these factors are inextricably related and to varying degrees come into play, as they did in the formation of biblical Israelite identity, and as they often do in similar group-identity formation.

The Role of Christianity in the Depiction of the Other

At this juncture, we may want to examine more closely the extent to which Christian claims played a role in the rabbinic separation between Israel and Other. In *Judaism and Its Social Metaphors*, Jacob Neusner traces the diachronic development of the concept "Israel" from the mishnaic period through the talmudic period.[89] He argues that the concept of Israel in the Mishnah had taxonomic significance, that it was a category and not a social reality. In the "second phase," the period between 300 and 600 CE, Israel is a social entity, a group that must come to terms with the theological challenges, such as the spiritualizing of Israel, which Christianity presented after Constantine.[90]

Neusner deals, inter alia, with how the rise of Christianity elicited a reaction from the rabbis. He claims that the rabbis' concept of historical Israel was a response to a spiritualized Christian "Israel." "If Abraham, Isaac, and Jacob stand for Israel later on, then Ishmael, Edom, and Esau represent Rome. Hence whatever sages find out about those figures," Neusner contends, "tells them something about Rome and its character, history, and destiny."[91] Moreover, according to Neusner, this conceptualization must take into account the political vicissitudes that gave way to a new symbolization, namely Rome as Christianity. Thus, the reading of Rome in metaphoric terms as the differentiated outsider must consider Rome as Esau/or Ishmael, a generic outsider and Rome as specific Other.[92]

Furthermore, Neusner maintains that in order to detect the distinction between Rome as non-Israel, and Rome specifically as Christianity, we must differentiate among documents of the rabbinic period, for the documents read individually "yield insight that combining all their statements on a given topic does not bring to light."[93] And, if we were to read Genesis Rabbah, we would come to see that the sages "read the book of Genesis as if it portrayed the history of Israel and Rome."[94] Because Genesis Rabbah reached closure toward the end of the fourth century, Neusner avers, "Accordingly, we should not find surprising sages' recurrent references, in the reading of Genesis, to the struggle of two equal powers, Rome and Israel, Esau and Jacob, Ishmael and Isaac." "Now Rome," states Neusner, "plays a role in the Biblical narrative, with special reference to the counterpart and opposite of the partriarchs, first Ishmael, then Esau, and always Edom."[95]

According to Neusner, in amoraic texts even Ishmael represents Rome. In his earlier work *Judaism and Christianity in the Age of Constantine*, he writes:

> If Abraham, Isaac, and Jacob stand for Israel, later on, then Ishmael, Edom, and Esau represent Rome. Hence, whatever sages find out about those figures tells them something about Rome and its character, history, and destiny. So Genesis is read as a literal statement and also as an effort to prefigure the history of Israel's suffering and redemption. Ishmael, standing now for Christian Rome, claims God's blessing, but Isaac gets it, as Jacob will take it from Esau.[96]

Given our study of references to Ishmael and Isaac in Genesis Rabbah, the notion that Genesis Rabbah depicts the siblings as two struggling powers and the assertion that Ishmael represents Rome—metaphorically or otherwise—seem unfounded. While Neusner's theory does not require that all of Genesis Rabbah's statements about Ishmael contrast him unfavorably with Isaac, it does require greater substantiation.[97]

Be that as it may, in *Judaism and Its Social Metaphors*, Neusner provides two compelling illustrations of reading Rome behind references to Ishmael.[98] More importantly, Neusner's work, especially his articulation of the rabbinic metaphor of family enhances our understanding of the ways in which midrash functions as a means of establishing social identity within rabbinic literature. One can only hope to build on the groundwork he has firmly established.

Neusner notes that the metaphor of family originated not in the fourth century but in Scripture, and proved useful in light of the exigent political situation in which the Jews of Palestine found themselves. But to what extent are midrashim that mention Esau and Ishmael a polemic against Edom-Rome? Are they a response to Christianity's spiritualization of Israel?[99]

The social metaphor of Israel qua family in contrast to non-Israel indeed undergirds the rabbis' religious system. But while there are instances where non-Israel is a real Other, in the case of Israel's relation to Christianity, for example, as I have tried to demonstrate, this is far from always the case. Of course we would be remiss to ignore the nexus between rabbinic Judaism and early Christianity, indeed an exceedingly complex nexus of enduring interest especially to scholars of late antique Judaism and early Christianity.

Many contemporary studies highlight the fertile ground from which both groups cultivated literary produce and underscore the ways in which both partook in a broader context of mutual cultural exchange.[100] They have made persuasive arguments that the two communities' interest in Scripture as well as the competing claim to the Abrahamic covenant led them to take each other's arguments seriously, and may also have brought them in some kind of dialogue, such that we ought not see these communities as bounded, or in isolation, especially as they endeavor to create and maintain boundaries, in part by means of polemical discourse.[101]

The notion that the rabbis in emphasizing Israel's chosenness, particularly in the amoraic period, directly respond to Christian claims to being "true" Israel, may explain some midrashic texts, certainly those deemed apocalyptic, but must not be used as a hermeneutical model for explaining all midrashim that refer to Esau, Ishmael, and the children of Keturah vis-à-vis Israel and those that set Israel apart from the generic "nations of the world." In other words, we must allow for multicausal explanations of this genre of midrashim and, in doing so, consider the effects of the destruction of the Second Temple in light of ancient Jewish formulations of retribution theology, as well as the effects of outside hegemonic forces that were a constant reminder of Jewish minority status. Explanations for rabbinic renderings of Isreal's chosenness must not overlook internal and external, contemporaneous as well as past, stimuli and must take into account the precedence of an archetypal primordial Other.

Throughout the biblical period and well into premodernity, chosenness was inextricable to the very character of Israelite/Jewish identity. Election was conceived in numerous ways, not the least of which as the righteous status of Jacob and his sons vis-à-vis the unfit status of the marginalized descendants of Abraham. Clearly competing claims to the Abrahamic covenant may have factored into the formulation of many midrashim, but as intuitively sound as this may be, we must nevertheless be careful to avoid eisegetical explanations and look for rabbinic hermeneutical markers that allow us to distinguish between midrashim that refer to a real Other, such as Christianity, and those that have to do with a fabricated antipode, keeping in mind of course that even the real Other is based on perception and thus in a sense is also fabricated.

One interpretive marker that cuts across the rabbinic corpus is the reference to the end days, a characteristic of apocalyptic midrashim as well as the pesharim of Qumran. These sources allude to a historical entity such as Rome, Christianity, and as we shall shortly see, Islam, but for now let us briefly look at one example.[102]

The following parable in Shir Ha-Shirim Rabbah 7:8 is convincing evidence of the rabbis' awareness of Christian and perhaps Islamic assertions:

> A parable: The wheat, the chaff and the stubble were arguing with one another. The chaff said, "For my sake the ground had been sown." The stubble said, "For my sake the ground had been sown." The wheat said to them, "Wait until the threshing time comes and we will see for whom the ground had been sown." When the threshing time arrived and they were all brought to the floor, the farmer went out to winnow it. The chaff was scattered to the winds; he took the straw and threw it on the ground; he cast the stubble into the fire. He took the wheat and piled it in a heap and when all the passersby saw it they kissed it. . . . So, of the nations some say, "We are Israel and for our sake the world was created," and others say, "We are Israel, and for our sake the world was created." Israel says to them, "Wait for the day of the Holy One, Blessed be He and we will know for whom the world was created," as it is written, "For the day will come and burn like a furnace" (Mal. 3:19). And it is written, "You shall fan them, and the wind will carry them away," but of Israel it is said, "And you shall rejoice in the LORD; you shall glory in the Holy One of Israel" (Isa. 41:16).

At first glance, one cannot help but make an association between this midrash and Christianity, although it may be referring to other groups, such as the Samaritans and gnostics, in addition to (or rather than) Christians. Furthermore, even though Shir ha-Shirim Rabbah draws on earlier sources such as the Yerushalmi, Genesis Rabbah, and Leviticus Rabbah, its final redaction is quite likely the later part of the eighth century in which case the nations may also include Christianity as well as Islam.[103]

This midrash is strikingly apocalyptic in its orientation toward the future judgment of the unrighteous. Worth considering is the way in which midrashim that refer to Esau and other marginalized figures in light of what will happen in the future reflect a real encounter with Christian claims. Apocalyptic midrashim by nature deal with the actual present in the guise of prophesying the future destruction of Israel's enemy. Indeed, as noted above we see this phenomenon in post-seventh-century rabbinic texts that deal with the Ishmaelites, as well as in the pesharim of the Dead Sea Community, in particular in its use of the Kittim to symbolize Rome.[104]

At a time when Christianity was propounding supersessionist claims, one would expect to find other midrashim expressing a similar sentiment as in the midrashim just cited. This, however, is not the case. In amoraic literature, we find only a few examples, approximately twenty, where the marginalization of Israel's kin, the "illegitimate" children of Abraham, is emphasized. Regarding their content, they are very similar to tannaitic midrashim. That there are relatively more midrashim of this type in amoraic corpora is insufficient evidence to support the hypothesis that competing Christian claims had an appreciable bearing on the development of these midrashim.

Irrespective of whether or not Christianity was a significant factor in the development of midrash, the metaphorical expressions of Israel's election found in these sources lead one to conclude that the rabbis were internally asserting their unique status vis-à-vis the other nations. Moreover, the rabbinic attitude toward Other as it manifests itself in these midrashim is benign when compared to the vitriolic expressions of hate that one finds in later rabbinic texts.

The select status of Israel pervades rabbinic literature, yet at the same time the midrashim we have examined do not pronounce the Other as inherently wicked, but rather reiterate that only Israel is heir to Abraham. These texts reflect the rabbinic conceptualization of covenanted Israel vis-à-vis Other. Stephen Geller, for example, draws our attention to a similar phenomenon in biblical literature. In his reading of the defilement of Dinah, Genesis 34, he argues that the degree to which the Canaanites are an ideational projection is an attempt to assuage "Israel's deep apprehension, as an ancient people, of the real unnaturalness of its relationship to its land, and to nature in general, by reason of its conditional, mainly legal, connection to its God."[105] Geller avers, "In that story, and in biblical religion as a whole, the Canaanites are, in effect, a literary device, a use of imagery and typology to clarify the difficult idea of divine transcendence. Historical Canaanites are irrelevant."[106]

The sources examined above yield the following conclusions: in these amoraic texts, we find the theme of Israel's divine election, a theme that manifests itself in several midrashim where only the children of Jacob are righteous and the bearers of the covenant. Moreover, most of these midrashim, with the exception of those that are characteristically apocalyptic, ought not be read as direct responses to Christianity, but rather as reflective of the rabbis' affirmation of the Jewish notion of chosenness.

In post-seventh-century rabbinic corpora, we shall find that the depiction of Ishmael changes significantly. Islamic hegemony, as well as the development of the notion of Arab as a generic term associated with Islam, as opposed to individual tribes and peoples, was a contributing factor to this change in portrayal.

4

Ishmael in Later Midrashim

> Thus we find in the case of Ishmael; he and Abraham had affection for one another and he did not chastise him and he came to be bad so Abraham hated him and cast him out of his house empty-handed. What did Ishmael do? When he was fifteen years old he began to bring an idol from outside and he worshipped it, as it says, "And Sarah saw the son of Hagar the Egyptian, whom she had bore Abraham, making sport (*mĕṣaḥēq*)" (Gen. 21:9).
>
> —Exodus Rabbah 1:1

In our study of Gen. Rab. 48:13, the midrash on "and Abraham took a calf tender and good and gave it to one of his servants," we had the occasion to see that reading this midrash through a historical lens is difficult but not impossible.[1] We thus came to the conclusion that several figures could have been plausibly identified as the servant. What, then, made it possible for the rabbis to use Ishmael in this manner?

Moreover, in our discussion of Genesis 18:10, we also concluded that there are several ways to interpret "behind him," and yet the rabbis chose to identify "him" as Ishmael. The fact that in these midrashim they could use Ishmael in an innocuous or even mildly positive sense tells us something about the rabbinic attitude toward him in the pre-Islamic period.

Preceding the emergence of Islam in the seventh century, the rabbinic Ishmael was multivalent. But by the later medieval period, he became a more fully developed antagonist. From an investigation of how tannaitic and amoraic sources are reworked in later corpora, one can infer that the identification of Ishmael with Islam contributed to the retailoring of earlier sources.

Furthermore in later rabbinic sources, compilations of the period of and after the rise of Islam, we not only find earlier sources reworked but we also discover the creation of new midrashim that cast a negative light on Ishmael. There are about fifteen negative depictions in the later rabbinic works, but more importantly we note that the animus intensifies with the passage of time. Moreover, midrashim that contrast Isaac the chosen one with Ishmael the rejected Other were more common in earlier literature, whereas harsh, antagonistic portrayals are substantially more common in literature of this later period. Finally, with the exception of rabbinic anthologies such as Midrash Ha-Gadol and Yalquṭ Shimʿoni, as well as the depiction in PRE, there are only three positive portrayals, all of which are found in earlier, pre-Islamic sources. Other more subtle changes in the portrayal of Ishmael and his relationship to Abraham are also best elucidated in light of the rise of Islam.

The success of Islam as a real presence in the Middle East presented theological, social, and political challenges for Judaism. The conflicts arising from these challenges, particularly the theological, differed fundamentally from those Christianity had presented several centuries earlier. For unlike Islam, Christianity established its identity at the expense of Judaism.[2] Nonetheless, Judaism was now confronted with another viable monotheistic religion rooted in the Hebrew Scriptures that also asserted its political hegemony beyond the Near East.

Indeed, the emergence of Islam throws light on the portrayal of Ishmael in later midrashic compilations such as Deuteronomy Rabbah, Exodus Rabbah, Midrash Psalms, and the Tanḥuma literature.[3] Midrashim on Ishmael and the Ishmaelites found in later compilations continue several themes found in earlier corpora, themes such as the election of Israel, the unfit status of Ishmael and Esau, and the thievery of the Ishmaelites, but also introduce new elements such as the hatred of Ishmael for Isaac and Abraham's disdain for Ishmael. Moreover, in our discussion of PRE, we will take into account the mention of Ishmaelites in apocalyptic terms. Like midrashim that use Esau to refer to Rome in depicting future events, often, if not invariably, in PRE we find the Ishmaelites used in a similar manner to refer to Islam.[4]

In Tanḥuma, Toledot 1 (Buber), on "These are the generations of Isaac son of Abraham" (Gen. 25:19), we read:

> "Grandchildren are a crown for elders, and the glory of children is their parents" (Prov. 17:6). Who caused Abraham to be magnified? Jacob, as it is written, "Thus says the Lord unto the house of Jacob, which redeemed Abraham" (Isa. 29:22). . . . It is also written, "A wise son shall make a father glad" (Prov. 10:1)—this is Isaac, as it is said,

> "For in Isaac shall your seed be named" (Gen. 21:12). "But a foolish son" (Prov. 10:1)—this is Ishmael," as it is written, "Now these are the generations of Ishmael" (Gen. 25:12) . . . "Abraham fathered Isaac" (Gen. 25:19) Did he father no one but Isaac? It is written, "Hagar bore a son to Abram" (Gen. 16:15) and also, "These are the sons of Keturah: Zimran, Yokshan . . ." (Gen. 25:2). But it does not say that Abraham fathered anyone else but Isaac, because Isaac was righteous. It is therefore written, "Abraham fathered Isaac" (Gen. 25:19).

This midrash illustrates the importance placed on the righteousness of Israel through Isaac and Abraham. In other midrashim, Abraham had fathered unfit children, such as Ishmael and the children of Keturah. Here, however, Abraham fathers only Isaac. Ishmael and the children of Keturah are of no consequence. Notice, too, that Ishmael is a "foolish son"—an image starkly contrasting the image of Ishmael hastening to prepare the calf that Abraham gives him in order to make him quick in performing commandments. Moreover, labeling Ishmael a "foolish son" has no apparent textual grounding.

Further support for my claim that Ishmael's portrayal in the later literature is a response to the rise of Islam can be found in Deut. Rab. 4:5. We read there:

> The Holy One, Blessed be He said, "Listen to me, for no one who listens to me loses." The sages say, "You find that there is the man who listens to his wife and loses and there is the one who listens to his wife and profits. How? The first man listened to his wife and lost. From where do we know this?" Scripture says, "And to Adam He said, 'For you listened to your wife's voice' " (Gen. 3:17). . . . There is the man who listened to his wife and profited—this is Abraham. From where do we know this? Scripture says, "And Sarai said to Abram, 'Look, the LORD has kept me from bearing. Consort with my maid; perhaps I shall be built up [with sons] through her.' And Abram listened to Sarai's voice" (Gen. 16:2). R. Shemuel bar Nahman said, "To what does this matter compare? To one to whom a son was born. An astrologer saw him and said, 'This son will be a leader of robbers. His father needs to cast him out.' His father heard this and said, 'Am I to cast out my son?!' The father of the astrologer heard this and said, 'All that my son said to you, you listen to him.' So, Sarah saw Ishmael's depravity, and she said to Abraham, 'Cast out this maidservant and her son' " (Gen. 21:10). "The matter distressed Abraham greatly" (Gen. 21:11). The Holy One, Blessed be He

> appeared to him and said, "'Do not be distressed over the boy or your slave; whatever Sarah tells you, listen to her voice . . .'" (Gen. 21:12). He listened to her voice and profited, that the name of his seed is Isaac.[5]

Unlike other midrashim dealing with Gen. 21:10, this midrash is not found in Genesis Rabbah. Moreover, the justification for Ishmael's dismissal is qualitatively different. While other midrashim on this verse rationalize Sarah's request by attributing sinful behavior to Ishmael, this midrash foretells the future. That is, Sarah notices Ishmael's depravity and envisages its deleterious effect on Isaac; like the astrologer, she prognosticates his leadership of brigands.

The *mashal* in this midrash identifies him as the future father of robbers, which is no surprise since the Ishmaelites have been associated with robbery from as early as the tannaitic period. Indeed, in its discussion of the expulsion of Ishmael, this source has the Ishmaelites in mind. Unlike earlier midrashim on Genesis 21, here we find that the reference to Ishmael going bad is to the Ishmaelites. Ishmael is the source of children who stray, quite possibly by wrongly laying claim to the biblical heritage of the Jews.

Because he listened to Sarah, Abraham profited in that Isaac, not Ishmael, is the name of his seed. The suggestion that Abraham's dismissal of Ishmael profits him is an interpretation of the scriptural story unprecedented in earlier midrashic corpora. Just as important is the explicit claim that his seed is Isaac. These unique features seem to reflect a shift in the use of Ishmael from a biblical figure often used to symbolize a generic Other for the purposes of rabbinic self-identity to the eponymous prototype of Islam.

In Deut. Rab. Va-'Etḥanan[6] we read:

> He [God] said to him [Moses], "Behold, Abraham who sanctified my name in the world died." He said to Him, "Master of the world, Ishmael whose offspring provoke anger came forth from him," as it is written, "Robbers live untroubled in their tents, and those who provoke God are secure, those whom God's hands have produced" (Job 12:6).[7]

In this rather moving midrash where Moses pleads with God for immortality, Moses argues with God that Abraham deserved to die since he produced Ishmael whose "offspring provoke anger." As in PRE, Ishmael's offspring, not Ishmael himself, are faulted. In earlier sources such as PT.

Taʿanit 3:4 and BT. Sukkah 52b[8] where the Ishmaelites are depicted as robbers, the prooftext from Job is used in order to illustrate why God regretted having made the Ishmaelites. In this midrash, the prooftext serves to buttress Moses's comment, "whose offspring provoke anger," a strong, if not distinctive, expression of antagonism.

Unlike earlier sources that make no explicit statements regarding Ishmael's attitude toward Isaac and vice versa, later compilations contain several midrashim expressing Ishmael's hatred for Isaac. Pesiqta de Rab Kahana 16:5 reads:

> "If only it could be as with a brother" (Song of Songs 8:1). Like which brother? Like Cain and Abel? Cain killed Abel. Like Ishmael and Isaac? Ishmael hated Isaac. Like Esau and Jacob? Esau hated Jacob. Like Joseph's brothers and Joseph? Joseph's brothers hated Joseph.

This midrash is found also in three later midrashic compilations: Exod. Rab. 5:1, Tan. Shemot 27 (Warsaw) and Pes. Rab. 29. A noteworthy version is Tan. Shemot 24 (Buber):

> Like which brother? From the beginning of the creation of the world until now, brothers hate each other. Cain hated Abel and killed him, as it is written, "And Cain rose against Abel his brother and killed him" (Gen. 4:8). Ishmael hated Isaac, "And Sarah saw the son of the Egyptian whom she bore for Abraham playing" (Gen. 21:9). "Playing" can only mean that he sought to kill him, as it is written, "Let the young men, I pray thee, arise and play before us" (2 Sam. 2:14).

The proof text for the assertion that Ishmael hated Isaac is significant. As previously noted, in early rabbinic exegesis Genesis 21:9 is interpreted in several ways, one of which is R. Shimon's interpretation that playing had to do with inheritance. Here, however, the verse supports the idea that Ishmael hated Isaac, so much so that he attempted to kill him. The word "playing" does not mean inheritance, but rather unequivocally the shedding of blood—murder.

Thus in Exod. Rab. 1:1, we read:

> "Now these are the names [of the sons of Israel, who came to Egypt with Jacob, each came with his household]" (Exod. 1:1). "He who spares the rod hates his son, but he who loves him disciplines him early" (Prov. 13:24). This is how it is in the world: if a man says to his

> fellow, "So and so, hit your son," all his life he bears ill will towards him [out of resentment for the advice he gave him]. Then why does Scripture say, "He who spares the rod hates his son?" To teach you that anyone who refrains from chastising his son, he will come to evil behavior and hate him. Thus we find in the case of Ishmael; he and Abraham had affection for one another and he did not chastise him and he came to be bad so Abraham hated him and cast him out of his house empty-handed. What did Ishmael do? When he was fifteen years old he began to bring an idol from outside and he worshipped it, as it says, "And Sarah saw the son of Hagar the Egyptian, whom she had bore Abraham, making sport (*mĕṣaḥēq*)" (Gen. 21:9). "Making sport" is nothing other than idol worship, as it says, "And they rose up to worship idols (*lĕṣaḥēq*)" (Exod. 32:6). Making sport is nothing other than the shedding of blood, "Let the young men . . ." (2 Sam. 2:14). "Making sport" is nothing other than forbidden sexual acts, as it is written, ". . . the Hebrew servant, whom you have brought to me . . ." (Gen. 39:17). At that moment Sarah said, " 'Cast out this maidservant and her son' (Gen. 21:10), lest my son will learn from his ways." Immediately, "the matter distressed Abraham greatly, for it concerned a son of his" (Gen. 21:11) *because of his wicked behavior* [emphasis added]. "And God said to Abraham, 'Do not be distressed [over the boy or your slave; whatever Sarah tells you, do as she says . . .]' " (Gen. 21:12). From this you learn that Abraham was second to Sarah in prophecy.[9]

Before citing the rest of the midrash, a few observations are in order. To begin with, Abraham and Ishmael had mutual affection but Abraham's affection prevented him from disciplining his son who, as a result, turned to evil ways such as idol worship at the age of fifteen. Except for R. Shimon's interpretation, the other interpretations of Genesis 21:9 describing Ishmael's most egregious behavior, such as those found in T. Soṭah 6:6, Sifre Deut. 31 and Gen. Rab. 53:11, are rehearsed here in Exod. Rab. 1:1 and in Tan. Shemot 1 (Warsaw). In fact, here, Genesis 21:10 is quoted partially. Tan. Shemot 1 reads:[10] "At that moment, Sarah said, 'Cast out this maidservant and her son, lest my son will learn from his ways.' " Genesis 21:10, however, reads, "Cast out this maidservant and her son, for the son of this maidservant shall not inherit with my son." The statement about inheritance is omitted and replaced with a cautionary comment. Ishmael must leave because of his wicked ways.

Exod. Rab. 1:1 continues:

> "And Abraham rose early" (Gen. 21:14) to teach you that he hated Ishmael because he behaved wickedly and expelled him and his

> mother Hagar empty-handed from out of his house. Do you think that Abraham acted this way? "And Abram was very rich in cattle [and silver and gold]" (Gen. 13:2). Would he really send his wife and son empty, without food and sustenance? Rather, it is to teach you that when he [Ishmael] began to behave wickedly, Abraham turned away from him. What eventually happened to him? When he grew up, Ishmael sat at the intersection and robbed people, as it says, "And he shall be a wild ass of a man [his hand against everyone]" (Gen. 16:12).

Abraham was "distressed over the matter" not because he had to expel his son but because of his son's "wicked behavior." Furthermore, he cast out Ishmael and Hagar empty-handed, not because Abraham could not afford to give them food. On the contrary, Abraham's household was abundant, "very rich in cattle and silver and gold." It is rather to indicate that Abraham hated Ishmael because Ishmael went morally astray; thus Abraham "turned away from him."

The midrash proceeds with Esau:

> In the same manner, "And Isaac loved Esau . . ." (Gen. 25:28). Esau went bad because he [Isaac] did not chastise him. As we have learned, on that very day [the day he sold his birthright][11] Esau the wicked committed five transgressions: he had sex with an engaged woman, he killed a person, he denied the resurrection of the dead, he denied the principle of the unity of God, and he despised his birthright. All of these sins are indicated in specific verses in Scripture or by gezerah shavah [analogy with other verses in Scripture]. Furthermore, he longed for the death of his father and sought to kill his brother, as it is said, "Let but the mourning period of my father come and I will kill Jacob my brother" (Gen. 27:41). He caused Jacob to flee from his father's home and he went to Ishmael to learn wicked ways and to add to his wickedness, as it is said, "Esau went to Ishmael . . ."(Gen. 28:9).[12]

This final section of the midrash demonstrates a striking shift in earlier midrashim dealing with Genesis 28:9. That Esau the wicked commits five transgressions is no surprise since we already read this in BT. Baba Batra 16b. Why Esau went to Ishmael, however, is certainly curious. Unlike in PT. Bikkurim 3:3 and Gen. Rab. 67:13 that expound the meaning of Mahalath and Basemath, in Exod. Rab. 1:1 Esau goes to Ishmael to learn wicked ways and "to add to his wickedness." In the earlier sources, there is discussion of Esau's repentance. But more to the point, comments about

Ishmael are absent in PT. Bikkurim 3:3 and Gen. Rab. 67:13, although the end of Gen. Rab. 67:13 mentions the rebellion of both Esau and Ishmael. In contradistinction, this midrash implies that Ishmael is more wicked than Esau, or at least Esau can learn from Ishmael's wickedness, a surprising development when considering the rabbinic portrayal of Esau's ignominious character and our examination of the amoraic treatment of both figures.

Additionally, in Midrash Tehillim 11:4 Ishmael is deemed wicked: " 'The LORD tries the righteous; but the wicked and he who loves violence His soul hates'(Ps. 11:5). The wicked is Ishmael, and the one who loves violence is Esau." And in Midrash Tehillim 71:3, we read: " 'Rescue me, O my God, out of the hand of the wicked, out of the hand of the unrighteous and cruel man' (Ps. 71:4) . . . the unrighteous man—Ishmael; the cruel man—Edom whose enactments against me are as bitter as vinegar."[13]

Furthermore, the *mashal* of the king with the orchard that is found in Gen. Rab. 61:6 is also found in Tan. Naso 17 (Buber) and Num. Rab. 11:2. In Genesis Rabbah, the *mashal* interprets Genesis 25:5, "And everything Abraham had he gave to Isaac." In Tan. Naso 17, however, it interprets Gen. 12:2, "And I will make your name great and it shall be a blessing." But this is not the only difference:

> What did Abraham do? He gave birth to two, Ishmael and Isaac but he did not bless them. The matter may be compared to a king who had an orchard that he gave to a tenant. . . . The king is the Holy One, Blessed be He and his orchard is the world. He handed it to Abraham and said, "Bless." What did he do? Abraham had two children, one righteous and the other wicked—Isaac and Ishmael. Said Abraham, "If I bless Isaac then Ishmael will seek a blessing and he is wicked." . . . When Abraham died, the Holy One, Blessed be He appeared to Isaac and blessed him.[14]

In this later midrash, the two trees represent Isaac and Ishmael whereas in Gen. Rab. 61:6, they represent Isaac and the children of Ishmael and Keturah.[15] In Genesis Rabbah, Ishmael is not put in opposition with Isaac, but in this midrash not only is he in conflict with Isaac, he is also deemed wicked twice, once by the narrator and once by Abraham himself. The significance of the transformation of Gen. Rab. 61:6 cannot be overemphasized. For here we have a superb example of how the emergence of Islam effected a modification in the portrayal of Ishmael. In Gen. Rab. 61:6, the children of Ishmael and Keturah do not represent an observable reality but rather are part of the rabbinic process of self-identification. In other words, they are fictitious and the only reality they mirror is the rabbinic understanding of the chosenness of Israel vis-à-vis the other nations.

This transformation in Tan. Naso 17 and Num. Rab. 11:2 in all likelihood reflects one way in which the rabbis dealt with the relative prominence of Islam. No longer is Ishmael only a collateral member of Abraham's family toward whom the rabbis are at times indifferent or even at times favorably inclined. Now, he is one vying directly against Isaac, and the rabbinic attitude toward him becomes increasingly hostile. In fact, Tan. Toledot 5 (Buber) interprets the verse to mean that Ishmael sought to kill Isaac.[16]

It is important to note that despite this transformation, the later corpora retain three earlier midrashim that are neutral or positive. Take, for example, Exod. Rab. 3:2 and Midrash Tehillim 5:8, also found in Gen. Rab. 53:14, where the ministering angels seek to prosecute Ishmael on account of what he will do in the future to the Israelites, that is, destroy them with thirst. God, however, responds by asking, "Right now, is he righteous or wicked?" They respond, "Righteous." And God states, "I judge someone only where he is at the moment."

Similarly, Gen. Rab. 55:7, a midrash that explicitly expresses Abraham's love for Ishmael, is found also in Tan-Yelamdenu, Wayyera 42.[17] Both Gen. Rab. 55:7 and Tan-Yelamdenu, Wayyera 42[18] read:

> "After these things, God put Abraham to the test. He said to him, 'Take now, I pray you (*na*), your son, your only son, the one whom you love, Isaac . . .'" (Gen. 22:1). "I pray you" is nothing more than entreaty. "Your son"—He [Abraham] asked, "Which son?" "Your only son"—He said to Him, "This one is the only son of his mother, and this one is the only son of his mother." He said to him, "The one whom you love." He said to Him, "Is there a limit to the affection?" He said to him, "Isaac."[19]

Clearly then later compilations, certainly medieval rabbinic anthologies, retain earlier material that adduces Abraham's love for Ishmael, but this is more the exception than the rule.

In Pesiqta Rabbati 11[20] we find a midrash which portrays the marginalized children of Abraham as unfit, similar to those discussed in a later section of this chapter:

> "And the children of Israel will number as the sands of the sea" (Hos. 2:1). They are compared to the sand; they are compared to dust; they are compared to stars. Why are they compared to the stars? Abraham

> is like the sun and Isaac is like the sun,[21] but Jacob is like the stars, for in the future, the sun and the moon will be ashamed but the stars have no shame. Thus, the faces of Abraham and Isaac are pale on account of their sons—Abraham on account of Ishmael and the children of Keturah, and Isaac on account of Esau and his chieftains. The stars have no shame, thus Jacob is not ashamed, "For the LORD of Hosts will reign on Mount Zion and in Jerusalem, and the Presence will be revealed to the elders" (Isa. 24:23).[22]

As in other midrashim dealing with the status of Esau, Ishmael, and the children of Keturah, we have here an example of demarcating between the unfit Other and righteous Israel who merits revelation of the divine Presence.[23] What we find more frequently, however, are midrashim that denigrate Ishmael.

An unequivocal example of the rabbinic identification of Ishmael as Islam is found in Lam. Rab. 1:42:

> "The yoke of my offences is bound fast, lashed tight by his hand, imposed upon my neck, it saps my strength . . ." (Lam. 1:14). . . . Another interpretation of "bound" (*niśqad*): The congregation of Israel said, "I was trained by means of my transgressions and I thought that He would forgive me for all my transgressions and did not know that He would bring them all upon me, rather, 'they are lashed tight (*yiś-targû*)'; He made them come intermittently (*śerigût*)."[24] Another interpretation of "bound": The congregation of Israel said, "I was trained by means of the kingdoms and thought that He would bring them upon me one after the other and I did not know that he would bring them upon me in pairs [double]—Babylon and the Chaldeans, Media and Persia, Greece and Macedon, Edom and Ishmael. He made them come upon me intermittently, Babylon was hard but Media was lenient, Greece was severe but Edom lenient, the Chaldeans severe but Persia lenient, Macedon severe but Ishmael lenient."

For the sake of historical accuracy, Radal (Rabbi David Luria)[25] would emend the text as follows: The Chaldeans were severe but Babylon lenient, Persia severe but Media lenient, Greece severe but Macedon lenient, Edom severe but Ishmael lenient. Ishmael, however, is found in one manuscript family and in the printed edition, whereas Seir is found in the other manuscript family that Paul Mandel argues is earlier. As he points out, the pairs of nations are actually one nation. That is to say, the second nation in the pair is a synonym for the first. Persia, for example, is another name for Media, Macedon for Greece, Seir for Edom. The use of Ishmael to represent another nation, however, is found only in the later manuscript family and in the printed edition,[26] that is, well after the emergence of Islam. This change seems to reflect a shift in the use of Ishmael. The later manuscript family and the printed edition irrefutably reflect the use of Ishmael to represent Islam.

One ought not envision a direct, consistent correlation between Ishmael and Islam at this juncture. As we have seen, there are instances where Ishmael does not represent Islam. Nonetheless, several midrashim amply attest to the use of Ishmael to discuss Islam. The animus toward Ishmael was a way in which the rabbis confronted the swiftly emerging political force in the Near East, essentially identified with Arabs. It was also a means of dispelling Islamic claims as rightful heir to Abraham. In other words, by taking a swipe at their Arab progenitor, the rabbis in a sense protest against Islamic hegemony as well as contend with perceived theological supersession.

The tendency to malign Ishmael in later rabbinic compilations discloses a contentious and adversarial attitude toward Islam. But was it toward Islamic political power or Muslim claims to the Abrahamic heritage?[27] At what point in Islamic theological and philosophical discourse does Ishmael play a significant role in its self-conceptualization, and when was it widely accepted? What was the extent of the rabbis' awareness of Islamic appropriation of Ishmael?

To begin with, as previously discussed, we have early Jewish sources such as *Josephus* and Jubilees that make the connection between Ishmael and Arabs. Moreover, the fifth-century church historian, Sozomen, a native of Gaza, informs us that the Arabs were descended from Ishmael and Hagar and, that being the case, they, like the Jews, abstain from eating pork, and observe other Jewish rites and customs. If they deviate from doing so, it should be ascribed to the lapse of time and to their contact with neighboring nations. Sozomen then tells us that because of contact with Jews who told the Arab tribes of their "true origin," some members of these tribes returned to the observance of the "laws of their forefathers," while others converted to Christianity.[28] According to Sozomen's account, the veracity of which there is no reason to question, by the fifth century, the Arabs themselves were aware of their genealogical descent from Ishmael.[29]

Be that as it may, the rabbis themselves, drawing on tannaitic material that identify Ishmael as an Arab, associate Ishmael with Islam. Thus, rather than understanding the change in the portrayal of Ishmael as a direct response to a specific Muslim claim, perhaps we ought to consider the rise of Islam—a broad complex phenomenon of interlocking political power and religious discourse—as an external factor generating an internal change in the rabbinic use of Ishmael in rabbinic interpretation.

In rabbinic texts as late as the ninth century, it is difficult to detect a direct correlation between Ishmael and Islam, although we find some evidence of it. Indeed, it is difficult to determine with great accuracy when in fact the transformation of Ishmael, the biblical figure, to Ishmael, symbol of Muslims/Islam, occurred. Nevertheless, by tracing the changes in midrashim found in earlier rabbinic corpora and by detecting later midrashim that treat Ishmael differently, we can conclude that the rabbis associated Ishmael with Islam.

The symbolization of Ishmael, however, is not fully developed in rabbinic texts but rather takes place later in the medieval period. As previously noted, rabbinic hermeneutics resists turning biblical figures into symbols, even though Esau and Ishmael are used metonymically in several midrashim, especially those characteristically apocalyptic.

In texts deemed part of the rabbinic corpus, no doubt we find a matrix of dyadic associations in many interpretations: Israel and the nations of the world, Israel and Other, clean and unclean, the righteous and wicked, the world-to-come and this world, insider and outsider. At the same time there is fluidity as to how and when a biblical character or historical personage is used in dyadic discourse. While the midrashic mindset maintains a fixed system of such relationships, for the most part it eschews symbolization, thus allowing the rabbis to read out multiple meanings of biblical verses. Thus, in our efforts to highlight the effects of historical events on rabbinic interpretation, our foregrounding must always take into account the methodological characteristics of rabbinic exegesis and the very interplay of both history and hermeneutics.

The Treatment of Ishmael in Pirke de Rabbi Eliezer

The portrayal of Ishmael in PRE is one of the most elaborate and complex portrayals of Ishmael in the midrashic corpus.[30] Ishmael and the Ishmaelites are mentioned in a total of nine chapters, one of which is a relatively long account of Abraham's visit to Ishmael. On the one hand, the author depicts Ishmael as the beloved son of Abraham, yet on the other, he characterizes him, as we have seen elsewhere, as the marginalized, rejected firstborn. Furthermore, while the author of PRE maintains an ambivalent approach to Ishmael, he invariably depicts the Ishmaelites as Israel's enemies.

Modern scholars have made assertions about the relationship between the Islamic and Jewish versions of Abraham's visits to Ishmael, which are based on the assumption that Ishmael represents Islam in the Jewish version. We will therefore look at the story of Abraham's visits as it is found in PRE and in Islamic sources in order to test the accuracy of these assertions.

In his portrayal of Ishmael and the Ishmaelites, the author of PRE significantly reworks two earlier rabbinic sources—the midrashim on those who were called before they were born and the attempt to offer the Torah to the nations of the world. As we shall see presently, throughout PRE the author[31] distinguishes between Ishmael and his descendants, *beney Yishmael*. Why he makes this distinction is unclear. What is apparent, however, is the paucity of evidence to support the fact that the midrashim on Ishmael in PRE are generated by extratextual concerns such as the rise of Islam. Rather, these midrashim foster the notion that only Israel is the chosen people. On the other hand, the Ishmaelites, described in apocalyptic terms, are used to represent Islam.

Chapter 32 of PRE opens with the following:[32]

> Six were called by their names before they were born and they are: Isaac, Ishmael, Moses our master, Solomon, Josiah and the name of the Messiah whom the Holy One, Blessed be He will bring immediately in our days. . . . How do we know about Ishmael? Scripture says, "And you shall call his name Ishmael" (Gen. 16:11). Why was his name called Ishmael? In the future the Holy One, Blessed be He will hear[33] the voice of the groaning of the people from what in the future the Ishmaelites will do, therefore his name is called Ishmael, as it is said, "God will hear (*yišmaʿ ʾēl*) [what the Ishmaelites will do] and afflicts (vb. *ʿanâh*) them" (Ps. 55:20).[34]

Here, as in PT. Berakot, Ishmael is named among prominent biblical characters of Jewish history. In the earlier sources, however, the prooftext is Genesis 16:11, "Behold, you are with child, and shall bear a son; you shall call his name Ishmael." In PRE the author uses an additional prooftext: "In the future the Holy One, Blessed be He will hear the voice of the groaning of the people from what in the future the Ishmaelites will do, therefore his name is called Ishmael, as it is said, 'God hears and afflicts them'" (Ps. 55: 20). The midrash plays with the meaning of *ʿanâh*—to humble, to afflict, and also to answer. That is, God hears the groaning of his people and answers them by humbling or afflicting the Ishmaelites.

PRE's reworking of this midrash found in the earlier texts reflects a deliberate attempt on the part of the author to distinguish between Ishmael and the Ishmaelites, while at the same time maintaining their ancestral connection. The earlier midrashim are neutral, whereas PRE indicts the Ishmaelites for their treacherous treatment of the Israelites. In this case, the use of an additional prooftext, Psalm 55:20, as well as PRE's explicit statement, enhances one's understanding of the midrash. Whereas PT. Berakot 1:6 does not compromise Ishmael's position vis-à-vis the other named figures, PRE depicts the Ishmaelites negatively.

And as previously mentioned, Mekhilta, Pisḥa 16, and Gen. Rab. 45:8 do not include Ishmael with the others, for to include Ishmael, who is not part of the covenant, with Isaac, Solomon, and Josiah would give him equal status. The negative portrayal of the Ishmaelites in PRE, on the other hand, is a means by which the author refers to Islam. Let us first investigate images of Ishmael in PRE.[35]

In chapter 29 of PRE, Abraham sends for Shem[36] and he circumcises Abraham and Ishmael:

> The eighth trial: When Abraham was ninety-nine years old, the Holy One, Blessed be He said to him, "Walk before me and be blameless" (Gen. 17:1). The Holy One, Blessed be He said to him, "Until now you have not been blameless before me, but circumcise the flesh of your foreskin and walk before me and be blameless." . . . R. Gamliel said, "He sent and called for Shem, the son of Noah, and Shem circumcised the flesh of his foreskin and the flesh of the foreskin of Ishmael his son," as it is said, "On the same day Abraham was circumcised and his son" (Gen. 17:26).

Shem circumcises Abraham and Ishmael, but there is no mention of all the members of his household having been circumcised "on the same day." The fact that they are not mentioned emphasizes Ishmael's relationship to Abraham. The rest of the chapter discusses circumcision, distinguishing between the circumcised and uncircumcised. Although there is no explicit reference made to Ishmael, he is implicitly referred to in the following:

> Rabbi Zerika taught: If they do not cut off [to not use at all] from the tree its fruit of the first three years, all the fruit that it produces will be fit to be plucked but not good in appearance and its wine will be unfit for the altar. But if they cut the fruit of its first three years

> (*ʿorlâh*), all the fruit it produces will have good appearance, and their wine will be chosen as libation for the altar. So, too, with our father Abraham. Before he was circumcised, the fruit that he produced was not good in its deeds, and was unfit for the altar. But when he was circumcised, the fruit which he produced was good and its deeds were good and it was chosen to be brought to the altar like wine for libation, as it is said, "And wine for the drink offering" (Num. 15:5).

By playing on the word *ʿorlâh*, the midrash differentiates between the status of Ishmael and Isaac. The pun on *ʿorlâh*, which means both "foreskin" and "the first three years of the fruit of trees," creates an analogy whereby Isaac is singled out as the chosen son of Abraham. Ishmael is the unfit son, unworthy of sacrifice on the altar. Like the tree whose first three years of fruit are unharvested (not cut off), Abraham who is uncircumcised (*ʿārēl*) produces unfit fruit—Ishmael. But, like the tree whose first three years of fruit is harvested (cut off), Abraham produces fruit, Isaac, worthy of being offered on the sacrificial altar.

As we have noticed elsewhere, setting Israel apart from the other nations is a prevalent theme in rabbinic literature. The analogy in this case, however, is not fully, or at least not explicitly, worked out regarding the children of Keturah who were produced after Abraham's circumcision. One could make the case that Isaac is unique since he is the son of an elderly barren wife. More likely, the idea that the first fruit after the initial years is fit, or "holy" as in Levitcus 19:24 underlies the midrash.[37]

Chapter 29 consists of a collection of comments made by various rabbis concerning circumcision and Israel's unique status as the truly circumcised, the sui generis one among the nations. When, for example, the midrash discusses Genesis 17:27, "All the men of his house, those born in his house, and those bought with money of a foreigner were circumcised with him," it claims that they and their descendants were not "valid" converts. According to the midrash, Abraham circumcised them because of purity, "so that they should not defile their masters with their food and drink." In fact, a convert is not considered a true convert until seven generations have passed in order to test whether or not they return to their idolatrous ways. The midrash continues: "and in their death they are like corpses of the field and their prayers do not come before the Holy One, Blessed be He, as it is said, 'The dead do not praise the Lord'" (Ps. 115:17). As in the case with Ishmael, a distinction is drawn between Israel and those who are not part of the covenant. And yet it should be noted that Ishmael's status is greater than theirs, for he is not included among the converts.

A similar distinction is made between Israel and Esau, about whom the midrash states:

> Rabbi said, "Isaac circumcised Jacob and Esau. Esau despised the covenant just as he despised his birthright. Unlike Esau, Jacob is faithful to the covenant which is maintained through his seed, but Jacob clung to the covenant of circumcision and he circumcised his sons and grandsons. . . . The sons of Jacob circumcised their sons and their grandsons."[38]

Rabbi Zerika's play on *ʿorlâh* and the distinction he makes in essence between Ishmael and Isaac (see above) must be understood in light of the thrust of the chapter, which emphasizes Israel's status as the chosen people with whom God has made a covenant. It is therefore not surprising that at the beginning of the chapter we read that Shem circumcised Abraham and Ishmael, that "in that same day Abraham and his son Ishmael were circumcised" (Gen. 17:26). The tension created by including Ishmael with Abraham and then excluding him is paradigmatic of how the author of PRE deals with Ishmael in general, and thus generates an overall ambivalence toward Ishmael. At the same time, however, it is important to note that, with the possible exception of one instance, the author never disparages Ishmael.[39]

Abraham's love for Ishmael is most pronounced in chapter 30, which we will examine shortly, but is also found in chapter 31:

> The tenth trial: "And after these things God tested Abraham" (Gen. 22). . . . And Ishmael went out from the desert to see Abraham his father. R. Yehudah said, "That night, the Holy One, Blessed be He appeared to Abraham and said to him, 'Take now your son, your only son whom you love, Isaac' (Gen. 22:2). Abraham, having pity on Isaac, said before the Master of the Universe, 'Which son, the son born before circumcision or the son of circumcision?' He said to him, 'Your only son.' He said to Him, 'This one is the only son of his mother, and the other is the only son of his mother.' He said to him, 'The one whom you love.' He said, 'I love this one and I love that one.' He said to him, 'Isaac.' "

Expanding the biblical narrative and serving to address the issue of the manner in which God commands Abraham to sacrifice Isaac, the dialogue between God and Abraham is not unique to PRE.[40] From the dialogue we learn of Abraham's equal love for both sons. What is unique to PRE, however, is

Ishmael's visit to his father Abraham. As we will soon see, the image of Ishmael visiting his father[41] complements the image of Abraham traveling in the desert to visit him in chapter 30.

The reference to the precircumcision son and the postcircumcised son is another feature of this midrash that we do not find in the other sources. This differentiation reinforces the notion of unfit and fit "fruit" in chapter 29. So, too, even in this example where Abraham avers his love for Ishmael, he is nonetheless marginalized.

Indeed, the mutual affection between father and son can never take precedence over the chosenness of Isaac:

> Abraham got up in the morning and took Ishmael and Eliezer and Isaac his son and saddled the ass. . . . Rivalry entered between Eliezer and Ishmael. Ishmael said to Eliezer, "Now Abraham will offer Isaac his son for a burnt offering kindled upon the altar, and I am his first-born son and I will inherit Abraham." Eliezer replied, and said to him, "He has already driven you out like a woman divorced from her husband, and he sent you away to the wilderness, but I am his servant, serving his house day and night and I shall be the heir of Abraham." The Holy Spirit replied to them and said to them, "Neither this one nor that one will inherit."[42]

Here, according to Heinemann, the author uses rabbinic material to create a midrash relevant to the eighth century. Like Heller, Heinemann maintains that the issue has to do with the question of which of the three monotheistic religions is the legitimate heir of the Abrahamic covenant.[43]

Heinemann asserts that an eighth-century audience introduced to this midrash would immediately associate Ishmael with Islam. Furthermore, while admitting that Eliezer does not represent Christianity any place in the rabbinic corpus, he nonetheless states, "In the context before us there is no doubt who the third side is in the great dispute revolving around the question, which of the three is the true monotheistic religion."[44]

In part, Heinemann's thesis is persuasive. It seems likely that in this case Ishmael represents Islam, but which of the many groups laying claim to the biblical heritage does Eliezer represent? Christians? Samaritans?[45] Maybe non-Jews in general? That there is a definitive correlation between Eliezer and Christianity is doubtful. That Ishmael represents Islam, however, is likely given the ways in which the midrash is altered. PRE, for example, adds a rivalry between Eliezer and Ishmael, which is not found in other sources.

Neither Eliezer nor Ishmael will inherit because Isaac is the chosen child. Heinemann points out that we do not have the argument between Ishmael and Isaac found in other sources such as Targum Ps. Jonathan, Tan. Wayyera 42 (Buber), and Gen. Rab. 55:4.[46] This, I think, is significant because in the debate over who will inherit, Isaac, meaning Israel, is silent. It is not Isaac who claims that he is more beloved, but rather, it is the Shekhinah, divine ordinance, that affirms Israel's chosenness. In a subtle sense, Judaism does not participate in this theological debate, yet ironically it makes a stronger claim for divine favoritism; the Shekhinah itself chooses.

That Ishmael represents Islam in this reworking of an earlier midrash does not attenuate the contention that the author of PRE uses the Ishmaelites rather than Ishmael to represent Islam, for when dealing with rabbinic texts such consistency is rare.

In the continuation of chapter 31, the author asserts Israel's status as the true inheritor of the covenant between God and Abraham's offspring:

> On the third day they reached Zophim and when they reached Zophim, Abraham saw the glory of the Shekhinah standing on the top of the mountain, as it is said, "On the third day Abraham lifted up his eyes, and saw the place from a distance" (Gen. 22:4). What did he see? He saw a pillar of fire standing from the earth to the heavens. He said to Isaac his son, "My son, do you see anything on one of these mountains?" He replied, "Yes, I see a pillar of fire standing from the earth to the heavens." He said to Ishmael and Eliezer, "Do you see anything on one of these mountains?" They responded, "No." He considered them asses and said to them, " 'Remain here with the ass' (Gen. 22:5)—just as the ass does not see anything, so too you do not see anything," as it is said, "And Abraham said to the youths, Remain here with the ass" (Gen. 22:5), a people resembling an ass.

According to Heinemann the motif of a people resembling a donkey began as an anti-Christian polemic.[47] He asserts that in Gen. Rab. 56:2,[48] the earliest source of this midrash, we find no mention of "a nation resembling a donkey," but several parallel sources such as Tanḥuma and Leviticus Rabbah include the phrase, which is a play on "*ʿim*—(with) the ass" and "*ʿam*—(people or nation) of asses."[49] The rabbis, Heinemann maintains, were not concerned only with biblical exegesis or with explaining the Aqedah, but rather with other issues, namely with God's revelation to Israel at the exclusion of the other nations of the world. The midrash in Gen. Rab. 56:2 was retailored, thus giving rise to other midrashim that address Israel's chosenness. The ability to "see," better yet, to understand, is exclusively reserved for Israel and not for the nations of the world.[50] The anti-Christian polemic here, Heinemann contends, is thus a later development not found in Gen. Rab. 56:2. Nevertheless, noteworthy is the fact that the rest of Gen. Rab. 56:2, while not polemically charged, makes an exclusivist claim to the Torah, which Israel received as a reward for worshiping God.[51] Rather than assuming the change in Tanḥuma and Lev. Rab. as indicative of anti-Christian polemic, we might consider it a clever play on "with" and "people" that comments on Israel's chosenness preserved in later texts. In this instance, it is difficult to argue that the change reflects specifically an anti-Christian polemic. Moreover, according to Chaim Milikowsky,[52] most MSS of Lev. Rab. 20:2 have Ishmael and Eliezer's names, but the Munich and Oxford 51 MSS (before emendation) do not. Instead, "his servants" (*ʿăbādāyw*) is found. It is therefore unclear whether or not to attribute the insertion of the names to the editor of Lev. Rab. since the change may have occurred during the transmission of the text when the rabbis were in engaged in staking a claim to Abraham vis-à-vis both Christianity and Islam.

Heinemann does not explicitly discuss how this midrash plays itself out in PRE. Given his conception of the development of midrashim, however, one could construct his position as follows: In PRE the polemic is not only anti-Christian but also anti-Islamic. Both nations cannot "see." Whereas in Leviticus Rabbah the phrase "nations resembling a donkey," was used as anti-Christian polemic, it is now used against Islam as well as Christianity. Indeed, as in the other midrashim found in chapter 31 of PRE, the midrash is used to set Israel apart from the other nations. In the midrash describing the argument between Ishmael and Eliezer, there too, we find that only Israel "sees," and therefore only Israel is the chosen one.

Furthermore, that only Israel "sees," should not lead us to assume that Ishmael represents Islam throughout PRE. Take, for example, the beginning of chapter 31 where Abraham professes his love for both his sons. Perhaps to comprehend the attitude toward Ishmael in this chapter, one must keep in mind the constant tension between Abraham's love for Ishmael and Israel's divinely decreed status. The author, fully cognizant, or so it seems, of the theological claims of Christians, Samaritans, and Muslims may have these faith traditions in mind when espousing Israel's chosenness, however this does not imply that every mention of Ishmael is a reference to Islam.

In this case, Ishmael may symbolize Islam but in PRE he is more frequently depicted as Abraham's circumcised son, yet distinguished from Isaac, the son through whom God will maintain his covenant with Abraham. The author of PRE acknowledges Ishmael's role in Israelite history. In a sense, he is reclaiming Ishmael for the Jewish tradition. Although Ishmael is not the bearer of the covenant, he is nevertheless a member of Abraham's household. Whether the author's position is prevalent among members of the Jewish community or whether he is debating them is difficult to know. It could be that he is disputing Muslim claims with real or imagined Muslims—perhaps Jewish converts—in mind. Given the dearth of evidence we must refrain from dealing with these issues in a manner exceeding the bounds of suggestion.

Our examination illustrates the nature of midrash qua interpretation. At every turn, we find ourselves in the midst of rabbinic discourse that treats biblical figures with precious few restrictions, sources that illumine the inextricable relationship between text and context. Paralleling the ambiguity of Ishmael's ambivalent status in the biblical narrative, PRE depicts both Ishmael's inferior status to Isaac and Abraham's love for Ishmael. PRE reclaims his role in the Jewish metanarrative and at the same time maintains his marginalized status.

Abraham's Visits to Ishmael in Pirke de Rabbi Eliezer

> Abraham stood and he prayed before the Holy One, Blessed be He for his son and as a result the house of Ishmael was filled with all the good things of blessings. When Ishmael returned, his wife told him what happened and Ishmael knew that his father still loved him, as it is said, "As a father loves his children" (Ps. 103:13).
>
> —Pirke de Rabbi Eliezer, Chapter 30

Studies of Abraham's visits to Ishmael in both Jewish and Islamic sources have been significantly overshadowed by the debate among scholars as to whether or not the Jewish version predates the Muslim, or vice versa. Contrary to the regnant view among scholars[53] of the story, which is often mistakenly deemed polemical, the Ishmaelites, not Ishmael, represent Islam. The response of the author of PRE to the rise of Islam lies not in the story of Abraham's visit to Ishmael itself but elsewhere in the book, in his depiction of the sons of Ishmael. The depiction of Ishmael and his sons in chapters 28–32, 41, 43, and 45 must be viewed together with the relatively positive portrayal of Ishmael in other chapters. According to PRE, Ishmael is Abraham's legitimate son, deserving of his father's blessing and love, but he will not inherit the Abrahamic covenant, whereas the Ishmaelites are the fourth and final kingdom that will be destroyed in the end days "by the finger of God."

To establish the claim that modern scholars err in equating Ishmael with Islam in the story of Abraham's visits to Ishmael, it will be helpful to examine their arguments in detail. The striking similarities between the Jewish and Muslim renditions[54] of Abraham's visits to Ishmael have drawn scholars to the field of literary archaeology, so to speak. Their endeavor to discern the earliest layer, to uncover the original literary kernel, however, reduces the dynamic of intercultural relations to facile alternatives—either the story was original or borrowed.[55] This unrefined schema belies the complex web of interchange, be it oral, written, social, or cultural,[56] between Muslims and Jews and makes it futile to posit a unidirectional influence. As Lazarus-Yafeh writes:

> One should not think in terms of influences or cultural borrowing only, however. It has been said that the Near East resembles a palimpsest, layer upon layer, tradition upon tradition, intertwined to the extent that one cannot really grasp one without the other, certainly not the later without the earlier, but often also not the earlier without considering the shapes it took later.[57]

The issue of locating the original source of the narrative is indeed highly speculative and ignores the oral nature of these texts. The story might have originated in rabbinic circles and then been reworked by Muslims and again later refashioned in PRE, the earliest extant version of the story.[58] On the other hand, it is also quite possible that the story originated in the Muslim tradition, which used both Arab folklore and Jewish legends. Alternatively, both traditions may have drawn from a written or oral source of which we have no trace.

Scholars in the past have described the nature of these texts in terms of polemical rhetoric,[59] literary expressions attacking and maligning one's antagonist to varying degrees, or apologetic, defensive rhetoric. They have examined the Jewish version in light of its Arab counterparts, but have ignored both the question of how the story works within each tradition and the nonpolemical nature of intercommunal literary relations. The presence of the story in both traditions reflects a cross-cultural diffusion in which external sources contribute to the shaping of literary expression, religious identity, and theological development. It seems more advantageous therefore to use this similarity as a means of examining this phenomenon.

Let us begin our study by turning to chapter 30 of PRE, which relates the ninth of Abraham's ten trials,[60] his expulsion of Hagar and Ishmael:

The ninth trial: Ishmael was born with the bow and grew up with the bow, as it is said, "And he became an archer" (Gen. 21:20).[61] He used to take bow and arrows and shoot at the birds. One time he saw Isaac sitting by himself and he shot an arrow to kill him. Sarah related the incident to Abraham and said, "Write to Isaac all that the Holy One, Blessed be He promised to give you and your seed. By your life, the son of this maidservant shall not inherit with my son, with Isaac," as it is written, "And she said to Abraham, 'Cast out this bondwoman and her son' " (Gen. 21:10). Ben Tema[62] said: Sarah said to Abraham, "Write a bill of divorce and send away this maidservant and her son from me and my son."[63] And of all the misfortunes that came upon Abraham, this thing was difficult and very evil in his eyes, as it is said, "And the thing was very evil in the eyes of Abraham on account of his son" (Gen. 21:11).

R. Yehuda said: That same night, the Holy One, Blessed be He appeared to Abraham our father. He said to him, "Abraham, do you know that Sarah was fit for you as wife [from her mother's womb]?[64] She is your companion and wife of your youth. Hagar is not called your wife nor is Sarah called your maidservant, as it is written, "But Sarah your wife shall bear you a son" (Gen. 17:19). Hagar is not called your wife but rather your maidservant. And all that Sarah spoke, she spoke in truth. Let it not be evil in your eyes about the boy and your maidservant," as it is written, "And God said to Abraham, 'Do not let it be evil in your eyes about the boy . . . ' " (Gen 21:12).

Abraham got up in the morning and wrote a bill of divorce, gave it to her and sent her away from him and from Isaac his son—from this world and the world to come, as it is said, "Abraham got up in the morning and took some bread and a bottle of water" (Gen. 21:14). He sent her away with a bill of divorce and he took the water bottle[65] and tied it around her waist so it would drag behind her and make it known that she is a maidservant. But, moreover, Abraham wanted to see Ishmael his son and to see the road on which they were walking.[66] On account of Abraham's merit, the bottle did not lose any water. When she arrived in the desert, she began to go astray after worship of the idols in the house of Pharaoh [her father],[67] and immediately the bottle lost water. Therefore [it is said], "And she cast the child" (Gen. 21:15).

Ishmael was seventeen[68] years old when he went out from his father's house and Isaac was ten[69] years old. [What is the meaning of] "And she departed and wandered" (Gen. 21:14)? "Wandered" can only mean idol worship, as it is written, "They are vanity, a work of errors" (Jer. 10:15).[70] And Ishmael was tired with thirst. He walked and he cast himself under the desert brambles and said, "Master of the Universe, if you desire to give me water, give it to me so that my soul will not go out in thirst, for death by thirst is unusual and the hardest of all deaths. The Holy One, Blessed be He heard his prayer, as it is said, "For God heard the voice of the boy" (Gen. 21:17) and it is written, "For God heard the voice of the boy where he is." The well that was created at twilight[71] opened and they drank and filled the bottle with water, as it is said, "And God opened her eyes" (Gen. 21:19). They left the well and from there they walked the entire desert until they reached the desert in Paran where they found streams of water so they dwelt there, as it is said, "And he dwelt in the desert of Paran" (Gen. 21:21). Ishmael sent and took for himself a wife from the daughters[72] of Moab and her name was ʿAyeshah.[73]

After three years Abraham went to see Ishmael his son and he swore to Sarah that he would not go down from the camel at the place where Ishmael dwelt. He arrived there at midday and found Ishmael's wife. He said to her, "Where is Ishmael?" She said to him, "He and his mother went to bring fruit and dates from the desert." He said to her, "Give me a little water and bread and refreshments for I am tired from the desert journey." She said to him, "There is no bread and there is no water." He said to her, "When Ishmael returns tell him these things and say to him that an old man came from the land of Canaan to see you and said that the doorsill of the house is not good."[74] When Ishmael returned his wife told him what had happened. He sent her away and his mother sent and took for him a wife from her father's house and her name was Fatimah. Again after three years Abraham went to see his son Ishmael and swore to Sarah like the first time that he would not go down from the camel at the place where Ishmael dwelt. He arrived there at midday and found Ishmael's wife. He asked about Ishmael's whereabouts, to which she replied, "He and his mother went to pasture the camels in the desert." Since he was exhausted from the journey, he asked for some bread and water. She brought it out and gave it to him. Abraham stood and he prayed before the Holy One, Blessed be He for his son and as a result the house of Ishmael was filled with all the good things of blessings. When Ishmael returned, his wife told him what happened and Ishmael knew that his father still loved him, as it is said, "As a father loves his children" (Ps. 103:13).

After the death of Sarah Abraham took his divorced [wife], as it is said, "And Abraham again took a wife and her name was Keturah" (Gen. 25:1). Why does Scripture say, "And Abraham again"? Because the first time she was his wife and again he had sex with her. Her name was Keturah because she was perfumed with all kinds of spices. [This is a play on "perfumed," *mĕqûṭeret*, and Keturah, *qĕṭûrâh*.] Another explanation: her name was Keturah because her deeds were as beautiful as incense, and she bore him six children: Zimran, Yokshan, Medan, Midian, Yishbak and Shuah, as it is said, "and she bore him Zimran . . ." (Gen. 25:2).

Like a woman divorced from her husband thus Abraham stood and sent them away from Isaac his son, in this world and in the world to come, as it is said, "But to the children of the concubines of Abraham, he gave gifts and sent them away from Isaac his son" (Gen. 25:6) by a bill of divorce.

According to the name of Ishmael's sons, Kedar, they were called the sons of Kedar, as it is said, "Of Kedar and the kingdoms of Hazor" (Jer. 49:28). And Kedemah were called the children of Kedem, as it is said, "the Kedemites" (ibid.). Because they dwelt in the territory of Cain, they were called the sons of Cain: "And Heber the Kenite had separated himself from Cain" (Judges 4:11). Did not all the children of Cain separate at the generation of the flood? But because they dwelt in the territory of Cain, they were called the children of Cain, as it is said, "Cain shall be wasted, as long as Asshur shall dwell in thy place" (Num. 24:22). Asshur is from the seed of Ishmael. They shall cause the kingdom of Asshur to cease.[75]

Balaam said: Of the seventy languages the Holy One, Blessed be He created in His world, he did not put His name on one of them except for Isra*el*. Since He made the name of Ishma*el* similar to the name of Israel, woe to him who shall live in his days, as it is said, 'Woe to one who shall live when God establishes him' (Num. 24:23). [emphasis added]

R. Ishmael said:[76] There are fifteen things that the children of Ishmael will do in the future in the land [of Israel] in the latter days. These are: they will measure the land with ropes[77] and they will make a cemetery into a resting place for sheep dunghills;[78] they will measure with them and from them on the tops of the mountains; lying will increase and truth will be hidden; law will be distanced from Israel; sins will increase in Israel, scarlet thread like wool, and paper and pen will dry up[79] and he will hew down the rock of the kingdom and he will rebuild the destroyed cities and clear the roads;[80] they will plant gardens and orchards; they will fence in the broken walls of the Temple and they will build a building in the Temple.[81] And two brothers will stand, princes in the end.[82] In their days the branch, the son of David, will stand over them, as it is said, "And in the days of those kings shall the God of heaven set up a kingdom, which shall never be destroyed" (Dan. 2:44).

R. Ishmael also said: Three wars of trouble will the Ishmaelites in the future wage in the land in the final days, as it is said, "From the

> swords they fled" (Isa. 21:15). "Swords" can only mean wars—one in the forest of Arabia, as it is said, "From the drawn sword" (ibid.), one in the sea, as it is said, "From the bent bow" (ibid.) and one in the great city which is in Rome which will be weightier than the other two, as it is said, "From the weightiness of war" (ibid.). From there the son of David will flourish and see the destruction of these and these. And from there he will come to the land of Israel, as it is said, "Who is this coming from Edom with crimsoned garments from Bozrah? . . . this in his glorious apparel, pressing forward in his great strength? It is I who speaks in righteousness, mighty to save" (Isa. 63:1).

Before dealing with various approaches Jewish scholars have taken to the narrative, and then offering an alternative approach, one that takes into account how the narrative functions within the larger framework of each tradition, let us set the stage by retelling the story as it is found in al-Ṭabarī's *Ta'rīkh al-Rusūl wal-Mulūk* (*Prophets and Patriarchs*):[83]

> At that time, there were Jurhumites in the valley near Mecca. Some birds had stayed in the valley because they saw water. When the Jurhumites saw the birds, they said, "They would not be there if there was no water." They came to Hagar and said, "If you want, we will stay with you and keep you company for as long as the water is yours." She said, "Yes." They were with her until Ishmael grew up. Hagar died and Ishmael married a woman from the Jurhum tribe.
>
> Abraham asked Sarah's permission to leave in order to visit Hagar and Sarah permitted him, stipulating that he not settle down.[84] When Abraham came to Ishmael's house, Hagar had already died. He said to his [Ishmael's] wife, "Where is your master?" She said, "He is not here. He went hunting." Ishmael used to leave al-Ḥarām[85] to go hunting. Abraham said, "Do you have any hospitality? Do you have any food or drink?" She said, "I don't have anything and no one is here with me."[86] Abraham said, "When your husband comes, greet him with peace and tell him that he should change the threshold of his door." Abraham left and when Ishmael came, he found his father's smell. He said to his wife, "Did anyone come to you?" She said, "An old man came to me whose description was such and such," as though she were making light of him. He said, "What did he say to you?" She said, "He said to me: 'Greet your husband with peace and tell him that he should change the threshold of his door.'" He divorced her and married another.[87] Abraham stayed as long as God willed and then he asked Sarah's permission to visit Ishmael. She permitted him,

> stipulating that he not reside there. Abraham came to Ishmael's door and said to his wife, "Where is your master?" She said, "He went hunting but will return soon, God willing. Stay here and may God be merciful on you." He said to her, "Do you have hospitality?" She said, "Yes." He said to her, "Do you have bread, wheat, barley or dates?" She brought milk and meat[88] and he prayed for a blessing on both of them. Had she brought bread or wheat or barely, God's land would have the most wheat, barley and figs.[89] She said, "Come down so I may wash your head," but he would not so she brought him the maqām[90] and put it at his right side. He placed his foot on it and his footprint remained on it. She washed the right side of his head, then she moved the maqām to his left and washed the left side.[91] He said to her, "When your husband comes, greet him with peace and tell him, The threshold of your door is sound." When Ishmael came, he smelled his father's scent and said to his wife, "Did anyone come to you?" She said, "Yes, an old man, the handsomest and best-smelling in the world. He said to me such and such and I said to him this and that. I washed his head and this is the place of his foot on the standing place." He said, "What did he say to you?" She said, "He said to me, 'When your husband comes, greet him with peace and tell him the threshold of your door is sound.' " Ishmael said, "That was Abraham."
>
> Abraham stayed as long as God willed it and then God commanded him to build the House. So he and Ishmael built it.[92]

Bernard Heller, Joseph Heinemann, and Haim Schwartzbaum assert that the story of Abraham's visit to Ishmael originated in Islamic sources and claim that Ishmael in PRE equals Islam and that in the reworking of this story, the author of PRE introduced anti-Islamic polemic.[93] Heller reads the story in light of the Islamic accounts and in doing so loses sight of the story's positive portrayal of Ishmael. Heller claims, for example, that unlike Ishmael's occupation in PRE, in the Islamic sources Ishmael's profession is highly esteemed, for Ishmael is a hunter and horseman, whereas according to PRE, he gathers dates and pastures camels.

To begin with, although it is not unanimous, most versions mention hunting. For example, al-Yaʿqūbī, al-Kisāʾī, and al-Masʿūdī either mention hunting and shepherding or no occupation. In al-Thaʿlabī we read that Ishmael was excited about hunting, was trained in hunting birds, and was a rider of horses. He shot targets and liked to compete and wrestle. In Ibn Kathīr and al-Bukharī, version a, the first woman says to Abraham, "He left to get food," whereas in version b of al-Bukharī, both the first and second wife respond, "He went hunting." This response is attributed to only the second wife in al-Ṭabarī, version a. Also, in Ibn al-Athīr, al-Thaʿlabī, and al-Ṭabarī, version b, we learn that Ishmael frequently leaves al-ḥarām to go hunting.

Even the Jewish sources do not agree. In Sefer ha-Yashar, the first wife says that Ishmael went out to hunt and the second wife says that he went to hunt and to shepherd the camels.[94] In Yalquṭ, he was in the desert gathering fruit and dates (an unusual desert activity), whereas in Midrash ha-Gadol, he was out shepherding the camels.

Heller's observation, however, seems to work against him. That is, had the author described Ishmael as a hunter or horseman, one might argue that the author was tainting Ishmael's character since the rabbis looked askance at hunters and horsemen.[95] The author of PRE, rather, portrays Ishmael as a shepherd of camels, a common occupation of desert life.[96] Moreover, when Abraham inquires about Ishmael's whereabouts, in both instances he is with his mother either taking care of the camels or gathering food to eat. The image is of a provider, tending to camels and to his family. PRE's description of Ishmael's occupation is slighting only if we read it as a deliberate distortion of an Islamic account of Abraham's visit and as a direct polemic against Islam for whom such occupations as horseman and hunter are esteemed. But can we presume that the intended audience was fairly familiar with the Arabic version? It seems highly unlikely.

But if we read the story in PRE in light of rabbinic culture and the overall portrayal of Ishmael, casting Ishmael as a gatherer of fruits and dates and a shepherd of camels contributes to his favorable portrayal. If we assume that the author was familiar with one of the Islamic accounts and used it to create his account, then one could argue that he intentionally chose to cast Ishmael in a less negative light. Because hunting and horse riding were not highly respected activities in the rabbinic world, the author chose to portray Ishmael as a man of the land, as a shepherd—an image associated with the biblical Patriarchs. To be sure, even casting him as a hunter should not be taken as an attempt to tarnish his character. Whether a hunter, a gatherer of fruit, or a shepherd of camels, the Ishmael who dwelt in Paran is associated with desert life.

Heller also observes, for example, that in the Islamic version the second wife offers Abraham "meat and milk" (in some versions she offers "meat and water"), whereas in the Jewish version she offers only "bread and water." He argues that this is a deliberate alteration of the Islamic text used to diminish the generosity of the second wife. The rabbinic author, however, may have been bothered by the thought of Abraham mixing meat and milk. Furthermore, "bread and water" in the biblical tradition means food in general,[97] and in the rabbinic tradition, it expresses hospitality, *hakhnasat orkhim*.[98] It is also important to note that the Arabic word for meat is *laḥm*, which may have been translated to the Hebrew *laḥem*, bread. It is therefore likely that the depiction of the second wife is not derogatory.

Heller argues that compliments to the second wife that are found in the Muslim text are omitted and therefore the midrashic depiction is negative. If read on its own, however, the portrayal of the second wife is positive. Neither the narrator nor Abraham comments on her character. Indeed, the point of the story in part is to illustrate the connection between father and son, one that is based on mutual respect and affection. Ishmael seeks paternal approval and gets it. The very fact that Abraham prays for his son after the second wife brought bread and water and that, because of the prayer, Ishmael's house was replete with "good things," says a great deal about the second wife. Unlike the first wife, the second was hospitable and she therefore found favor in Abraham's eyes.

He contends furthermore that the author of PRE used a Muslim text that did not have the names of the two wives and therefore was free to use the names of ʿAyeshah and Fatima.[99] The use of these names, according to Heller, also points to the story's Islamic origins and anti-Islamic overtones. That is, the use of the name of Muhammad's favored daughter, Fatima, and beloved wife ʿAyeshah,[100] bespeaks antipathy. This is indeed a curious claim.[101] The characterization of Fatima as hospitable perhaps reflects the author's predisposed attitude toward Fatima, Muhammad's beloved daughter. Finally, Gordon Newby argues that the use of Fatima may be the author's way of supporting the Fatimid dynasty, named for Fatima, from whom the ruler claimed descent.[102]

Heller concludes that all the legends in PRE pertaining to Ishmael debase his character because of the hardship the Jews faced under Islamic rule. Thus, according to Heller, in PRE Ishmael equals Islam and the author uses the biblical character to attack Islam. One, however, must be careful in making such blanket statements about the fate of Jews under Islamic rule. Mark Cohen, for example, argues that despite the articulation of legislation such as *saghar* (humiliation), Jews had potential for security under Muslim rule. Moreover, fragments from the Genizah illustrate joint Jewish and Islamic economic ventures as well as social relations. He states as follows:

> In Islam, Jews and Christians, though protected as *dhimmīs*, were considered infidels and suffered humiliation and contemptuous treatment from the dominant group. This was in keeping with their

> religious inferiority and lowly rank in the hierarchy of Muslim society. Nonetheless, in day-to-day life, the Jews of Islam regularly crossed boundaries in the hierarchy to participate—however temporarily and, at times, tenuously—as virtual equals with Muslims of similar category. Though always at risk of incurring Muslim wrath and even persecution, Jews, nonetheless, enjoyed substantial security during the formative and classical periods of Islam.
>
> In the economic sphere, the Jews of Islam apparently enjoyed parity with their counterparts belonging to the Islamic *ummah*.[103]

Furthermore, as Wasserstrom illustrates rather convincingly in his work on the very notion of Jewish-Muslim symbiosis under early Islam, the situation is exceedingly complicated.[104]

For the most part, Schwartzbaum supports Heller's argument that the story in PRE is polemical. Like Heller, he maintains that the story in PRE draws on Arabic sources, which employ the well-known motif of taboos associated with getting off one's horse and touching foreign soil.[105] He, however, notes that the story emphasizes Sarah's prohibition against Abraham to descend from his camel because it is mentioned in both visits to Ishmael. Schwartzbaum thus concludes that the prohibition is actually a statement against the Islamic idea that Abraham built the Kaʿba with Ishmael and is therefore the spiritual father of Islam. Yet, it is important to bear in mind that in the Arabic versions, Sarah also prohibits Abraham to go down or reside there on both occasions.[106]

Joseph Heinemann agrees partially with Heller. Not all the references to Ishmael in PRE, he argues, have a clear anti-Islamic agenda. The attitude of the author toward Islam is polemical; indeed some of the references to Ishmael may be polemical but there are those that are apologetic. The author for instance expresses conciliation in his version of Abraham's visit to Ishmael. Heinemann cites as evidence the example of PRE's description of Abraham's dismissal of Hagar and Ishmael: "Of all the misfortunes that have come upon Abraham this was a difficult and very bad matter." According to Heinemann this is indicative of a favorable attitude toward Islam because Abraham does not reject Ishmael. Moreover, of all the rabbinic reasons given for Ishmael's expulsion, the author of PRE chose the least egregious so as to avoid associating Ishmael with idol worship.[107] This last point of Heinemann's is the least convincing; nevertheless it should not divert our attention from the positive portrayal of the relationship between Ishmael and Abraham.

Schussman concurs with Heinemann in locating both apologetic and polemical tendencies in PRE's rendition of Abraham's visits to Ishmael. PRE is apologetic in its positive portrayal of Abraham. He *reluctantly* expels his son permanently from his house despite Divine directive; he visits him twice; he shows great concern for his son's well-being, and he blesses him. At the same time, she argues that in order to illustrate the unworthiness of Ishmael as successor to Abraham, thus the unworthiness of Islam as the inheritor of the Abrahamic covenant, Ishmael is portrayed negatively. Ishmael's unworthiness as successor, she suggests, is found throughout chapter 30, which reiterates Judaism's exclusive rights to the Abrahamic heritage.

Schussman, however, disagrees with these scholars as to the Islamic origin of the story, emphasizing that the contents and orientation of the story in both PRE and Islamic sources prove that the story is an original Hebrew composition. Her major argument is that the story was originally an exegesis of Genesis 21:21, "He lived in the wilderness of Paran; and his mother got a wife for him from the land of Egypt."[108]

As for the Islamic sources, Schussman maintains, innovations were introduced in order to aggrandize the image of Ishmael, to identify Abraham and Ishmael with the holy city, Mecca, and to affirm Abraham's role in the Islamic heritage. She also asserts that the Islamic version of the story is used in hadiths to connect two events—the expulsion of Hagar and Ishmael from Abraham's house and the building of the Kaʿba by Abraham and Ishmael. Schussman asks, why would the author create a story that disparages Ishmael, depicting him as unable to choose a good wife for himself? Rather, it appears that the author did not create the story but once it was given to him, he reshaped it according to his own needs.[109]

To her mind, the story is characteristic of Jewish exegesis to the extent that it explains Genesis 21:21, yet she overlooks the fact that the story also explains several verses in Genesis 21 such as Genesis 21:20, "And he became an archer," and Genesis 21:10, "Cast out this bondwoman and her son." The connection between the story and Genesis 21:21, as well as other verses in Genesis 21, is much more apparent in Midrash Ha-Gadol than in PRE:

> "And she said to Abraham, 'Cast out this bondwoman'" (Gen. 21:10). This is the eighth trial, that Sarah told him to cast out this bondwoman after she was built up by her. The ninth trial is the expulsion of his son, Ishmael, and this was very difficult for him—more than anything else, as it is said, "And the thing was very evil in the eyes of Abraham on account of his son" (Gen. 21:11). Not in the eyes of his mother . . . "And Abraham got up in the morning" (Gen.

> 21:14) . . . "And he dwelt in the wilderness of Paran" (Gen. 21:21). In the beginning, Ishmael took a wife from the daughters of Moab. After some time, our father Abraham went to the desert to see his son.[110]

Unlike in PRE where verses from Genesis 21 are used as prooftexts, in Midrash Ha-Gadol the biblical verses provide the organizing framework for the story. For the most part, the story of Abraham's visits is the same. Ishmael takes a wife from Moab who treats Abraham as persona non grata; he divorces her and marries a gracious woman whom his mother chooses for him from Egypt. The story serves many functions: it expounds several verses of Genesis, especially Genesis 21; it vindicates Sarah and Abraham; it establishes a connection between Abraham and Ishmael.

Schussman's thesis that the story originated as an exegesis of Genesis 21:21 is therefore unlikely. It may have originated as an exegesis of any one of the verses in Gen. 21 mentioned in the story, or even as an exegesis of the entire chapter. Or, it may have been adapted from an Islamic source because of its exegetical value.

She also discusses Ishmael's occupation and contends that had the author of PRE adapted the story from an Islamic source, the author would have retained the Islamic source's version of Ishmael's occupations because they reflect the biblical description that he was an archer and a *pereʾ ʾādām*, a wild ass of a man. The author furthermore would have retained the image of horseman and hunter. Rather, Schussman asserts, the description of his occupation in some of the Islamic sources arose from the original account of PRE. That is, the Islamic sources derived the story from Judaism and Islamicized it as in the case of Ishmael's occupation. Schussman suggests that al-Thaʿlabī's account of Ishmael's gallantry as hunter and horseman was an Islamic polemic against the negative Jewish portrayal of Ishmael as *pereʾ ʾādām* and archer in the Jewish tradition. But as she herself points out, in Arabian circles, archery was not frowned upon.

With respect to the names of the wives, Schussman asserts that the story was older than the Islamic period and in the Islamic period the names were added. Even though the author of PRE clearly used the names with a particular intent, she maintains this does not lead to Heller's conclusion as to the story's Islamic origin. Needless to say, the author's use of the names was more than superficial and insignificant. She points to the fact that in Islam itself the Shiʿa-Sunni tensions regarding ʿAyeshah and Fatima were widespread. That is, the Shiʿa denigrated ʿAyeshah due to the political oppression against them, whereas the Sunni favored ʿAyeshah over Fatima.[111]

Schussman moreover sees a hidden polemic behind the beginning and end of chapter 30 where an apocalyptic vision of the three wars that the Ishmaelites will wage is described. She states that chapter 30 opens with Ishmael behaving wickedly and ends with his sons following in his footsteps. The author attributes violence to the father, the bowman, and his sons who will inherit wars by sword and "bow." The use of the same motif conjures up the impression at the beginning and at the end in order to convey the notion that Islamic rule is not accidentally violent but rather flows naturally from father to son.[112] Thus for Schussman, the author of PRE portrays both Ishmael and the Ishmaelites negatively in order to polemicize against Islam. Yet, in making her case, Schussman ignores the other images of Ishmael and the Ishmaelites found in chapter 30, let alone throughout PRE. To begin with, Ishmael's occupation as gatherer of fruit and shepherd of camels is peaceful and also typifies Arab ethnicity. Second, the depiction of the Ishmaelites at the end of the chapter as well as throughout PRE represents them as powerful.

Furthermore, Schussman contends that while the depiction of Ishmael is not entirely derogatory, the overall picture is negative. The most obvious case in point is Ishmael's inability to find a suitable wife for himself, that the wife he had chosen was not proper and that his mother, Hagar, had to choose a wife for him. Not only did he choose an inadequate wife for himself but he chose a Moabite, which tarnishes Ishmael's character because of the biblical associations with Moabites.[113]

As Abraham is concerned for Isaac's well-being in the biblical story, so too, we find in PRE Abraham's concern for Ishmael. Choosing a wife for Isaac and making sure that Ishmael marries a more suitable wife are both expressions of parental love. Moreover, even in the Islamic sources the first wife is inadequate. Rather, the fact that Ishmael knew that his father came to visit, that he understood his father's language, that he obeyed his father, and that he was worthy of Abraham's blessing and love all point to a positive portrayal of Ishmael.

Abraham's Visits to Ishmael in Arabic Sources

In the Islamic sources, the story serves also to establish a bond between Abraham and Ishmael, one which leads to God's command to Abraham[114] to build the Kaʿba with Ishmael, and it functions as the raison d'etre for the arabization of Ishmael and his descendants.[115]

Unlike in PRE, of course, there is no direct association with the Genesis verse in the Islamic texts. Rather, the purpose of the Islamic renditions appears to be the establishment of Ishmael and his progeny among the Arab people. To quote Reuven Firestone, "If Ishmael had taken a wife from Egypt in the Islamic version of the legend as in the biblical story and its Biblicist[116] exegesis, Ishmael's arabization would not have been accomplished. Moreover, the story would hardly have held any relevance in an Arabian context."[117] The identity of Ishmael's wife therefore is an important feature of the story because it obviously contradicts Genesis 21:21: "And he dwelt in the wilderness of Paran and his mother took for him a wife out of the land of Eygpt."

All Arab tribes, according to traditional genealogists, are derived from one of two great ancestors, Qahtan or ʿAdnan, the former associated with the true or original Arabs, the latter associated with the Northern Arabs.[118] And the Jurhum is one of the ancient true Arab tribes derived from Qahtan.

The Islamic version claims that Ishmael married into the Jurhum tribe, one of the legendary pre-Islamic Arab tribes associated with the holy city of Mecca. The Jurhum emigrated from Yemen and settled in Mecca where they eventually gained control of the Kaʿba after a lengthy struggle with another tribe, Qatura. The tribe became extinct well before the inception of Islam. Nonetheless a connection was made between Ishmael and the tribe in the Qur'an, which says that the Jurhum protected Ishmael and Hagar.[119] Yet, noteworthy is the fact that the Qur'an does not mention Arab descent from Ishmael.

Fred Donner's hypothesis that the first community of believers, *mu'minūn*, was a multiconfessional monotheism that included among its ranks "Christians, Jews and perhaps other monotheists,"[120] might explain why the Ishmael-Arab identity is absent in the Qur'an. If, as Donner argues, the early community was not a community of muslimun, a community with clearly defined confessional boundaries and beliefs, but rather of *mu'minūn*, of believers independent of confessional identities, then exclusionary claims would undermine the multiconfessional character of the community of believers. The tradition passed on from Josephus via the Church fathers and the ecclesiastical historian Sozomen (of Gaza, mid-fifth cent.) may have been well known to the early community of Muhammad's followers, but might have been rejected for purposes of attenuating exclusivity. It was therefore only after a more fully defined Islam qua religion distinctly separate from other monotheisms that the need to emphasize Ishmael's Arabness emerged. Thus a further and more important association is made in the hadith account where Ishmael marries a Jurhumite.

According to Ibn al-Kalbī's genealogical system (its form was finalized around 800 CE), the descendants of ʿAdnan are the Northern Arabs. They are associated with the nonindigenous tribes who became arabized when they migrated into the Arabian Peninsula. The most important of these tribes are the Quraysh, from which Muhammad and the Umayyad and Abbasid dynasties, as well as the imams of the Shiʿites, all derive. Ishmael, the progenitor of both the Northern Arabs and Muhammad, is considered an ancestor of the tribal descendants of ʿAdnan,[121] who are Arabized but are regarded as the true Arabs.

According to I. Ephʿal, the classical Arab genealogies of the early Islamic period combine two genealogical systems: "the 'actual' Arab genealogies of the pre-Islamic period . . . and the biblical genealogies, introduced for purely ethnological and cultural interest. This incorporation of biblical sources in Arabic genealogical concepts is part of the broader process of absorbing Jewish elements into early Islamic culture."[122]

In order to appreciate the importance of the ancestry of Ishmael's wife and the role it plays in the Islamic account of Abraham's visit, we must keep in mind the role genealogy plays in Arab society, a role that not only maintains continuity with the past, but also provides social cohesion and order. Furthermore, geneological systems are an expression of sociopolitical matters.[123]

Here Abraham's visit to Ishmael in the Arab sources legitimizes Ishmael both as Abraham's son and as an Arab; it serves to establish Ishmael's role as patriarch of the Northern Arabs and thus also progenitor of Muhammad. And, it brings Abraham to the vicinity of Mecca so he and Ishmael can build the Kaʿba (Qur'an 2:124–127), thus affirming Abraham as the first hanīf, who built the sanctuary for the one true God.

That Muhammad is a descendant of Ishmael becomes especially significant as Islam's hegemony began rapidly to extend beyond the confines of the Arabian Peninsula and its environs, that is, as Islam encountered other peoples and in the process developed its distinctive characteristics. "The Muslims," writes Hoyland, "were entering a land of very ancient peoples with venerable traditions, and they needed to make some reply when questioned about their own particular history and their defining characteristics."[124]

The narrative of Abraham's visit to Ishmael must be viewed in light of the larger narrative of PRE.[125] It must be viewed also in light of Islam's theological and socio-political history, external factors that effected an inner-directed Jewish response. Inquiry into the cross-cultural exchange of literature must therefore consider how the texts take shape within the parameters of each tradition. Of course we do not wish to deny naively the possibility of polemics in reintertextual relationships. In this case, however, we find little, if any, evidence for reading these texts polemically.

Revisiting the Visits

Chapter 30 opens with an explanation of why Abraham must cast out his firstborn son, Ishmael:

> The ninth trial: Ishmael was born with the bow and grew up with the bow, as it said, "And he became an archer" (Gen. 21:20). He used to take bow and arrows and shoot at the birds. One time he saw Isaac sitting by himself and he shot an arrow to kill him. Sarah saw and told Abraham, "This and that Ishmael did to Isaac, but stand and write to Isaac all that the Holy One, Blessed be He promised to give you and your seed. By your life, the son of this maidservant shall not inherit with my son, with Isaac," as it is written, "And she said to Abraham, 'Cast out this bondwoman and her son'" (Gen. 21:10). Ben Tema said: "Sarah said to Abraham, 'Write a bill of divorce and send away this maidservant and her son from me and my son, [from this world and from the world to come].'" And of all the misfortunes that came upon Abraham, this thing was difficult and very evil in his eyes, as it is said, "And the thing was very evil in the eyes of Abraham on account of his son" (Gen. 21:11).

It is unclear what is meant by "born with the bow." As Friedlander points out, "Perhaps the version should read, 'Ishmael was born under (the constellation) Sagittarius.' The word *qaššāt* sometimes means this constellation, or it might indicate harshness."[126] Radal is of the opinion that "born with the bow" is better understood in light of what the angel told Hagar in Genesis 16:12, "And he [Ishmael] shall be a wild ass of a man: his hand shall be against everyone and everyone's hand against him; and he shall live in the face of all his brothers." According to Radal, "his hand against everyone" connotes the use of the bow.[127] Indeed it seems likely the rabbis, adept punsters, played with the words *nitrabâh*, "to grow up," and *rōbeh*, "archer." Moreover, the description in Genesis 16:12 is similar to the angel's prognostication in the biblical story. Ishmael is destined to be a hunter in the Bible and also in PRE. It is his nature as an archer to shoot birds and animals of the field; he is a *pere' 'ādām*. In offering a reason for Sarah's request, the author of PRE offers one of the classic rabbinic reasons. The portrayal, albeit damaging, is the only rabbinic suggestion that does not cast him as a thief, rapist, or idol worshiper.[128] Heinemann claims that the author of

PRE deliberately avoided affiliating Ishmael with idol worship. That is, shooting arrows at Isaac is less of an indictment against the father of Islam than engaging in idol worship. Heinemann's opinion is based on two assumptions: the author of PRE was aware of the important role Ishmael plays in Islam,[129] and Muslims would be exposed to PRE. While the first assumption is reasonable given the dating of PRE and the success of the Muslim Empire in the Middle East by this time, the validity of the second is more difficult to assess.

To be sure, it is important to note Abraham's reaction to Sarah's order: "And of all the misfortunes that came upon Abraham, this thing was difficult and very evil in his eyes." Despite his son's aggressive nature and despite the fact that Ishmael, if he remained in Abraham's home, would share in Isaac's inheritance, Abraham was reluctant to cast out his son.

The next paragraph of chapter 30 throws light on another reason for Ishmael's dismissal:

> R. Yehuda said: That same night, the Holy One, Blessed be He appeared to Abraham our father. He said to him, "Abraham, do you know that Sarah was fit for you as wife [from her mother's womb]. She is your companion and wife of your youth. Hagar is not called your wife nor is Sarah called your maidservant, as it its written, 'But Sarah your wife shall bear you a son' (Gen. 17:19). Hagar is not called your wife but rather your maidservant. And all that Sarah spoke, she spoke in truth. Let it not be evil in your eyes about the boy and your maidservant, as it is written, 'And God said to Abraham, Do not let it be evil in your eyes about the boy . . . ' " (Gen. 21: 12).

When God appears to Abraham, he tells Abraham to listen to Sarah, not because Ishmael tried to kill Isaac, but because she is the "wife of his youth." God tells Abraham that what Sarah spoke, she spoke in truth. And what did Sarah speak? She does not say that Ishmael attempted to kill Isaac but rather "this and that Ishmael did to Isaac," and therefore only Isaac should inherit. The son of "this maidservant" should not inherit with her son, therefore Abraham should "write a bill of divorce and send away this maidservant and her son from me and my son." As in the biblical narrative, Sarah is threatened by both Hagar and Ishmael.[130]

Abraham obeys Sarah. He gets up early, takes bread and a bottle of water, and sends Hagar away with a bill of divorce. He also takes a water bottle and binds it on her waist to indicate her slave status and to mark the path they would take so he could later visit Ishmael.

Ishmael was twenty-four years old when he departed from his father's house. The next line of the story is a quotation from Genesis 21:14 referring to Hagar, "And she departed and wandered." The midrash explains, "'[She] wandered,' *tēta*ʿ, can only mean idol worship, as it is written, 'They are vanity, a work of errors' (*taʿtūʿîm*)" (Jer. 10:15). It is important to note that in the desert, Hagar, not Ishmael, strays after idols. Ishmael leaves his father's house, whereas his mother "departed and wandered"; she strays after idols. Moreover, while Hagar is straying after idols, Ishmael prays to the Holy One, blessed be He:

> And Ishmael was tired with thirst. He walked and he cast himself under the desert brambles and said, "Master of the Universe, if you desire to give me water, give it to me so that my soul will not go out in thirst, for death by thirst is unusual and the hardest of all deaths." The Holy One, Blessed be He heard his prayer, as it is said, "For God heard the voice of the boy" (Gen. 21:17) as it is written, "For God heard the voice of the boy where he is." There was opened to them the well that was created at twilight.

The depiction of Ishmael is contrasted with that of Hagar who strays after idols. Ishmael prays to God and He hears "the voice of the boy," interpreted by the author of PRE to mean "his prayer."[131] God responds to Ishmael and because of this Hagar is brought back: "And God opened her eyes (and she saw a well of water)" Genesis 21:19. That is, she saw the greatness of God and no longer strayed or wandered: "There they left the well and from there they walked the entire desert until they reached the desert Paran and there they found streams of water and they dwelt there."

PRE's portrayal of Ishmael in the desert is sympathetic. Unlike his mother who strays, Ishmael remains faithful to God and when he faces death he cries out to God not out of anger for his lot in life but rather out of sheer desperation. God so cares for Ishmael that he opens the well that he created on the eve of the first Sabbath in the week of Creation. But it is not only God who loves Ishmael. After they settle in Paran and Ishmael marries a Moabite named ʿAyesha, three years later Abraham visits Ishmael, swearing to Sarah that he would not descend from the camel in the place where Ishmael dwells. The implication is that Sarah worries that if Abraham descends, he might be convinced to favor Ishmael or he might have sexual relations with Hagar.

The story of the visit ends with Abraham content that his son remarried, according to his wishes. The second wife is hospitable and Abraham blesses Ishmael's household. The story of Abraham's visit ends with the following: "Ishmael knew that his father's mercy was still on him, as it is said, 'As a father has mercy on his children'" (Ps. 103:13).

The chapter, however, continues with a discussion of the children of Ishmael[132] and what they will do in the future. They, for example, will measure the land with ropes and make a cemetery into a place for sheep dunghills. Moreover, "lying will increase and truth will be hidden." At the same time, "they will hew down the rock of the kingdom and they will rebuild the destroyed cities and clear the roads; they will plant gardens and orchards; they will fence in the broken walls of the Temple and they will build an edifice in the Temple."

The fifteen things mentioned quite probably reflect concrete changes as well as perceived changes that may have taken place in Jerusalem during Islamic rule, such as land measurement, which was an innovation of the Islamic administration that took place during Muʿawiyya's reign.[133] Furthermore, according to H. Graetz and Z. Fraenkel,[134] the reference to the two princes—"And two brothers will stand, princes in the end"—refers to the two Caliphs, Mohammad al-Amin (809–813 CE) and Abdallah al-Ma'mnm (813–833 CE), the sons of Harun al-Rashid who battled for the caliphate.

Ma'mun's decree that any ten Jews can elect their own leadership created dissension within the Jewish community. A. Grossman argues al-Ma'mun attempted to bring about the demise of central leadership among the *dhimmī*, protected people.[135] The change in attitude toward the Jewish community may have given rise to the messianic sentiment that follows: "In their days the branch, the son of David, will stand over them, as it is said, 'And in the days of those kings shall the God of heaven set up a kingdom, which shall never be destroyed'" (Dan. 2:44). The author aptly quotes Daniel, an apocalyptic work par excellence, as prooftext for his eschatological vision: all foreign rule shall be vanquished; the Davidic covenant shall be fulfilled.

The contrast drawn between the story of Abraham's visit to Ishmael and what the sons of Ishmael will do in the future is overlooked by scholars who focus only on the relationship between the story of Abraham's visit to Ishmael found in Jewish sources and that found in Islamic sources.

The assumption of previous scholars has been to equate Ishmael with Islam but the equation, rather, is between Islam and his sons, *beney* Ishmael. On its own, the story of Abraham's visits to Ishmael in PRE is not anti-Islamic. Abraham and Ishmael are depicted in a mutually loving relationship. Ishmael, though not the chosen son, is nevertheless Abraham's son and must not be completely disparaged. The author of PRE, on the other hand, depicts the children of Ishmael in a less favorable light and foreshadows their demise in terms of apocalyptic imagery.

THE ISHMAELITES IN PIRKE DE RABBI ELIEZER

A significant reference to the children of Esau and Ishmael is found in chapter 41 of PRE, where God offers the Torah to them:[136]

> R. Tarphon said: The Holy One, Blessed be He rose from Mount Seir and appeared to the people of Esau, as it is said, "And he said, 'The LORD came from Sinai and rose from Seir unto them' " (Deut. 33:2) And "Seir" can only mean the children of Esau, as it is said, "And Esau dwelt in Mount Seir" (Gen. 36:8). The Holy One, Blessed be He said to them, "Do you accept the Torah?" They said to Him, "What is written in it?" He said to them, "You shall not murder" (Exod. 20:13, Deut. 5:17). They said to him, "We are unable to abandon the blessing that Isaac gave Esau our father for he said to him, "By your sword you shall live" (Gen. 27:40). And from there he returned and appeared to the Ishmaelites, as it is said, "He appeared from Mount Paran" (Deut. 33:2).[137] He said to them, "Do you accept the Torah?" They said to him, "What is written in it?" He said to them, "You shall not steal" (Exod. 20:15). They said to him, "We are unable to abandon the thing that our fathers did for they stole Joseph and brought him down to Egypt, for it is written, 'For indeed I was stolen from the land of the Hebrews' " (Gen. 40:15). And from there he sent [messengers] to all the nations of the world and said to them, "Do you accept for yourselves the Torah?" They said to him, "What is written in it?" "You shall have no other gods before me" (Exod. 20:3). They said to Him, "We are unable to abandon the law of our fathers who served idols. We have no delight in the Torah but give your Torah to your people, as it is said, 'The LORD will give strength to His people, the LORD will bless his people with peace' " (Ps. 29:11).

Unlike all other references to the Ishmaelites in PRE, this reference comes from earlier sources such as the Mekhilta and Sifre. The author incorporated the ancient sources, some of which already mention the Ishmaelites, but altered some of the details. Unlike the earlier sources where God offers the Torah to the Moabites and Ammonites, in PRE God offers it to the children of Esau, the children of Ishmael, and to all the other nations.

Furthermore, the response to God's offer in PRE is different. In the Mekhilta, God appears to "the people of Esau the wicked" and offers the

Torah to them. When they learn that it states, "Do not murder," they respond, "This is the inheritance that our father left us, 'And by your sword you shall live' " (Gen. 27:40). He then offers it to the people of Ammon and Moab,[138] to which they respond: "What is written in it?" God answers, "Do not commit adultery" (Deut. 5:17). They refuse the Torah because "they were all children of adulterers, as it is written, 'And the two daughters of Lot were pregnant by their father' " (Gen. 19:36). Finally, God offers the Torah to the Ishmaelites and when they find out that it says, "Do not steal," they reply, "This was the blessing said to our father, 'And he shall be a wild ass of a man and his hand shall be upon all' (Gen. 16:2). And it is written, 'For I was stolen out of the land of the Hebrews' (Gen. 40:15)."[139] In Sifre, Z'ot Ha-Brakhah 343, the reason the Ishmaelites cannot accept the Torah is also because "the very essence of their father is a robber."

In Tanna debe Eliyyahu,[140] Pirke Hayyaridot, chapter 3 and in PRE we have a slightly different version[141] whereby the other nations offer different reasons for not accepting the Torah.[142] In the earlier midrashim, the nations cannot accept the Torah because of the nature of "our father," whereas in the later texts the nations cannot accept it because they must maintain the law or custom of "our fathers." They are unable to accept because, like the Jews who throughout history were offered alternative ethical and religious systems, they must remain faithful to their ancestral ways, even if these ways are socially unacceptable.[143] As Heinemann points out, the Jews under Muslim rule were reticent about denouncing the new religion as false and therefore made a nontheological claim: "We are unable to abandon the traditions of our fathers." According to Heinemann, in the eyes of the author of PRE, this was also a legitimate claim not only for the Jews, but also for the other nations.[144]

There is some merit to Heinemann's contention but ultimately it is unpersuasive. The change in the midrashic text in PRE may have been influenced by an effort on the part of the author to deal as evenhandedly as possible with theological claims made by Christianity and Islam, but there is no evidence to support this notion. If we assume that the Ishmaelites represent Muslims, then the text establishes them as robbers, no doubt an offensive charge. Furthermore, as we shall see, even though the augury in chapter 38 that God will destroy "the people of Esau who are the foes of the Israelites and likewise the Ishmaelites who are their enemies," may not overtly attest to hostile relations between the Israelites and Ishmaelites, the ultimate destruction of the Ishmaelites calls into question the idea that the author maintains an apologetic attitude toward Islam. Heinemann's investigation, a delving into the text in order to detect extratextual concerns and issues, models the type of work scholars of midrash must do, yet at the same time it seems quite unlikely that the aforementioned midrashim disclose the author's well-disposed attitude toward Islam; we must therefore beware of ad hoc explanations, and be careful of reading too much history into these particular texts. Having said as much, as I have noted throughout, apocalyptic references are more often than not telltale indicators of rabbinic preoccupation with the larger political and religious forces dominating their vision of the world at large.

The midrashim associated with Ishmael are connected to the biblical story and to the notion that only Israel is the chosen people, whereas most of the midrashim associated with the Ishmaelites are used to represent Islam by means of apocalyptic imagery.[145] Most scholars have equated Ishmael with Islam in chapter 30 of PRE and in doing so not only have ignored other references to Ishmael but have also treated lightly references to the Ishmaelites, *beney Yishmael*, in PRE.

References to the Ishmaelites exemplify apocalyptic fantasy, a genre of midrash which H. A. Wolfson characterizes as historical and eschatological predictive scriptural interpretation. The historical interpretation seeks predictions of future events in scriptural texts that refer to events that have already taken place. The eschatological interpretation, on the other hand, seeks nonliteral reference, which may be applied to the events occurring in the end days, such as the coming of the Messiah.[146] In chapter 28, for example, which discusses Abraham's eighth trial (Gen. 15:1), four kingdoms—Rome, Greek, Media and Persia, and Islam—are mentioned:[147]

> R. Aqiba said: The Holy One, Blessed be He showed Abraham our father the four kingdoms between the pieces[148] ruling and perishing, as it is said, "And He said, 'Take me a heifer of three years old'" (Gen. 15:9). This is the fourth kingdom, that is the kingdom of Edom [Rome] which is like a threshing heifer. "And a she-goat of three years old" (ibid.) refers to the Greek kingdom, as it is said, "And the he-goat magnified himself exceedingly" (Dan. 8:8). "And a ram of three years old" (Gen. 15:9) refers to the kingdom of Media and Persia. "And a turtle-dove" (ibid.)—these are the sons of Ishmael. It does not say "*tōr*," "turtle-dove" in the language of the Torah, rather in Aramaic. "*Tōr*" means the "ox." When the male ox is harnessed to the female, they will open and break all the valleys. "And a young pigeon" (Gen. 15:9)—this is Israel who is compared to a young pigeon, as it is said, "O my dove you are in the clefts of the rock" (Song of Songs 2:14). . . .

> Abraham stood and prayed before the Holy One, Blessed be He so that the four kingdoms should not enslave his children. A deep sleep fell upon him and he slept, as it is said, "A deep sleep fell upon Abram" (Gen. 15:12). Is it possible for a person to lie down and sleep and yet be able to pray? From this you learn that Abraham lay down and slept from the strength of the prayer that his children might enslave[149] these four kingdoms, as it is said, "And behold a dread, a great darkness fell upon him" (ibid.). "Dread" refers to the fourth kingdom as it is written, "And behold a fourth beast, terrible and powerful and exceedingly strong" (Dan. 7:7). "Darkness" refers to the kingdom of Greece that darkened the eyes of Israel from all the commandments of the Torah. "Mighty" is the kingdom of Media and Persia which was mighty in selling Israel for nothing. "Fell" is the kingdom of Babylon for by their hand the crown of Israel fell. "On him" refers to the Ishmaelites upon whom the Son of David will flourish, as it is said, "His enemies I will clothe with shame but on him shall his crown flourish" (Ps. 132:18).

The order of the kingdoms is peculiar and five proper names are mentioned, although the fifth, the Ishmaelites, is not a kingdom. As Elbaum notes,[150] the author of PRE embellishes Gen. Rab. 44:15 by substituting the Ishmaelites, who represent Islam, for Babylon and emends Gen. Rab. 44:17[151] by including the Ishmaelites, though not referring to them as a kingdom. It may be that an earlier version named only the kingdoms of Edom, Greece, Media, and Persia and the author of PRE added the sons of Ishmael. Or, the case may be that he used a midrash that already included them. It is also possible that Media and Persia are considered one kingdom. That is, the version of this midrash in Yalquṭ Shimʿoni 76 includes the following prooftext for Media and Persia: "The two-horned ram that you saw [the kings of Media and Persia]" (Dan. 8:20). Furthermore, let us recall that in all likelihood the reference to Media and Persia in Lam. Rab. 1:42 is to one kingdom. This passage nonetheless illustrates that throughout PRE the Ishmaelites, except for one midrash, are depicted in apocalyptic terms whereby in the future the Son of David will rise against them.[152]

As many scholars have already noted,[153] the rise of Islam ignited messianic fervor among Jews, so it is of no surprise that PRE depicts the Ishmaelites in apocalyptic terms. In chapter 38 the fate of the Ishmaelites is described in apocalyptic imagery: " . . . R. Ishmael said: The five fingers of the right hand of the Holy One, Blessed be He, all of them are the secret of redemption . . . with the thumb and the entire hand in the future the Holy One, Blessed be He will destroy the people of Esau who are the foes of the

Israelites and likewise the Ishmaelites who are their enemies, as it is said, 'Your hand shall prevail over your foes, and all your enemies shall be cut down' " (Micah 5:8). It is not so clear to whom "their" refers. It may be that the Christians are called enemies of the Jews and the Muslims the enemies of the Christians, but not of the Jews. Alternatively, "their" may refer to the Ishmaelites who are also the enemies of Israel. In either case, they, too, will be destroyed in the end.

One could argue that if the children of Ishmael indisputably represent Islam then surely by extension Ishmael, too, refers to Islam. But a study of the midrashim pertaining to Ishmael in PRE proves otherwise. There are several possible reasons for the distinction between Ishmael and the children of Ishmael. It could be that the author was using earlier sources in which Ishmael did not symbolize Islam.[154] But, in creating midrashim on the Ishmaelites, the author used them to depict Islam.

Another more likely explanation for this phenomenon may have to do with the author's attempt to resituate Ishmael within the Jewish tradition. That is to say, Ishmael, albeit Abraham's marginalized son, is a member of his family and thus plays a role in Judaism's metanarrative. Clearly the author distinguishes between Abraham's sons, but he nevertheless maintains a place for him within Judaism. The author contests the Muslim belief that Islam is the true monotheistic religion, superseding Judaism by depicting the Ishmaelites as a vanquished kingdom in the end days.

PRE's response to Islam's claim to Abraham via Ishmael is to maintain Abraham's dignity, to acknowledge the neutral role Ishmael plays in the biblical narrative, and to portray Islam as the Ishmaelites, thus removed farther from Abraham. Ishmael's depiction in the Bible and in the early rabbinic sources is less definitive, which may in part have contributed to his complex depiction in PRE. In other words, the tradition itself was inconsistently disparaging. The characterization of Ishmael in PRE represents a stage in the transformation of Ishmael from the biblical figure and from the rabbinic Other to the eponymous prototype of Islam.[155] In PRE his descendants represent Islam, but for the most part he himself does not.

To be sure, we cannot underestimate the value of previous studies of the story of Abraham's visit to Ishmael in PRE, studies that have paid serious attention to philological and textual concerns. Their work directs our attention to the intertextual parallels in Jewish and Muslim folklore and the need to explore the shared reservoir of types, genres, and traditions. Schussman is correct to understand the story in Islamic folklore as one that merges the expulsion of Hagar and Ishmael with the building of the Kaʿba. The assertion that the story in PRE predates the Islamic sources, however, is difficult to determine, and the focus on concerns pertaining to origin undermines the very intertextual nature of the relationship between the Jewish and Muslim versions of the story of Abraham's visits to Ishmael. The stories, each taking shape within a different religious milieu, emerge from an intertwined world of religious and cultural discourse, from a complex web of social interchange.

Conclusions

This examination of midrashim on Ishmael, and to a lesser degree on Esau, the Ishmaelites, and the children of Keturah, gives us the opportunity to make several significant observations about rabbinic biblical interpretation and the interfacing of historical phenomena and exegetical concerns. To begin with, the rabbinic portrayal of Ishmael is multifarious. He is depicted as a beloved yet displaced son, a sibling rival and the Arab forefather of robbers. Moreover, he, along with Esau, the Ishmaelites, and the children of Keturah, represents Other.

In closely looking at the biblical account of Ishmael's life, we discover a tension between his membership in and expulsion from Abraham's household. In Genesis 17 he is circumcised, yet because of divine favoritism, a few chapters later in Genesis 21 he is expelled from his father's home. Banished into the desert, he is no longer a collateral member of Abraham's household. As I have tried to illustrate, however, the biblical narrative does not entirely cast him in a negative light. I have also tried to show that the ambiguity in the biblical narrative surrounding Ishmael in many ways affects the ways in which Ishmael is depicted in rabbinic literature. For example, one concern for the rabbis was to distinguish between Ishmael, the unfit, and Isaac, the chosen.

We find in very few sources of the tannaitic and amoraic periods that Ishmael's descendants are characterized as Arab, but more often like Esau, and the children of Keturah, Ishmael and the Ishmaelites are depicted as Israel's imagined antipode. That is, these marginalized figures, representing a rabbinic conceptualization of Other that serves to reaffirm Jewish identity, were used as a means for the rabbis to affirm Judaism's status as chosen Israel.

Islam's emergence as a hegemonic power in the Near East played a role in transforming the significance of Ishmael from a representative of Other to the eponymous prototype of Islam. Drawing on a longstanding tradition of associating Ishmaelites with Arabs, the rabbis used Ishmael metonymically to refer to Islam. As Islam's genealogical and theological contentions became more widespread in tandem with the swiftly shifting political landscape of the Near East, it is quite reasonable to assume that the rabbis addressed these challenging sociopolitical and religious matters much the same way they confronted foreign rule in times past. Much like the rabbinic treatment of Esau/Edom as Rome, the treatment of Ishmael in post-seventh-century sources exemplifies specific rabbinic hermeneutical devices and conceptual strictures, and generally speaking reflects a concern for both textual and extratextual issues.

References to Ishmael after the rise of Islam are not always about the Arabs or Islamic rule. As in the case of Esau, each reference to these characters must be understood contextually, and not necessarily as an insight to rabbinic attitudes toward real historical Others. At best we can conclude that historical events such as the rise of Islam influenced the development of midrashim, but we cannot assume that every reference to a marginalized biblical figure is a direct reference to Muslims, Christians, or Samaritans, for the very nature of rabbinic exegesis as textual interplay resists such constrictions. The rabbinic exhortation, "Turn it over again and again, for everything is in it" (Pirke Avot 5:22) best captures the rabbis' belief in the unity, truth, and efficacy of their sacred text, while recognizing—even celebrating—its multivocality. Underlying rabbinic exegetical discourse is the fundamental notion that a verse, a word (*davar*, which also means "thing") of Scripture is what Gadamer says of Truth, that it is the sum total of its interpretation.

In midrashic compilations redacted prior to the seventh century, the rabbinic portrayal of Ishmael varied according to textual and extratextual concerns. With the emergence of Islam, however, he is depicted negatively much more consistently. To be sure, some compilations retain earlier midrashim that present Ishmael favorably, but more often than not we uncover negative depictions. In fact, earlier midrashim are reworked so as to emphasize Ishmael's wickedness as a reaction to the Muslim claim as Abraham's rightful heir. That is to say, the rabbis disparaged Ishmael who in their eyes was Abraham's illegitimate son.

Ishmael's identity as an Arab, albeit sufficiently established in the Hellenistic period, was insignificant in classical rabbinic texts, but later midrashim draw on the earlier association in identifying Ishmael with Islam. That is to say, earlier traditions already associated Ishmael with the

Arabs such that regardless of whatever role Ishmael played in Islam's theological-genealogical formulations, the rabbis themselves associated Ishmael with Islam. Needless to say, whether via Ishmael or not, Muslim claims to Abraham were a relevant concern, and thus at times were also a source of polemical discourse.

It is difficult to determine with any accuracy when precisely rabbinic use of Ishmael to symbolize Islam became normative. We discover in PRE that the Ishmaelites represent Islam. This being the case, how then do our rabbinic sources contribute to our understanding of "rabbinic Judaism"? While we cannot use these midrashim as sources that detail rabbinic history with precision, we can use them to tell us how, for example, the rabbis reacted to the emergence of Islamic hegemony and also to its claim to the Abrahamic covenant.

This inquiry into rabbinic portrayals of Ishmael has provided us with a framework for studying midrash, one that undeniably underscores the need for a multilayered approach to midrashic studies. While I borrow from standard interpretive methods, I find no single approach adequate. Analyzing midrashim from the tannaitic period through the early medieval period, detecting attitudinal differences toward Ishmael in the later midrashim even though early and later works share rhetorical and terminological similarities, contributes potentially to a historical analysis of rabbinic texts. Indeed this approach takes into consideration the historical and literary aspects of midrash. By looking at individual midrashim and tracing how they are transformed in later corpora and by analyzing midrashim of the period of the rise of Islam, we are able to gain insight into how the rabbis dealt with contemporary concerns and issues. There are times when midrashic texts elucidate history, but again, this is not always the case. Each source must be assessed with an eye to what it can and cannot tell us about historical, social, and cultural phenomenon.

An approach that examined only the exegetical significance of these midrashim, or one that only focused on their historical import, would have been less than adequate. Moreover, in this case, examining the differences between Babylonian and Palestinian statements on these marginalized figures would also not have been helpful, very likely because there were not many Babylonian statements. On the other hand, dividing the material not by compilation (except for PRE, which is an authored work rather than a compilation) but by chronology—amoraic and postamoraic (post-rise of Islam)—was especially fruitful.

The material presented here provides the groundwork for future research in midrash and other related fields. This study, for example, may contribute to research dealing with the relationship between medieval biblical commentaries and midrash. While the later rabbinic sources, such as Exodus Rabbah and Midrash Tanḥuma, do not always depict Ishmael as Islam, later Jewish works of the eleventh and twelfth centuries, such as the liturgical poems, *piyyutim*, of Ibn Gabirol and Judah Halevi make references to Ishmael that no doubt refer to Islam. In the works of the medieval commentators, as well as comments found in the Genizah fragments,[1] Ishmael is synonymous with Islam. Why only rarely in later midrashic compilations do we find a direct correspondence between Ishmael and Islam, but in the work of Saadia Gaon, for example, Ishmael indubitably refers to Islam? Perhaps a comparative study of the use of Ishmael in midrash and in other types of medieval Jewish literature would shed greater light on the nature of rabbinic biblical interpretation and on how Ishmael (the biblical figure) was transformed into the eponymous prototype of Islam.

Other pertinent questions and issues remain. For example, did other factors contribute to the rabbinic portrayal of Ishmael? It is also worth exploring how Jewish apocalyptic literature, particularly Midrashei Ge'ulah, portray Ishmael. Is there a difference and, if so, what might that tell us about the relationship between these different types of literature and the communities that produced them?

My attempt to weave the work of distinct disciplines, albeit it subtly so, is best described by Carl E. Schorske in the introduction of *Fin-a-siècle Vienna: Politics and Culture:*

> Yet the historian will not share to the full the aim of the humanist textual analyst. The latter aims at the greatest possible illumination of a cultural product, relativizing all principles of analysis to its particular content. The historian seeks rather to locate and interpret the artifact temporally in a field where two lines intersect. One line is vertical, or diachronic, by which he establishes the relation of a text or a system of thought to previous expressions in the same branch of cultural activity (painting, politics, etc.). The other is horizontal, or synchronic, by it he assesses the relation of the content of the intellectual object at the same time. The diachronic thread is the warp, the synchronic is the woof in the fabric of cultural history. The historian is the weaver, but the quality of his cloth depends on the strength of the color of the thread. He must learn something of spinning from the specialized disciplines whose scholars have in fact lost interest in using history as one of their primary modes of understanding, but who still know better than the historian what in their metier constitutes stout yarn of true color. The historian's homespun will be less fine than theirs,

> but if he emulates their method in its making, he should spin yarn serviceable enough for the kind of bold-patterned fabric he is called upon to produce.[2]

My use of Schorske's vivid imagery attempts not to criticize historians but rather to highlight the way in which the scholarly pursuit of understanding rabbinic literature is a multifaceted enterprise that must account for historical phenomena that shape the very literariness of our sources. That is, it is my hope that this study will demonstrate the importance of recognizing the use of midrashim as literary artifacts, as historical documents not only embedded in history but also conveyors of that history, a history of rabbinic theological beliefs, cultural concepts, and attitudes, however varied they may be.

Endeavors to maintain the longstanding notion of chosen Israel in light of competing theologies of politically dominant forces reflect the multidirectional nature of rabbinic exegesis. The rabbis, very much aware of the larger world of their inhabitance, had to contend with the interfacing of theological claims and political power of both Christians and Muslims, which were by and large inextricably interlaced. Yet they did so by reverting back into their polychromatic world of scriptural exegesis, a world of intertwined discourse, stitched of familiar fabric—a world where marginalized figures reflect rabbinic anxieties and aspirations, history and fancy, and real and imagined Others. Within this vastly rich, deeply hued world of midrash we thus discover Ishmael, the beloved firstborn son of Abraham, the marginalized sibling of Isaac, the progenitor of Arabs, and indeed the Ishmael of Judaism and the Ishmael of Islam.

Notes

Introduction

1. M. Heidegger, *Being and Time*, trans. John Macquarrie and Edward Robbinson (New York: Harper and Row, 1962), 192–93.

2. G. Bruns, *Hermeneutics Ancient and Modern* (New Haven: Yale University Press, 1992), 4.

3. Ibid.

4. Y. Heinemann, *Darkhei ha'aggadah* (Jerusalem: Magnes, 1970).

5. J. Kugel, in "Two Introductions to Midrash," *Midrash and Literature*, Hartman and Budick, eds. (New Haven: Yale University Press, 1986), 91, offers the following definition of midrash: "Suffice it to say that the Hebrew word *midrash* might be best translated as 'research,' a translation that incorporates the word's root meaning of 'search out, inquire'. . . . The word has been used to designate both the activity of interpretation and the fruits of that activity. . . . At bottom midrash is not a genre of interpretation but an interpretative stance, a way of reading the sacred text." For Kugel, then, the term primarily designates an exegetical posture and not "the fruits of that activity."

See also Boyarin, *Carnal Israel* (Berkeley: University of California Press, 1993), 9, who concisely states that midrash is "the hermeneutic system of rabbinic Judaism." He also asserts: " 'midrash' is the type of biblical interpretation which is found in the Jewish biblical commentaries which the Jews call 'midrash.' " (*Intertextuality and the Reading of Midrash* [Bloomington: Indiana University Press, 1990], ix). Neither Boyarin nor Kugel, however, ignores the multifaceted nature of midrashic literature.

I would be remiss not to mention Jonah Fraenkel's *Darkhei ha'aggada vehamidrash* (Masada: Yad Letalmud, 1991), a groundbreaking work in its systematic and exhaustive attempt to analyze the literary quality of midrash. See Fraenkel's "Hermeneutic Problems in the Study of the Aggadic Narrative," *Tarbiz* 47 (1978): 139–72 (Hebrew), and "Chiasmus in Talmudic-Aggadic Narrative," in *Chiasmus in Antiquity: Structures, Analyses, Exegesis*, John W. Welch, ed. (Hildesheim: Gerstenberg, 1981), 183–97. Ofra Meir is also a leading Israeli New Critic scholar of midrash. See Meir, *The Poetics of Rabbinic Stories* (Tel Aviv: Sifriyat Po'alim, 1993)

(Hebrew), *The Darshanic Story in Genesis Rabba* (Tel Aviv: Hakibbutz Hameuhad, 1987) (Hebrew), and "Hasipur Hadarshani Bemidrash Qadum Ume'uchar," in *Sinai* 86 (1980). Both authors emphasize the importance of understanding rabbinic stories on the literary level. See, too, the work of Arnold Goldberg, in particular those in *Frankfurter Judaistische Beiträge* (vol. 2 [1974], vol. 5 [1977], vol. 6 [1978], vol. 8 [1980], vol. 9 [1981], vol. 10 [1982], vol. 12 [1984], vol. 13 [1985], vol. 14 [1986], vol. 15 [1987], vol. 16 [1988], vol. 17, [1989], vol. 18 [1990]), where he treats rabbinic literature qua literature and explores the basic forms and functions of literary units. Although he is very much aware of different approaches to the study of rabbinic literature, his own work is marked by a fundamental appreciation of the synchronicity of texts.

6. J. Heinemann, "The Nature of Aggadah," 49. In stressing this aspect of folkoric midrashim, *aggadot*, he nonetheless acknowledges two levels of meaning, "one overt, the other covert." He writes: "The first deals openly with the explication of the biblical text and the clarification of the biblical narrative, while the second deals much more subtly with contemporary problems that engaged the attention of the homilists and their audience. . . . The aggadists do not mean so much to clarify difficult passages in the biblical text as to take a stand on the burning questions of the day, to guide the people and to strengthen their faith" (49). See my discussion in chapter 4 of Heinemann's interpretation of midrashim in Pirke de Rabbi Eliezer, passim. For a discussion of the work of both Y. Heinemann and J. Heinemann, see D. Boyarin, *Intertextuality and the Reading of Midrash*, 1–21, who succinctly summarizes each author's methodological presuppositions: "I would begin by saying that if the school which I have synecdochically represented by Joseph Heinemann places midrash aggada too firmly in its own historical circumstances and considers it a mere reflection of them, Yizhaq Heinemann removes aggada too extremely from any historical and social meanings. What is common to these theories is that they both assume the opposition between 'objective' and 'subjective,' one privileging the objective and the other the subjective. The assumption of this distinction forces one view to assume that the rabbis did not intend to interpret at all and the other to suppose a romantic, near mystical understanding of historical interpretation" (11).

7. Heinemann, "The Nature of Aggadah," 43.

8. S. Fraade, *From Tradition to Commentary: Torah and Its Interpretation in the Midrash Sifre to Deuteronomy* (Albany: State University of New York Press, 1991), 14–15.

9. In *The Sage in Jewish Society of Late Antiquity* (London: Routledge, 1999), Kalmin argues that Babylonian rabbis, because their organizational structure was influenced by Persian models, were more distant from nonrabbinic society, whereas Palestinian rabbis interacted with others in both formal and informal settings. This difference, in turn, explains the differing depictions of King David, for example. The Palestinian rabbis tend to extol him; they gloss over his sins and portray him as a rabbi whose behavior conforms to rabbinic halakhah. The Babylonian Amoraim, on the other hand, explicitly mention his sins, making the slightest effort to whitewash them and to reconcile discrepancies between his behavior and rabbinic law. This difference, according to Kalmin, is attributed to their differing relationships

to nonrabbis. He states the following: "Palestinian rabbis . . . in keeping with their greater involvement with non-rabbis and their weaker position in society, tend to depict David as sinless and saintly. They portray him positively to defend him, and by extension themselves, against the scorn or criticism of non-rabbinic Jews. Babylonian rabbis, in contrast, kept their distance from non-rabbinic Jews and occupied a strong position in society. They therefore felt little need to defend David, and by extension themselves, from attack by non-rabbinic Jews" (83).

10. Kalmin also demonstrates this in his article, "Rabbinic Portrayals of Biblical and Postbiblical Heroes," in Shaye Cohen, ed., *The Synoptic Problem in Rabbinic Literature* (Providence: Brown University, 2000), 119–41. He examines several Palestinian and Babylonian traditions regarding rabbinic assertions of equality and greatness vis-à-vis biblical figures, and concludes that there are distinct attitudinal differences among sayings of tannaitic, Babylonian amoraic, and Palestinian amoraic provenance.

11. C. Hayes, *Between the Babylonian and Palestinian Talmuds* (New York: Oxford University Press, 1997), 4.

12. Ibid., 9.

13. Daniel Boyarin, *Carnal Israel*, 15.

14. See Kugel, *In Potiphar's House: The Interpretive Life of Biblical Texts* (New York: Harper Collins, 1990), *The Bible as It Was* (Cambridge: Belknap Press of Harvard University Press, 1997), and *Traditions of the Bible: A Guide to the Bible as It Was at the Start of the Common Era* (Cambridge: Harvard University Press, 1998).

15. See Heinemann, *Aggadot Ve-Toldotehen* (Jerusalem: Keter, 1974) and *Derashot be-tsibur bi-tekufat ha-Talmud* (Jerusalem: Mosad Byalik, 1970). For a survey of contemporary approaches to the study of midrash, see C. Bakhos, ed., *Current Trends in the Study of Midrash* (Leiden: Brill, 2006).

16. Boyarin, *Carnal Israel*, 14. See his most recent work, *Border Lines: The Partition of Judeo-Christianity* (Philadelphia: University of Pennsylvania Press, 2004) and "De/Re Constructing Midrash," in C. Bakhos, ed., *Current Trends in the Study of Midrash.*

17. Rubenstein, *Talmudic Stories: Narrative Art, Composition, and Culture* (Baltimore: Johns Hopkins University Press, 1999).

18. Rubenstein writes: "Geonic sources call the sages of the sixth and seventh centuries 'Saboraim' and attribute to them various types of editorial activity. Did the Stammaim flourish in the fifth century and precede the Saboraim? Or should the Stammaim be identified with the Saboraim? In the case of aggada, the potential distinction between Stammaim and Saboraim becomes less certain. . . . *I use the term* Stammaim *for all post-Amoraic sages, who composed, redacted and edited the talmudic text in the fifth through seventh centuries.* It was during this time that the Babylonian Talmud text took shape" (*Talmudic Stories*, 17–18, emphasis in original). Rubenstein's most recent book, *The Culture of the Babylonian Talmud* (Baltimore:

Johns Hopkins University Press, 2003), attempts to depict more comprehensively and vividly the "wider cultural context of the rabbis."

19. See the exchange between P. Schäfer, "Research into Rabbinic Literature: An Attempt to Define the *Status Quaestionis*," *JJS* 37 (1986): 139–52, C. Milikowsky, "The *Status Quaestionis* of Research in Rabbinic Literature," *JJS* 39 (1988): 201–11, and P. Schäfer, "Once Again the *Status Quaestionis* of Research in Rabbinic Literature: An answer to Chaim Milikowsky," in *JJS* 40 (1989): 89–94. See also the collection of essays edited by P. Alexander and A. Samely in *Bulletin of the John Rylands University Library of Manchester* 75:3 (1993) [Theme Issue, Artefact and Text: The Recreation of Jewish Literature in Medieval Hebrew Manuscripts]. For our purposes, the following articles of this collection are of special interest: Malachi Beit-Arie, "Transmission of Texts by Scribes and Copyists: Unconscious and Critical Interferences," 32–52, Israel M. Ta-Shma, "The 'Open' Book in Medieval Hebrew Literature: The Problem of Authorized Editions," 17–42, and Philip Alexander, "Textual Criticism and Rabbinic Literature: The Case of the Targum of the Song of Songs," 159–74.

20. S. Stern, *Jewish Identity in Early Rabbinic Writings* (Leiden: Brill, 1994), xxiii.

21. Even though it has been, and may always be, impossible to determine approximately when a midrashic work was compiled, by establishing the relationship of one compilation to another, we can arrive at a relative date. According to M. Herr: "one cannot rely on the historical allusions alone or merely on the names of the sages mentioned in the Midrash, nor can one rely on the first mentions of the Midrash and its first citations, since all the Midrashim contain much material from extended eras. The lack of historical allusions alone after a definite period do not suffice to testify to its compilation immediately after that period, just as the lack of mention of a Midrash and of its citation until a certain period does not prove that it was edited at the date nearest to the beginning of that period. In neither case can one rely on the *argumentum a silentio*. A more reliable method for determining priority and lateness among Midrashim is the relationship between the various Midrashim—the use one makes of another—as well as their relationship to other sources. Thus, for instance, where Midrash A and Midrash B contain parallels, it is possible to determine whether A drew on B, or B on A, or whether both drew on a third common source, extant or not. After one arrives by use of this method, though *with great caution* [emphasis mine], at a determination of precedence, it becomes clear that other additional indications exist (literary forms, language, style, etc.)" (M. Herr, "Midrash," *Encyclopedia Judaica*, vol. 11 [Jerusalem: Keter, 1972], 1509).

22. Alon Goshen-Gottstein, *The Sinner and the Amnesiac: The Rabbinic Invention of Elisha Ben Abuya and Eleazar Ben Arach* (Stanford: Standford University Press, 2000), 4.

23. See, for example, E. Said's seminal work, *Orientalism* (New York: Vintage, 1978) which, in demonstrating how the Western notion of Orientalism has been a means by which the West has harnessed hegemonic power over the Occident, provocatively articulates this phenomenon. See also J. Clifford, ed., *Writing Culture:*

The Poetics and Politics of Ethnography (Berkeley: University of California Press, 1986), F. Barth, ed., *Ethnic Groups and Boundaries: The Social Organization of Culture Difference* (Boston: Little Brown, 1969), who in the introduction to the work identifies primary strategies communities employ to define self vis-à-vis the imagined Other, real strategies that must be understood within the context of how a community objectifies itself. See, too, C. Geertz, *The Interpretation of Cultures: Selected Essays* (New York: Basic, 1974), and P. Cushman, *Constructing the Self, Constructing America: A Cultural History of Psychotherapy* (New York: Addison Wesley, 1995), esp. 345–48. Many philosophical works, too numerous to cite here, deal with the Other. See J. Satre, *Being and Nothingness: A Phenomenological Essay on Ontology* (New York: Pocket Books, 1956). For an analysis of the development of stereotypes in group cultures, see W. Jansen, "The Esoteric-Exoteric Factor in Folklore," in A. Dundes, ed., *The Study of Folklore* (Englewood Cliffs: Prentice Hall, 1965), 43–51. In addition, for works related more specifically to the topic at hand, see J. Neusner and Ernest Frerichs, eds., *To See Ourselves as Others See Us: Christians, Jews and "Others" in Late Antiquity* (Chico: Scholars Press, 1985), and E. P. Sanders, *Jewish and Christian Self-Definition* (Philadelphia: Fortress, 1980). See, too, J. Neusner, *Judaism and Its Social Metaphors* (Cambridge: Cambridge University Press, 1989), and E. Hall, *Inventing the Barbarian: Greek Self-definition through Tragedy* (New York: Oxford University Press, 1989). Also see Miriam Taylor, *Anti-Judaism and Early Christian Identity: A Critique of the Scholarly Consensus* (Leiden: Brill, 1995), whose work demonstrates that the Jews in the writings of the Church Fathers are symbolic figures who "play an essential role in the communication and development of the Church's own distinctive conception of God's plans for His chosen people, and in the formation of the Church's cultural identity" (4). Also, M. Niehoff, *Philo on Jewish Identity and Culture*, Texts and Studies in Ancient Judaism 86 (Tübingen: Mohr Siebeck, 2001), examines Philo's individual construction of Jewish identity and culture not only vis-à-vis Greek culture "but also in relation to the discourse among Romans, Egyptians and other Jews of various political colours" (13). Regina Schwartz, *The Curse of Cain: The Violent Legacy of Monotheism* (Chicago: University of Chicago Press, 1997), examines the diverse ways in which Israelite collective indentity is constructed in antipodal terms.

24. Henceforth, PRE. With regard to transliteration, I have used the academic style (See Patrick Alexander, ed., *SBL Handbook of Style: For Ancient Near Eastern, Biblical, and Early Christian Studies* [Peabody: Hendrickon, 1999]). I have, however, retained the common spelling of several Hebrew and Aramaic words.

Chapter 1. Ishmael and Esau: Marginalized Men of the Bible

1. See R. Syren, *The Forsaken First-Born: A Study of a Recurrent Motif in the Patriarchal Narratives* (Sheffield: JSOT, 1993), for an examination of this motif (not including Leah and Rachel). Syren avers that the postexilic Jewish community is the historical *Sitz im Leben* for this phenomenon. Part of the narrative strategy of Genesis is to provide an understanding of the nations and races on earth under the providence of the God of Israel and at the same time to emphasize Israel's election, its signal fate as God's chosen people. "It seems also that the 'blessings' of the first-born

sons are worked out in deliberate reference to the concept of God's election of Israel," writes Syren. He further states that God's promise to Abraham to make Ishmael a people is a means of supplementing God's choice. That is, "by adding an idea of 'also-peoples' to the chain of 'also-sons' in the patriarchal narratives, God's choice is not challenged." Syren also asserts, "The scope of the stories themselves is broadened to take in the experiences of the postexilic circles who demonstrated an active interest in the world around Judah. Their experience of recent historical changes had taught that 'also-peoples' outside the tiny area of Judah had some standing in God's plans" (144–45). See also D. Steinmetz, *From Father to Son: Kinship, Conflict and Continuity in Genesis* (Louisville: Westminister, 1991), and F. Greenspahn, *When Brothers Dwell Together: The Preeminence of Younger Siblings in the Hebrew Bible* (New York: Oxford University Press, 1994).

2. N. Sarna, *Understanding Genesis* (New York: McGraw Hill, 1966), 181.

3. R. Alter, *The Art of Biblical Narrative* (New York: Basic, 1981), 6.

4. As J. Levenson, *The Death and Resurrection of the Beloved Son: The Transformation of Child Sacrifice in Judaism and Christianity* (New Haven: Yale University Press, 1993), 70, notes, "The list of non-first-borns who attain special eminence reads like a roster of the great names of early Israel: Isaac, Jacob, Levi, Judah, Joseph, Ephraim, Moses, Eleazar, Ithamar, Gideon, David, Solomon." I thank Joel Kaminsky for calling my attention to Samuel, who is also an important nonfirstborn Israelite.

5. In an attempt to be as comprehensive as possible, I will include a survey of form- and source-critical scholarship on the relevant biblical passages.

6. Gen. 16, with the exception of vv. 1a, 3, and 15–16, is generally considered part of the J narrative. As von Rad writes, "In many respects ch. 16 is typical of the Yahwist's narrative style. The expositor's first impression is that here he is introduced to an occurrence of great compactness and vividness. . . . The narrative here is very spacious, so to speak, with much to be read between the lines. . . . The emphasis is no longer on the aetiologies." G. von Rad, *Genesis: A Commentary*, trans. John H. Marks (London: SCM, 1972), 195–96. A. Bentzen, M. Noth, and W. Zimmerli, however, understand the chapter as an aetiological tribal story. To be sure, von Rad acknowledges the original aetiological intention of the narrative, which he attributes to "the deep south of Palestine," but once it is incorporated into narrative context, he claims that it takes on the purpose of heightening suspense. As Westermann, *Genesis 12–36: A Commentary*, trans. John J. Scullion S.J. (Minneapolis: Augsburg, 1981), 235, notes, von Rad and Zimmerli also "see in it an additional theological explanation coming from J's overall orientation. . . . Kilian sees the meaning of the narrative in the joining of Abraham and Sarah on the one side with Hagar and Ishmael on the other. . . . J. van Seters understands Gen. 16 as an anecdotal popular narrative (*Abraham in History* . . . [1975], 192–96): 'The focal point is on the struggle between the two women.'" While von Rad understands chapter 16 as originally an aetiological story, the Elohist version in chapter 21, Westermann claims, is not aetiological (229).

7. For *ʿal pĕnê*, cf. Exod. 20:3; Deut. 21:16; and Job 1:11. According to Speiser, *ʿal pĕnê*, literally "in the face of," should be translated as "in defiance, disregard of." Westermann translates it as "in confrontation with," von Rad renders it "over and

against," whereas Fox uses the more neutral, "in the presence of." Since the narrative does not necessitate using a negative, hostile term, I have chosen the JPS translation, "alongside." As Sarna notes, "The idea seems to be that the Ishmaelites and related tribes will live in close proximity to each other." N. Sarna, *Genesis* (Jewish Publication Society Torah Commentary; Philadelphia: Jewish Publication Society, 1989), 121. Or, it could be that despite constant mutual depredation he will live among his kinsmen, which may very well be a curse since his fate would depend on his relatives.

8. Westermann, 246.

9. Ibid. Westermann further claims that 16:12 belongs to tribal sayings, as in the case of Gen. 9:25–27, which are not part of the patriarchal period but rather belong to a period when the tribes were coming into being: "Only at this time can the tribal saying of 16:12 have been shaped. The link is achieved in convincing manner in 16:12 by the figure of Ishmael's mother; the tribal life of the Ishmaelites was in accord with her character: 'This intractable Ishmael is an unruly son of his stubborn mother, who did not want to submit to the yoke' (H. Gunkel; similarly O. Procksch). It is this saying only, not the narrative as a whole that is directed to the origin of the tribe of Ishmael. The tribal saying with its jubilant, defiant affirmation of predatory bedouin life and which like others of the same kind, was once transmitted independently" (246). Syren supports Westermann's claim that Gen. 16:12 was probably part of an earlier tribal saying originally unconnected with Ishmael. H. Gunkel, Kilian, and W. Zimmerli also hold this view. Drawing on the work of Kilian, Syren states that Gen. 16:12 is an anonymous saying, that "the opening 'he' is determined more by form than content and could refer to anyone." Now part of the patriarchal narrative, however, Gen. 16:12 must be understood within this context.

10. G. J. Wenham, *Word Biblical Commentary*, 2 (Dallas: Word Books, 1994), 10–11.

11. Sarna, *Genesis (JPS Commentary)*, 121.

12. Syren, 22. For an illuminating comparison of Ishmael's expulsion from the promised land, on the one hand, and of Cain's expulsion from Eden, on the other, see Levenson, 91–92, and also 102 where he writes, "The terse narrative of Gen 21:9–13 looks, Janus-like, both back to the story of the primal family and forward to the next generation of Patriarchs." Furthermore, Levenson, 108, astutely draws our attention to the "intertextual connection between the supernatural deliverance of Ishmael in Gen 21 and another story of a first-born son whose life is spared, the story of Joseph."

13. von Rad, 194.

14. Speiser, *The Anchor Bible: Genesis* (Garden City: Doubleday, 1964), 118.

15. Rashbam (Rabbi Samuel ben Meir) claims that there might be a wordplay in the biblical text between *pere'* and Paran, the wilderness where Ishmael dwelt.

16. Speiser, *The Anchor Bible: Genesis*, 121.

17. According to biblical scholars, the entire chapter is from the hand of P. See Levenson, *The Death and Resurrection of the Beloved Son*, chapter 10, for an examination of the J, E, and P treatments of the disinheritance of Ishmael.

18. For a discussion of circumcision more generally, see Sarna, *The JPS Commentary: Genesis*, 125, and Excursus 12; Westermann, *Genesis 12–36*, 265; de Vaux, *Ancient Israel* (New York: McGraw Hill, 1961), 46–48.

19. Throughout the narrative, Ishmael is referred to as "son," "lad," or "child," but in this instance, Abraham refers to his son by his proper name.

20. See Gen. 25:12–16 for a list of Ishmael's descendants. According to I. Eph'al, " 'Ishmael' and 'Arab(s)': A Transformation of Ethnological Terms," *JNES* 35 (1976), this genealogical list mentions the Arab names found in Assyrian sources, that is, the compiler of the list uses the names of the nomadic tribes of his own time dwelling to the east and south of Palestine (i.e., the "Arabs"). See chapter 3 for a more detailed discussion of the Ishmaelites. For a discussion of the Hebrew *nasi* (Prince), see E. A. Speiser, "Background and Function of the Biblical Nasi," *CBQ* 25 (1963): 111–17. Speiser claims that the translation of the term would have to vary according to context. When referring to clans and tribes, however, "chieftain" is the more accurate translation.

21. Cf. Seth Daniel Kunin, *The Logic of Incest: A Structuralist Analysis of Hebrew Mythology*, Journal for the Study of the Old Testament Supplement Series 185 (Sheffield: Sheffield Academic Press, 1995), 77ff., contends that Isaac and Ishmael are in direct opposition, and that structurally Ishmael's value is negative while Isaac's (not surprisingly) is positive. Kunin states, "Thus in Genesis 22 and the preceding chapters there is a clear pattern of opposition between Isaac and Ishmael" (96). Indubitably, Isaac is the chosen bearer of the covenant, and that throughout Genesis, and for that matter all of TaNaKh, there is an opposition between Israel and the other nations. The opposition, however, is sometimes highlighted, other times attenuated. While Kunin's broad systematic, structuralist analysis sheds light on the relationship between Hebrew mythology and biblical narratives, the study often loses sight of textual nuances and tensions. To be sure, real or imagined binary opposition is created between Israel's distinctiveness as apart from the surrounding nations for the purposes of boundary formation; yet the Hebrew scriptures as a whole clearly reflect different attitudes to the very notion of maintaining those boundaries. On the other extreme, Mark Brett contends that the editors of Genesis intended covertly to undermine the ethnocentrism of the imperial governors of the Persian period. Genesis was designed to promulgate both "universal solidarity and the particulars of identities" (146). Brett writes, "There is no clear distinction between the divinely elected family and other nations, but rather, a complex and hybrid set of relationships" (146). Although Brett's analysis of genealogy as well as his comparison of endogamous and exogamous relationships is provocative, it is nonetheless difficult to ignore the exclusivist elements of the general story line of Genesis that pervade the entire narrative.

22. Westermann, 270.

23. Ibid., 268.

24. Vawter astutely comments: "It is very evident that in 17:15–21 'covenant' and even 'everlasting pact' is something different from what it is in vss. 1–14 . . . and

in vss. 23–27. In this intervening section 'my covenant' has ceased to be the covenant of circumcision which God entered into with the Hebrews (including Ishmael and his descendants) and has become instead the distinct inheritance through whom strict blood lines of a privilege that father could not transmit to son but could only deliver to legally acceptable candidates. Thus a Moabite and an Ammonite (cf. Gen. 19:30–38) could never become part of Israel (cf. Deut. 23:4) according to Israel's later law. The same is doubtless true of Ishmael. A people that once shared in its patriarchal covenant, in view of a theology that tended to exclude it from this covenant when the covenant became more and more identified with Israel, simply came to be reckoned as outside the covenant. In these verses, the 'covenant' means little more or less than the inheritance of 15:2–4; namely, those who are accepted in the direct line of Abraham-Isaac-Jacob and who will dominate the chapters that follow" (Bruce Vawter, *On Genesis: A New Reading* [Garden City: Doubleday, 1977], 224). Although Deut. 23:4 states that no Ammonite or Moabite shall become part of "the congregation of the LORD" ("even the tenth generation," meaning "forever"), it is worth mentioning that King David is the great-grandson of Ruth, a Moabite woman who eventually settled in Bethlehem. It could be that there is an internal biblical dispute, or that Deut. 23:4 only refers to men not women. For a stimulating reexamination of the issue of particularism and universalism in the Hebrew Bible, see Jon Levenson's "The Universal Horizon of Biblical Particularism," in Mark G. Brett, ed., *Ethnicity and the Bible* (Leiden: Brill, 1996), 143–69.

25. Syren explains the paradox as arising from postexilic conditions: "After the upheavals of the exile, the Israelite community had to come to terms with radically changed conditions affecting its life and institutions. At the same time, however, its old beliefs and time-honoured practices had to be safeguarded. The new prospects opening up in the outside world had to be understood by looking back within its own traditions and religious inheritance" (Syren, 41; see also 62–63). According to Syren, the inclusivity of Gen. 17:23–27 reflects a period of Israelite history when marginal groups were permitted to join the religious community; circumcision thus served as a prerequisite. Yet, Gen. 17:19–21 reflects a period when the national identity of Israel was threatened by foreigners, as in the case of Nehemiah 13. Gen. 17, therefore, holds two views in balance. While a universalistic outlook is maintained, it is limited in that Israel is indeed set apart from all other nations. Syren makes a clever, though not fully convincing, argument for understanding the postexilic community as the historical background for Gen. 17. There is no scholarly consensus that Gen. 17 is postexilic, and furthermore, even if his assertion were correct, this alone does not explain an acceptance of other groups. Can we assume that the postexilic period gave rise to openness to outsiders when in fact Ezra provides countervailing evidence? For a discussion of the attitude of postexilic writers toward foreigners during the time of restoration, see Daniel L. Smith-Christopher, "Between Ezra and Isaiah," in Mark G. Brett, ed., *Ethnicity and the Bible* (Leiden: Brill, 1996), 117–42. Smith-Christopher outlines three distinct options coexisting in postexilic biblical thought—exclusion, transformation, and inclusion. See also M. Weinfeld, "The Universalist Trend and the Isolationist Trend in the Period of the Restoration to Zion," (Hebrew) *Tarbiz* 23 (1964): 228–42, who argues that Isa. 40–66 envisages a Judaism open to all during the period of restoration.

26. With the exception of Westermann, Gen. 21 is commonly assigned to E.

27. See note 12, sup.

28. Both the Septuagint and the Vulgate include "with her son Isaac," which is not in the Masoretic Text. In Targum Onkelos and Neofiti, *mĕṣaḥēq* is translated as "idolatrous behavior."

29. As in the case of Exod. 32:6.

30. Joshua Schwartz, "Ishmael at Play: On Exegesis and Jewish Society," *HUCA* 66 (1995): 203–221. See especially note 2 (204), where he gives a bibliographic listing of scholars dealing with this issue. One example of sexual connotation is masturbation. See Phyllis Trible, *Texts of Terror* (Philadelphia: Fortress, 1984), 33. As we will have occasion to see in the next chapter, since the verb *zḥq* in this verse is the same verb used in Gen. 39:17, in which Potiphar's wife accuses Joseph of trying to seduce her, the rabbis also consider the notion that Ishmael's behavior was sexually immoral. See also, Naomi Steinberg, *Kinship and Marriage in Genesis: A Household Economics Perspective* (Minneapolis: Augsburg, 1993), 79–80, who also holds the opinion that Ishmael was masturbating, that his "actions prompt Sarah to remember that in order to insure Isaac's place as next of kin to Abraham, Ishmael must be removed from the household. Ishmael's sexual actions have a direct bearing on the genealogical concerns of the family stories in Genesis" (80).

31. Schwartz, 204.

32. Westermann, 339.

33. Much has been written on the dating of Jubilees. For a survey of literature, see J. C. Vanderkam, *Textual and Historical Studies in the Book of Jubilees*, HSM 14 (Missoula: Scholars, 1977), 207–13, and D. Mendels, *The Land of Israel as a Political Concept in Hasmonean Literature*, Texte und Studien zum Antiken Judentum 15 (Tübingen: Mohr Siebeck, 1987), 148–49.

34. For a comparison of the treatment of Ishmael and Isaac in Jubilees, see Roger Syren, "Ishmael and Esau in the Book of Jubilees and Targum Pseudo-Jonathan," *The Aramaic Bible: Targums in Their Historical Context*, D. R. G. Beattie and M. J. McNamara, eds. (Sheffield: JSOT, 1994), 310–15. Syren demonstrates that *Jubilees*, as well as Josephus and Targum Ps. Jonathan, exhibits "a fair and generous attitude towards Ishmael" before the birth of Isaac. He also points to the parity between Ishmael and Isaac in Jubilees, however, he does not subscribe to an "extremely positive view" of Ishmael as propounded by D. Mendels, 150, and, in a similar vein, by M. Ohana, "La Polemique judeo-islamique et l'image d'Ismaël dans Targum Pseudo-Jonathan," *Augustinianum* 15 (1975): 371.

35. J. C. Vanderkam, trans. and ed., *The Book of Jubilees: A Critical Text* (Lovanii: Peeters, 1989), 102–103.

36. For a discussion on this topic, see J. Schwartz, "A Child's Wagon," in *Tarbiz* 63 (1993): 375–92 (Hebrew).

37. J. Schwartz, "Ishmael at Play," 209.

38. Drawing on Ovadiah Seforno, an Italian rabbi of the late fifteenth century, Levenson, 101, writes: "The precise nature of the 'playing' (*mĕṣaḥēq*, v 9) that calls forth the matriarch's jealousy is unclear, though the term is obviously yet another turn on Isaac's name (*yiṣḥāq*). The likelihood is that the passage in question is a variant of some sort to 16:4–6, in which Hagar's pregnancy motivates Sarah's complaint, 'I am lowered in her esteem.' If this is the case, then 21:9 refers not to the innocent play of children, but to Ishmael's mockery, presumably of Sarah herself. As Seforno comments on this verse, Sarah 'thought he was aroused to such ridicule because he heard it from his mother.' "

39. von Rad, 232.

40. Speiser, *Anchor Bible*: Genesis, 155. Westermann notes: "It is not to be assumed that the verb (*mĕṣaḥēq*) is a play on the name of Isaac, because Ishmael is its subject apart from the fact that all previous uses derive from the Qal [form of the verb]" (339). Westermann's argument is unconvincing. Most scholars claim that it is an allusion to the name Isaac—an obvious pun.

41. In Gal. 4:28–29, Paul interprets "playing" in negative terms: "Now you, my friends, are children of the promise, like Isaac. But just as at that time, the child born according to the flesh persecuted the child who was born according to the Spirit, so it is now also" (NSRV trans.).

42. J. A. Hackett, "Rehabilitating Hagar: Fragments of an Epic Pattern," in *Gender and Difference in Ancient Israel*, Peggy Day, ed. (Minneapolis: Fortress, 1989), 20.

43. See Schwartz, "Ishmael at Play," 205 n.5, where he makes a similiar argument and writes: "In a mother's eyes, with a greater agenda on her mind, such play or jesting might have been construed as threatening." Similarly, Coats writes, "Ishmael was acting like Isaac, claiming Isaac's spot." G. W. Coats, "Strife without Reconciliation: A Narrative Theme in the Jacob Traditions," in *Werden und Wirken des Alten Testaments*, ed. R. Albertz, et al. (Göttingen: Vandenhoeck and Ruprecht, 1980), 97. See, too, J. Kaminsky, "Humor and the Theology of Hope: Isaac as a Humorous Figure," *Interpretation* 54 (2000): 366, and L. H. Silberman, "Listening to the Text," *JBL* 102 (1983): 21, who writes, "Its real meaning, hidden under a series of wordplays, may be that Sarah sees the son of her rival, Hagar, has been and may continue to be *mshq*, the joy of his father to the exclusion of her son *yshq* who is for her the joy-giver." And, Esther Fuchs, *Sexual Politics in the Biblical Narrative: Reading the Hebrew Bible as a Woman*, JSOTS Sup 310 (Sheffield: Sheffield Academic Press, 2000), 150–52, compares the strife between Sarah and Hagar with that of Rachel and Leah and categorizes these stories under "contest type-scene."

44. Since Gen. 21:9–21 is generally recognized as belonging to E, this is more likely the case. For a literary critical analysis of Gen. 21, see L. Lyke, "Where Does the Boy Belong? Compositional Strategy in Genesis 21:14," *CBQ* 56 (1994): 637–48.

45. Schwartz, 206.

46. Ibid., 207.

47. Ibid.

48. In Gen 16:6 Sarai (Sarah) treats Hagar harshly. As Sarna notes, "The Hebrew verb used here implies that Sarai subjected Hagar to physical and psychological abuse. It carries with it the nuance of critical judgment of her actions. According to Ramban, 'the matriarch sinned by such maltreatment, and Abraham too by permitting it'" (Sarna, *JPS Commentary*, 120).

49. Trible, 20–21. See also N. Steinberg, *Kinship and Marriage*, 78ff.

50. Hackett, 26 n.19.

51. See also Deut. 21:15–17 where the firstborn son, even though he is from the unloved wife, receives double portion of the father's possessions. For a discussion of the special status of the firstborn male offspring and the law of Deut. 21:15–17, see Levenson, chapter 7. See also F. Greenspahn, *When Brothers Dwell Together*, 57–59. Steinberg writes, "Through kinship studies the legal situation becomes clear: the son borne by the primary wife is automatically entitled as his father's heir. The son who will not inherit from his father is expected to leave home, something that Ishmael has not done" (78). The narrative suggests otherwise. If this were the case, then why must Sarah demand Ishmael's dismissal? Why does Abraham express reservations, and why must God intervene?

52. James B. Pritchard, ed., *The Ancient Near East: An Anthology of Texts and Pictures* (Princeton: Princeton University Press, 1958), 157.

53. N. Sarna, *Understanding Genesis*, 156. As Sarna illustrates, the biblical text "repeatedly emphasizes the fact of sonship." For example, Gen. 17:23, 25, 26 read: "Then Abraham took his son Ishmael . . . and his son Ishmael was thirteen years old when he was circumcised. . . . Thus Abraham and his son Ishmael were circumcised." When Sarah demanded the eviction of Hagar and Ishmael, one learns, "the matter distressed Abraham greatly, for it concerned a son of his" (Gen. 21:11). Abraham was buried by both sons: "His sons Isaac and Ishmael buried him in the cave of Machpelah" (Gen. 25:9). Finally, Ishmael's genealogy begins as follows: "This is the line of Ishmael, Abraham's son, whom Hagar the Egyptian, Sarah's slave, bore to Abraham" (Gen. 25:12). Cf. Philo who disqualifies Ishmael by highlighting the menial status of Hagar, a slave woman from Egypt. See M. Niefhoff, *Philo on Jewish Identity and Culture*, Texts and Studies in Ancient Judaism 86 (Tübingen: Mohr Siebeck, 2001), 24–27.

54. Sarna, 156.

55. Ibid.

56. See Speiser's discussion of Nuzi text No. 67 in relation to Gen. 16:2 in *The Anchor Bible*, 120. See T. Thompson, *The Historicity of the Patriarchal Narratives: The Quest for the Historical Abraham* (Berlin: Walter de Gruyter, 1974), 252–58, for a discussion dealing with the use of the Nuzi texts to illumine Gen. 16, 21:1–21, and 29:31–30:24. See also H. Donner, "Adoption Oder Legitimation? Erwagungen Zur Adoption Im Alten Testament Auf Dem Hintergrund Der Altorientalischen Rechte," in *Oriens Antiquus* 8 (1969): 87–119, where he states that Gen. 16:21 deals

not with adoption but rather with a type of legitimation (106ff.). S. Teubal, "Sarah and Hagar," in A. Brenner, ed., *A Feminist Companion to Genesis* (Sheffield: Sheffield Academic Press, 1997), 236, curiously and far less convincingly maintains that Ishmael's banishment had nothing to do with material wealth but rather with religious ethics: "Sarah was a religious woman and a woman of religion, a priestess. Isaac's religious upbringing must have been Sarah's foremost consideration."

57. Greenspahn, 81. See also 30–83, where he argues contra von Rad, who asserts that the privileged status of the firstborn in the ancient Near East is "uncontested." Cf. Robert Alter, *The Art of Biblical Narrative*, 6, who uses the phrase "iron clad law of primogeniture," von Rad, *Genesis: A Commentary*, 416, and E. Neufeld, *Ancient Hebrew Marriage Laws, with Special Reference to Special Semitic Laws and Customs* (London: Longmans, Green, 1944), 263, who writes, "The right of the firstborn . . . is the only right in Israel of which there is any real historical record."

58. Greenspahn, 82.

59. Sarna, *Genesis*, 21. Cf. J. Rosenberg's description: "Ishmael will become a people apart, volatile and treacherous to all, yet used by all," *King and Kin: Political Allegory in the Hebrew Bible* (Bloomington: Indiana University Press, 1986), 90.

60. The Hebrew *'admōnî* does not necessarily have the negative connotations of redheadedness or impetuosity, which is associated with "the sinister and the dangerous." "More likely a ruddy complexion is intended. This may well be connected with the convention found in Egyptian and Cretan art, as well as in the Ugaritic texts, that equates red skin with heroic stature," Sarna, 180.

61. The etymology of Edom probably lies "in the characteristically reddish hue of the Nubian sandstone and crystalline rocks of that country," ibid.

62. Vawter, 288.

63. Sarna, 180.

64. Speiser, 196. See also Sarna, 180, and Vawter, 288.

65. As Speiser notes, the Hebrew *rōbe qaššāt* is "a combination of two agent nouns, hence a bowman (*qaššat*) who does something, not a person who uses a bow. Moreover, no such meaning as to shoot can be established for the first element, which might be connected at best with Heb. for 'great,' or Aram. for 'youth,' and not without some difficulties in either case. The general type of compound, however, recalls in its construction 'a wild colt of a man' (xvi 12), or Akk. 'hunter-man,' which is familiar from the Gilgamesh Epic. The present translation is conjectural" (156).

66. Ibid.

67. Vawter, 287.

68. Reference is made to this in Judg. 11:17.

69. Gen. Rab. 73:9 proffers two opposing interpretations of the verse. R. Shimon b. Eleazar contends, "He kissed him with all his heart," whereas R. Jannai states that Esau wanted to bite Jacob.

70. For a thorough discussion of the shifting biblical stances toward Edom, see Syren, 109–21. Syren disagrees with Dicou (*Jacob en Esau*, 186–88) who argues that Esau/Edom is one and the same in Genesis and the Prophets. Syren on the other hand asserts that Gen. 32–33 belongs to a different *Sitz im Leben*, as does Deut. 2, which is exceptionally favorable toward Edom. He writes: "Esau/Edom, to whom, according to Deut. 2, Yahweh himself gave their land, has become, by the exile, a mortal enemy. Consequently, Yahweh has retracted his gift, so that Edom has finally become a 'realm of wickedness, a people whom Yahweh has cursed forever' (Mal. 1)" (116). In line with his theory that the motif of the first-born is postexilic, he envisages Gen. 32–33 as developing from a Jewish community of the resettlement: "I submit that it was the reconsiderations forced upon the post-exilic community that influenced the final editing of the chapters. The new conditions that faced the community included the necessity of working out a *modus vivendi* in relation to foreigners" (121). Unlike the prophetic literature, Gen. 32–33 takes a moderate stance, which, claims Syren, may be "a covert criticism of the prophetic outrage" (ibid). Again, Syren offers sketchy support for his novel hypothesis.

71. Num. 21:4, 33:37, 34:3; Josh. 15:1; I Kgs. 9:26; 2 Kgs. 3:9 and Jer. 40:11. On the other hand, the book of Obadiah is a hymn of hate against Edom.

72. The Ishmaelites are mentioned in only five contexts in the Hebrew Scriptures. In Gen. 27:25, 27ff., and 39:1 the Ishmaelites bring Joseph to Egypt; 1 Chr. 2:17 identifies one of David's officials as an Ishmaelite, however, in 2 Sam. 17:25 he is identified as an Israelite. They are listed as Israel's antagonists along with the Amalekites, Hagarites, Edomites, and Moabites in Ps. 83:7. Finally, in 1 Chr. 27:30 an Ishmaelite tends to David's camels. In chapter 3, I will discuss the connection between Arabs and Ishmaelites.

73. In *Myth in Old Testament Interpretation*, BZAW, 134 (Berlin: de Gruyter, 1974) 101–105, J. W. Rogerson discusses the influence of Levi-Strauss's theory of binary oppositions on the study of folktales and the relevance structural theories may have for Hebrew Bible studies. In brief, "Following Jakobson," writes Rogerson, "Levi-Strauss seeks to reduce myths to systems of binary oppositions, which in turn reflect the basic functioning of the human mind, and its tendency to analyse the natural world in oppositions" (105). See Seth Kunin's *The Logic of Incest*, which examines Hebrew mythology from a structuralist perspective.

74. In Pirke de Rabbi Eliezer (PRE), an early ninth-century midrashic text, God tests Abraham ten times. The ninth trial is to cast out Ishmael and the tenth, of course, is the Aqedah, the binding of Isaac.

75. See his article, cited earlier, "Where Does the Boy Belong? Compositional Strategy in Genesis 21:14." In a recent article, "Parallel Lives: The Trials and Traumas of Isaac and Ishmael," *Bible Review* 15 (1999): 20–25, C. Leviant also draws our attention to the similarity and disparity between the Ishmael-Hagar narrative and the Isaac-Abraham story. Leviant, for example, pays close attention to the use of similar expressions and word ordering in both birth announcements.

76. Sarna, 174.

77. R. Alter, *Genesis: Translation and Commentary* (New York: Norton, 1996), 201.

78. See David Freedman, ed., *Anchor Bible Dictionary*, 1, 5 (New York: Doubleday, 1992), 162; 640.

79. I am grateful to Sarah Diamant for bringing this to my attention.

80. See the discussion in the next chapter on rabbinic sources, Mekhilta de Rabbi Ishmael, Pisha 16, PT. Bikkurim 1:6, Gen. Rab. 45:8, that deal with this similarity.

81. The use of *min* in Gen. 27:28 is partitive whereas in Gen 27:39 it is privative thus negating the blessing bestowed upon Jacob in v. 28 (Westermann, 443). Furthermore, v. 40, "you shall serve your brother," reverses v. 29, "Be lord over your brothers." To use Fokkelman's term, this is an "anti-blessing." Westermann, however, notes that it does not mean "virtually a curse" as J. Skinner and others contend. According to Westermann, 443, by saying, "you shall live," Isaac blesses Esau: "Esau is to have a hard life, but he is to live . . . it is rather a daring intimation of the later and extended meaning of the idea of the blessing, the blessing as the promise of vital power: 'you shall live!'" Cf. Ez. 16:6.

Chapter 2. Ishmael in Tannaitic and Amoraic Literature

1. All translations of rabbinic and Islamic texts are my own and are based on critical editions (see notes, passim, and bibliography). On my translation of PRE, see chapter 4, n. 32.

2. See J. Neusner, *From Enemy to Sibling: Rome and Israel in the First Century of Western Civilization*, The Ben Zion Bokser Memorial Lecture (New York: Queens College, 1986), 14ff. See the discussion of his hypothesis, inf.

3. Cf. Gen. Rab. 53:11: R. ʿAzariah said in R. Levi's name: "Ishmael said to Isaac, 'Let us go and see our portions in the field'; then pretending to be playing, Ishmael would take a bow and arrows and shoot them in Isaac's direction. Thus it is written, 'As a madman who casts deadly firebrands and arrows, so is the man who deceives his neighbor and says, I was only making sport.'" (Prov. 26:19).

4. See Finkelstein, *Sifre al Sefer Devarim* (New York: Jewish Theological Seminary, 1993), ad loc., who sets it as a Baraita.

5. As Levenson points out in *The Death and Resurrection of the Beloved Son*, 101, this midrash retrojects Deut. 21:15–17 anachronistically into the Patriarchal narrative.

6. The exception is T. Soṭah 6:6, where he refers to Gen. 18:19.

7. In Gen. Rab. 59:7 we find a variation of T. Qiddušin 5:17 that portrays Ishmael in a favorable light: "And the LORD had blessed Abraham in all things." R. Judah said: "It means that God gave him a daughter." Said R. Nehemiah to him: "Then she was the center of the king's household, yet no blessing is recorded of her! Rather, 'And the LORD blessed Abraham in all things' means that He had not

given him a daughter at all." R. Levi said: "It means, with three things: He had made him master of his evil inclination, Ishmael reformed, and his storehouse was never diminished in any way." R. Levi said in R. Hama b. R. Hanina's name: "It means that He did not test him again." Both sources assume that Ishmael sinned but then repented. The notion that Ishmael would repent is also found in Gen. Rab. 30:4 where the verse "You shall be buried in a good old age" (Gen. 15:15) is taken to mean that God informed Abraham that Ishmael would repent. Perhaps what is operating here is the belief that no father could die happily if he had a wicked son. Surely the son of Abraham, the righteous, would repent. Here, as in the case of Gen. Rab. 48:13, rabbinic notions of Abraham's character are a consideration in this midrash.

8. Because PT. Berakot 1:6 and Gen. Rab. 45:8 are, in my estimation, variations of a tannaitic source, a rabbinic source that is putatively compiled in the mid to late third century, I am including them in my discussion of Mekhilta, Pisha 16.

9. In his work, "*Torah le-khol ba'e ha-ʿolam*": *zerem universali be-sifrut ha-Tana'im ve-yahaso le-hokhmat he-ʿamim* (Tel Aviv: Hakibbutz Hameuchad, 1999), Marc Hirshman detects a strain of universalism peculiar to the school of R. Ishmael. He points to the observation that legal discussions, for example, in the corpus attributed to R. Ishmael as opposed to that of R. Aqiba, do not explicitly use the Noahide commandments, the *sheva mitzvot beney noah*. See also Hirshman, "Rabbinic Universalism in the Second and Third Centuries," *HTR* 93, 2 (2000): 101–15, which examines several tannaitic texts attesting to a form of universalism in rabbinic Judaism. The Mekhilta's recognition of the righteousness of Ishmael, deemed a Gentile, and its claim that the deeds of all the righteous will be rewarded, indeed point to its inclusivity.

10. A discussion of this midrash in PRE 32 is found in chapter 4.

11. See my article, "Figuring (Out) Esau: The Rabbis and Their Others," *Journal of Jewish Studies* (forthcoming).

12. See Gen. 17:16 where God doubles Abraham's stipend by promising him a second son whom Sarah will conceive.

13. All translations of Genesis Rabbah are based on the critical edition of J. Theodor and Ch. Albeck, *Midrash Bereshit Rabba: Critical Edition with Notes and Commentary*, 3 vols. (Jerusalem, 1965; repr. of Berlin 1912–36, with corrections).

14. On the *mashal*, the rabbinic parable, see D. Stern, *Parables in Midrash* (Cambridge: Harvard University Press, 1991), 1–45. As Stern points out, in the Bible *mashal* refers to metaphors, similes, proverbs, and allegories. In rabbinic literature, however, the *mashal* becomes a generic term for such literary devices as parables and fables.

15. The verse is translated "which was behind," but for the purposes of the midrash it is rendered "he was behind."

16. See Yalquṭ Shimʿoni, Wayyera 82.

17. See J. Theodor and Ch. Albeck, *Midrash Bereshit Rabba: Critical Edition with Notes and Commentary*, 3 vols. Berlin, 1912–36, with corrections; repr. Jerusalem, 1965, with corrections) ad loc., n.4, for manuscript variations and other interpretations. For example, see *Leqah Tov*, a twelfth-century midrashic commentary on the Pentateuch and the Five Scrolls. According to this interpretation, we learn that the angel looks like an Arab and that Abraham is concealing Sarah from him because Arabs are licentious. In another interpretation, Ishmael seems to be performing the same function as Abraham. The issue of modesty, *yiḥûd*, concerns Sarah with the angel, not Sarah with either Abraham or Ishmael.

18. Gen. Rab. 53:14 interprets Gen. 21:17–18: "And the angel of God called to Hagar from heaven, and said to her, 'What troubles you, Hagar? Fear not; for God has heard the voice of the lad where he is. Arise, lift up the lad, and hold him fast with your hand; for I will make him a great nation,'" and addresses the question of why the angel of God calls to Hagar. Abraham's merit is one reason given, another is the merit of Ishmael's prayer, for the midrash reads: "The prayer of a sick person is the most efficacious of all." The midrash also interprets the phrase "where he is": "The ministering angels jumped to prosecute him. They said before the Holy One, Blessed be He, 'Master of all ages, will you provide a well for a man who is destined to destroy your children with thirst?' He said to them, 'What is he now?' They replied, 'A righteous man.' He said to them, 'I judge someone only where he is at the moment.'"

19. On Gen. 21:14, Ibn Ezra writes: "How could he expel his son and send him away with his mother empty-handed? Where was his generosity? The surprise is at those who are surprised, for Abraham acted exactly as the LORD had commanded him. If Abraham had given money against Sarah's wishes, he would not have observed the commandment of the LORD. And in the end, after Sarah's death, he did indeed give gifts to Ishmael's sons" (See Gen. 25:6).

20. "Slaves" is found in some variants. Cf. Theodor-Albeck, vol. 2, 570 n.2.

21. For a discussion of the variation of Ishmael's age in other sources, see Theodor-Albeck, vol. 2, 570 n.3.

22. Cf. Theodor-Albeck, vol. 2, 574 n.3.

23. BT. Qiddušin 81b reads as follows: Every time R. Hiyya b. Ashi used to fall on his face, he used to say, "Merciful One, save us from the evil inclination." One day his wife heard him and said, "Let us see. It is many years since he has had sex with me, so why then should he pray this way?" One day he was studying in his garden and his wife adorned herself and walked in front of him. He said to her, "Who are you?" She said, "I am Harutha and I have returned today." He propositioned her. She said to him, "Bring me that pomegranate from the highest bough." He jumped up and brought it to her. When he returned to his house, his wife was heating the oven and he sat in it. She asked, "What does this mean?" He told her what happened. She said, "It was I." He did not believe her until she gave him proof [the pomegranate]. He said, "Still my intention was evil." That righteous man (R. Hiyya b. Ashi) fasted all his life until he died.

See T. Soṭah 15:11; B. Baba Batra 60b. For a thorough analysis of rabbinic attitudes toward fasting, see chapters 4, "The Asceticism of Fasting," and 5, "Saint or

Sinner? Rabbinic Attitudes towards Fasting and Asceticism in Palestine and Babylonia in Late Antiquity," of Eliezer Diamond, *Holy Men and Hunger Artists: Fasting and Asceticism in Rabbinic Culture* (New York: Oxford University Press, 2004).

24. For other examples of this phenomenon, see BT. Šabbat 56b and BT. Ta'anit 23a.

25. Cf. Gen. Rab. 62:5, BT. Megillah 16b–17a and BT. Yebamot 64a.

26. This negative midrash is attributed to an Amora.

27. Neusner, *Judaism and Its Social Metaphors*, 141. For a consideration of Neusner's theses, see discussion in chapter 3, 79–80, passim.

Chapter 3. The Rabbis and Their Others

1. See references in introduction, n.23.

2. It is important to point out that I am not dealing with explicit statements made about the Gentiles, the *goyim* (the nations of the world–*'ummot ha-ʿolam*), but rather with the use of marginalized biblical figures to define and describe non-Jews. Depending on the context, the use of *goyim* may imply a real referent. To make sweeping statements about the use of *goyim* without paying close attention to nuances in its use is careless. A future study of the relationship between the use of *goyim* in tannaitic and amoraic texts compared to the use of these biblical figures may yield greater insight into the nature of midrash and the extent to which the rabbis used midrash to reflect contemporary circumstances. See discussion of S. Stern's work on the portrayal of non-Jews inf. See, too, G. Porton, "Forbidden Transactions: Prohibited Commerce with Gentiles in Earliest Rabbinism," in *To See Ourselves as Others See Us*, J. Neusner and E. Frerichs, eds. (Chico, CA: Scholars Press, 1985). In his analysis of the Gentiles in Mishnah-Tosefta, Porton writes: "The gentile is always pictured from the rabbis' point of view and described in any context in ways which are consistent with the needs of a given passage or literary form or convention" (334). For a more detailed analysis of Gentiles in Mishnah-Tosefta, see G. Porton, *Goyim: Gentiles and Israelites in Mishnah-Tosefta* (Atlanta: Scholars Press, 1988).

3. Cf. D. Boyarin, *Dying for God: Martyrdom and the Making of Christianity and Judaism* (Stanford: Stanford University Press, 1999), where he writes: "The verse itself is explicitly about Esau, who (through his alternative name Edom) is always an eponym for Rome (and then for Rome as Christendom) in rabbinic literature" (46).

4. S. Stern, *Jewish Identity in Early Rabbinic Writings*, 18.

5. Ibid., 137. For a survey and discussion of Jewish attitudes toward the "nations" in ancient Judaism, see R. Goldenberg, *The Nations That Know Thee Not: Ancient Jewish Attitudes toward Other Religions* (New York: New York University Press, 1998).

6. Cf. S. Stern, *Jewish Identity in Early Rabbinic Writings*, 19, for several rabbinic references to Esau as Rome, which in turn, according to Stern typifies the

nations. Stern argues that the nations are a blurred, "amorphous, undifferentiated collectivity," 18. He writes: "Whereas in the Bible, Esau is no more than the ancestor and founder of the small kingdom of *Edom* (Idumaea), by the rabbinic period he is identified as the ancestor of the Romans or as the founder of their city. Rome is thus referred to as 'kingdom of Esau,' 'son of Esau,' 'Esau,' 'kingdom of *Edom*' and '*Edom*' *tout court*; the Romans themselves are said to identify with Esau. Consequently, the rabbinic exegesis of the Biblical account of Esau and Jacob constitutes a web of veiled references to Rome and Israel. The contrast between Jacob and Esau . . . is thus an embodied prefiguration of the polarized, dialectical contrast between the single entities of Israel and the nations. It must be stressed that in the same way as the Jewish people of the rabbinic period are equated in our sources with the 'Israel' of the Bible, as though they were one and the same people, rabbinic literature fails to distinguish between the non-Jews of the Bible and those of their contemporary reality. Israel and Rome, the avatars of Jacob and Esau, are thus current manifestations of a changeless structure, and ever-lasting reality. In this sense, the homogeneity of the nations, which mirrors that of Israel in a dialectical, contrastive way, transcends not only ethnic plurality but also the vicissitudes of historical change" (19–20).

7. "Who Are the 'Amorites,' and Why Must Their Ways Be Shunned?" (work in progress). The reference to Amorites here might be a way of referring to local pagans whose "ways" Jews would be inclined to follow.

8. A demon. See *Encyclopedia Judaica*, 14 (Jerusalem: Keter, 1972), 719–22, and Bernard Bamberger, *Fallen Angels* (Philadelphia: Jewish Publication Society, 1952).

9. See Yalquṭ Shimʿoni, Wayyera 101, BT. Sanhedrin 89b, Tanḥuma, Wayyera 23, and Pesiqta Rabbati, chap. 40.

10. Cf. Ps-Jonathan Gen. 22, Tanḥuma Wayyera 42, PRE 31, and BT. Sanhedrin 89b.

11. Cf. Neusner, *Judaism and Its Social Metaphors*, 141ff., where he contends that the midrash is an "effort to prefigure the history of Israel's suffering and redemption" (141). He continues: "Ishmael, standing now for Christian Rome, claims God's blessing, but Isaac gets it, as Jacob will take it from Esau. The following works the contrast of Ishmael as against Isaac, yielding the same polemic against Rome" (ibid.).

12. This is probably a scribal error. Either Shillum or Shalum is the correct version. In any case, there are only two interlocutors, not three.

13. PT. Nedarim 3:8: "Mishnah [If one says] *qonam* [a term used as a vow of abstinence] that I do not benefit from the seed of Abraham, the person is permitted to benefit from idol worshippers. What about the children of Ishmael who are part of the seed of Abraham? Ishmael is not the seed of Abraham, for 'in Isaac shall your seed be called' (Gen. 21:12). Is not Esau part of the seed of Isaac? R. Yudan b. Shalom, 'in Isaac' [means] in part." Cf. BT. Nedarim 31a. In both cases, the Hebrew *bĕ* of *bĕYiṣḥāq*, "through Isaac" or "in Isaac," serves as a partitive preposition. See also footnote 102, inf.

14. As noted above, the two, however, meet in midrash where they argue over the inheritance of Abraham. See Gen. Rab. 55:4, sup.

15. See my article, "Double Identity: Hagar and the Other Woman," forthcoming.

16. H. Strack and G. Stemberger, eds., *Introduction to the Talmud and Midrash* (Minneapolis: Fortress, 1992), 332. Cf. A. Kensky, *Midrash Tanhuma Shemot: A Critical Edition of "Midrash Tanhuma Shemot" (Standard Edition) through Beshallah* (Diss., JTS, 1990), introduction.

17. See A. Shinan, *Midrash Shemot Rabbah, Chapters I–XIV: A Critical Edition Based on a Jerusalem Manuscript, with Variants, Commentary and Introduction* (Hebrew) (Tel Aviv: Dvir, 1984), 23–24. See also Strack and Stemberger, 335.

18. Copious studies on Esau and Edom in rabbinic literature attribute tropological meaning to him such that it is taken for granted that Esau represents Rome, and later Christianity, although it is not always clear whether the reference is to Christianity or to Christian Rome. To be sure, rabbinic literature often uses Esau figuratively to represent Rome and its future demise in apocalyptic fashion, but this is not always the case. For a survey of rabbinic references to Esau, see Irit Aminoff, *The Figures of Esau and the Kingdom of Edom in Palestinian Midrashic-Talmudic Literature in the Tannaitic and Amoraic Periods* (Diss., Melbourne University, 1981).

19. See M. Margalioth, ed., *Encyclopedia of Talmudic and Geonic Literature, Being a Biographical Dictionary of the Tannaim, Amoraim and Geonim* (Hebrew), 2 vols. (Tel Aviv, 1960); A. Hyman, *Sefer Toldot Tannaim ve-Amoraim*, 3 vols. (London 1910; repr., Jerusalem: Kiryah Neʿemanah, 1964); R. Halperin, *Atlas Eytz Chayim: Tannaim wa-Amoraim*, 2 parts (Tel Aviv: Hekdesh Ruah, 1980).

20. In several midrashim, however, this is not the case. See examples, inf.

21. G. Cohen, "Esau as Symbol in Early Medieval Thought," in *Studies in the Variety of Rabbinic Cultures* (Philadelphia: Jewish Publication Society; repr., 1991), 244.

22. See Gen. Rab. 2:3, 66:4, 67:13, Lev. Rab. 36:5, inf. There is no indication in these and other midrashim that Esau is tantamount to Rome.

23. See the discussion of tannaitic literature, sup.

24. All translations of the Sifre are based on the edition of Louis Finkelstein, *Sifre al Sefer Devarim* (New York: Jewish Theological Seminary, 1993).

25. Cf. New Testament parallels: Mark 1:1–2, Luke 20:9–19, and Matthew 21:33–46.

26. They took from the produce of the field what they owed the king.

27. The word used is *pĕsolet*, "refuse, base metal, worthless matter" (Jastrow, *Dictionary of the Targumim, Talmud Babli, Yerushalmi and the Midrashic Literature* [New York: Judaica Press, 1992], 1193). In this context, the word carries the connotation of *pĕsûl*, "blemish, disqualification," also from the root, *pāsal*; thus, I have translated the word in order to reflect this meaning.

28. Also found in Midrash Tannaim to Deut. 32:9 and Yalquṭ Shimʿoni, Ha'azinu 942 (Jerusalem: Mossad Harav Kook, 1973), 633. The notion that Ishmael and Esau are unfit issue of Abraham and Isaac is found also in Sifre Deut. 31. R. Shimon b. Yohai's claim that he and R. Aqiba differ on four exegetical points is a digression from the exegesis of Deut. 6:4, "Hear O Israel the LORD is our God, the LORD is one." For an analysis of Sifre Deut. 32:9, Ha'azinu 312, see E. Mihaly, "A Rabbinic Defense of the Election of Israel," *HUCA* 35 (1964): 103–35, and I. Yuval, *Shene goyim be-vitnekh: Yehudim ve-Notsrim, dimuyim hadadiyim* (Tel Aviv: Am Oved, 2000), 31ff.

29. As Mihaly notes, 105, the rabbis use Gen. 25:27, "But Jacob was a mild man who stayed in camp," as prooftext for a variety of impeccable behavior they attribute to Jacob. Jacob, for example, was born circumcised, performed all the commandments, was righteous, innocent of unseemly conduct, and studied Torah.

30. See Neusner's elaborate discussion of the multiple meanings of "Israel" in *Judaism and Its Social Metaphors*, passim. I refer to Israel as an entity that defines itself vis-à-vis the real and imagined Other in terms of family, nation, and people, that is in real and metaphorical terms.

31. Cf. Sifre Deut. 31.

32. Cf. Yalquṭ Shimʿoni, Wayyera 93. For a discussion on the treatment of David in the Babylonian Talmud, see Kalmin, *The Sage of Jewish Society in Late Antiquity*, where he compares the Palestinian and Babylonian Amoraim's treatment of David.

33. This might serve as evidence that Ecclesiasticus was considered part of the canon. See Yalquṭ Shimʿoni, Toledot 116.

34. Cf. Num. Rab. 16:10 and Yalkut Shimʿoni, Wayyetze 119.

35. Cf. Yalquṭ Shimʿoni, Toledot 115 and Midrash Tehillim 14:2 (Vilna Edition), which reads: "And Esau said in his heart, 'Let the days of mourning for my father be at hand; then I will slay my brother Jacob.' What was he thinking? 'There is no way I can kill my father, rather, I will tell his brother, Ishmael, and he will kill him and I will kill my brother, Jacob. Then the two of us will inherit the world.' Thus he spoke to Ishmael but in his heart Esau thought, 'After Ishmael kills my father, and I my brother, I will come against Ishmael and also kill him and thus inherit the world alone.' "

36. Cf. Exod. Rab. 1:1 and Tanḥuma, Shemot 1.

37. See *Diqduqei Sopherim*, n.3 on 16b.

38. See detailed discussion of Gen. Rab. 59:17 and Tos. Qiddušin 5:17, sup. and of Eliyyahu Rab 13, inf. BT. Baba Batra 16b fleshes out the interpretations of Gen. 24:1 found in Tos. Qiddušin 5:17.

39. Esau seems to have symbolized Rome in the tannaitic period and Christianity in the Amoraic. For a detailed analysis of Esau as symbol of Rome and Christianity, see Adi Schremer, forthcoming. According to Boyarin, *Dying for God*,

3, "After 312, Esau, or Edom, his descendant, are most often read as the Christian Church, or as the Rabbis put it: 'The Principate turned to sectarianism' [TB Sotah 49b and parallels]." And he notes, "Esau, who (through his alternative name, Edom) is always an eponym for Rome (and then for Rome as Christendom) in rabbinic literature," (46).

40. Gershon Cohen, "Esau as Symbol in Early Medieval Thought," 245.

41. Ibid., 248.

42. See Neusner, *Judaism and Its Social Metaphors*, 126. In examining Gen. Rab. 63:3, he writes, "In the sages' typology, Esau always stands for Rome, and later we shall see that the representation of Esau as sibling, brother, and enemy distinguishes Esau-Rome from all other nations." As I hope to demonstrate, Esau equally represents an imagined other, not exclusively Rome.

43. In the late 1970s, Jacob Neusner first challenged the authenticity of rabbinic attributions and many scholars followed his vein of inquiry. His position is articulated in many publications. See, for example, *Reading and Believing: Ancient Judaism and Contemporary Gullibility* (Atlanta: Scholars Press, 1986); William Scott Green, "What's in a Name?—The Problematic of Rabbinic 'Biography'," in *Approaches to Ancient Judaism: Theory and Practice*, ed. William Scott Green (Missoula: Scholars Press, 1978), 77–96; David Kraemer, "On the Reliability of Attributions in the Babylonian Talmud" *HUCA* 60 (1989): 175–90, and Sacha Stern, "Attribution and Authorship in the Babylonian Talmud" *JJS* 45 (1994): 28–51. See also Richard Kalmin, *Sages, Stories, Authors and Editors in Rabbinic Babylonia* (Chico, CA: Scholars Press, 1994), 2–3 and 10–15, and the references cited, and Christine Hayes, *Between the Babylonian and Palestinian Talmuds*, 10–17, and especially n.17.

44. While there are pre- and postamoraic layers in these works, these distinctions do not affect my thesis. The midrashim dealing with Ishmael and the Ishmaelites in the Talmuds reflect the characteristics of those of the pre-Islamic period. I will, however, call attention to noteworthy exceptions and distinctions as they arise.

45. See L. Zunz, *Ha-Drashot Be-Yisrael*, C. Albeck, ed. (Jerusalem: Mossad Bialik, 1954), 42–47, G. Porton, "Defining Midrash," 77–78, Strack and Stemberger, 261–62. See also A. Urowitz-Freudenstein, *An Investigation of Exegetical Methods in the Tannaitic Midrashim: A Study of Texts That Mention Individual Women* (diss., JTS, 1997), who surveys scholarly works dealing with the nature of tannaitic midrashim and also examines the methods of exegesis used in tannaitic midrashim and their relationship to aggadic material.

46. Earlier we discussed four sources from the tannaitic period that dealt with the subject of the chosenness of Israel over and against the other nations, particularly the children of Ishmael and Esau. In the amoraic period, however, there are at least fourteen examples: Gen. Rab. 47:5, 53:12, 61:6, 61:7, 66:4, 68:11; Lev. Rab. 36:5; PT. Nedarim 3:8; BT. Nedarim 31a; BT. San. 59b; BT. Šabbat 145b; BT. Pesaḥim 56a, 119b; BT. Sotah 13a.

47. For a discussion on how this affected the relationship between Judaism and Christianity in late antiquity, see Rosemary Radford Reuther, *Faith and Fratricide: The Theological Roots of Anti-Semitism* (New York: WIPF and Stock, 1997) and J. Neusner, *Rabbinic Judaism: Structure and System* (Minneapolis: Fortress, 1995), 213–36.

48. The only exception is the use of Esau as a symbol of Rome. See the discussion below.

49. Cf. G. Cohen who writes: "Although the Jewish feelings of election are clearly enunciated in, and derived from, Scripture, the doctrine of the election of Israel was accorded renewed emphasis in the generation following the destruction" (247).

50. See C. Bakhos, "Figuring (out) Esau," *Journal of Jewish Studies* (forthcoming).

51. Gen. Rab. 38:10 on "So the LORD scattered them abroad" (Gen. 11:8) is the only case in which the children of Keturah seemingly serve solely an exegetical purpose: "The rabbis said, [*Wayyapeṣ* (scattered) is to be read] '*wayyaṣep* (swept away), that is, the sea came up and swept away thirty families from them.' R. Pinchas said in the name of R. Levi, 'A person's misfortune always profits others. From where were the thirty families replaced? From Abraham, sixteen from the people of Keturah and twelve from Ishmael, and as for the remaining two, 'And the LORD said to her, Two nations are in your womb' (Gen. 25:23)." R. Pinchas in the name of R. Levi cleverly uses the children of Keturah and the children of Ishmael to resolve the disappearance of the thirty families. With no restriction or condition, he includes the two nations—Jacob and Esau. In this midrash, no distinction is made between Jacob, that is Israel, and the other nations. Accounting for thirty families motivates this midrash but this is the only case where concerns beyond the explication of the verse seem to play no role in interpreting verses referring to the children of Ishmael and Keturah. In fact, as we will have occasion to see, even midrashim on Keturah take the rabbinic image of Abraham into account.

52. Jan Retsö, *The Arabs in Antiquity: Their History from the Assyrians to the Umayyads* (London; New York: RoutledgeCurzon, 2003), 212. According to James Montgomery, *Arabia and the Bible* (New York: Ktav, 1969), based on its resemblance to the Hebrew word "*arabah*," the term "Arab" is generally translated as "wilderness" or "desert." I.Ephʿal "'Ishmael' and 'Arab(s)': A Transformation of Ethnological Terms," *JNES* 35 (1976), however, disputes this claim (228). The different theories of the identity and genealogical history of Arabs are many, and are by their very nature exceedingly complicated. See the aforementioned works, as well as the following: René Dagorn, La Geste D'Ismaël (Genève: Librairie Droz, 1981), F. V. Winnett, "The Arabian Genealogies in the Book of Genesis," in *Translating and Understanding the Old Testament: Essays in Honor of Herbert Gordon May*, ed. H. T. Frank and W. I. Reed (Nashville: Abingdon, 1970), I. Ephʿal, *The Ancient Arabs: Nomads on the Borders of the Fertile Crescent, Ninth to Fifth Centuries BC* (Hebrew) (Jerusalem: Magnes, 1984), I. Shahîd, *Rome and the Arabs: A Prologomenon to the Study of Byzantium and the Arabs* (Washington, D.C.: Dumbarton Oaks, 1984), and idem, *Byzantium and the Arabs in the Fourth Century* (Washington, D.C.: Dumbarton Oaks, 1984).

53. Montgomery, 28ff.

54. JPS translates "Arab" as bandit.

55. Montgomery, 42.

56. I. Ephʿal, 231. Ephʿal draws on the Book of Judith (tentatively dated to the fourth century BCE), Josephus's *Jewish Antiquities* and PT. Taʿanit 4, 69b (discussed earlier) to illustrate the development of this concept in postbiblical Jewish sources.

57. F. Millar, "Hagar, Ishmael, Josephus and the Origins of Islam," *JJS* 44 (1993): 23–45.

58. While this study does not reveal a difference between the ways in which the two Talmuds depict Ishmael and the Ishmaelites, one must not assume that distinctions between how they portray biblical figures do not exist. See, for example, my discussion of R. Kalmin's work in the introduction, n.9.

59. This association is found also in BT. Sukkah 52b: R. Hana b. Aha said: (There are several name variants. Cf. the previously cited PT. Taʿanit 3:4.) "It was stated in the study house [of Rav]: The Holy One, Blessed be He regrets having made four things. They are: Exile, the Chaldeans, the Ishmaelites and the Evil Inclination . . .'Ishmaelites,' as it is written, 'Robbers live untroubled in their tents, and those who provoke God are secure, those whom God's hands have produced' " (Job 12:6).

60. Another early Jewish source is PT. Taʿanit 4:5 (4:69b) where the land of the Ishmaelites is called Arabia. See Sozomenus, HE VI, 38 [trans. C. D. Hartranft in *Nicene and Post-Nicene Fathers*, reprint 1976, 375a], a Christian writing in the early fifth century, who identifies Ishmael as the ancestor of the Saracens.

61. M. Jastrow, *A Dictionary of the Targumim, The Talmud Babli and the Yerushalmi, and the Midrashic Literature* (New York: Judaica Press, 1996), 1065.

62. Cf. T. Berakot 4:16; Gen. Rab. 84:17 reads: " 'And they lifted their eyes and looked . . . a caravan of Ishmaelites' (Gen. 37:25). R. Abba b. Kahana said, 'Is it not the way of the Ishmaelites to carry skins and *ʿiṭrān*? But see how on this occasion the Holy One, Blessed be He, prepared sacks filled with spices at that moment for that righteous man so that the wind might waft their scent to him because of the odor of the Arabs.' "

63. Cf. M. Aberbach and B. Grossfeld, *Targum Onkelos to Genesis: A Critical Analysis Together with an English Translation of the Text* (New York: Ktav, 1982), 9–16, and A. Shinan, *Mikra Ehad Ve-Targumim Harbeh* (Jerusalem: Hakibbutz Hameuchad, 1993), 38–40.

64. Gen. Rab. 53:14 gives another interpretation of "Fear not; for God has heard the voice of the lad where he is" (21: 17): " 'Where he is,' by his (Ishmael's) own merit, for the prayer of a sick person is the best of all." While the biblical story does not explicitly mention that Ishmael is sick, the rabbis infer this from verses 15–16: "When the water in the skin was gone, she cast the child under one of the

bushes. Then she went and sat down opposite him a good way off, about the distance of a bow shot; for she said, 'Do not let me look on the death of the child.' And as she sat opposite him, she lifted up her voice and wept." Cf. Tanḥuma, Yayyeze 5 and Tehilim 5:8.

65. Cf. Lam. Rab. 2:4 and Tanḥuma, Yethro 5 and Ps. Rab. 5:8.

66. It would be worth exploring how often and to what extent in rabbinic literature R. Shimon's opinion serves as the opposing opinion.

67. As will be discussed in the next chapter, this distinction between the righteous Ishmael and the wicked Ishmaelites is one that the author of PRE makes.

68. Tema, a well-known oasis on the ancient caravan route between the Red Sea and the Persian Gulf, is mentioned several times in the Bible. See especially the Book of Job which, according to Montgomery, has an "Arab flavor" (172ff.).

69. See chapter 3, "The Hebrews and Their Cousins," in Montgomery. Cf. chapter 8, "Old Testament and Arabia," in Retsö.

70. In the printed edition, "but a mere Tayaya, no." As Kalmin, *Sages, Stories, Authors, and Editors in Rabbinic Babylonia*, 270, indicates, not all versions have "Tayaya," the use of which may reflect a later layer of the Talmud that associates tayaya with Ishmael. Other versions have "Ishmael" or "an Ishmaelite." Kalmin shows on 264–71 that the depiction of tayaya according to the anonymous editors differs from that of the amoraim who portray them as "military men and desert guides" (267) located around Pumbedita or in either the Arabian or Sinai desert. The editors, on the other hand, view them as thieves who frequent Nehardea. Perhaps the meaning of Ishmael and the editors' understanding of tayaya are synonymous, or as Kalmin suggests, their meanings overlap. On the basis of this limited evidence, it is difficult to assess the significance of this later variation.

71. That is, your own son is an Arab who worships the dust of his feet.

72. Retsö, 531.

73. Aharon Oppenheimer, "The Attitude of the Sages towards the Arabs," in *Jewish Studies in a New Europe: Proceedings of the Fifth Congress of Jewish Studies in Copenhagen*, ed. Ulf Haxen, et al. (1994), 577.

74. I specifically note "stereotypical-like" because it is not evident, at least not yet to me, the extent to which this type is widespread beyond rabbinic literature such that we could call it stereotypical.

75. Oppenheimer, 579.

76. James H. Charlesworth, trans., *The Old Testament Pseudepigrapha* 2 (Garden City: Doubleday, 1985), 94. According to Millar, the discoveries at Qumran have "made it certain" that the Greek version of this passage from Jubilees, which comes to us from Latin and Ethiopic translations, was originally in Hebrew, and that it is missing among "the quite numerous Hebrew fragments." This leads Millar to the following conclusion: "As far as our evidence goes, therefore, it was Josephus alone who both emphasised the common genealogical origins of circumcision as

practiced by Jews and Arabs, and specifically identified the descendants of Ishmael among the peoples of the contemporary world, classifying them as 'Arabs,' the Nabataean inhabitants of the kingdom whose capital was Petra" (37). Millar claims that Josephus occupied "a central place in the construction of a genealogical and religious connection between Jews and Arabs" (44). Millar's dubious conclusions are based on insufficient evidence. To begin with, he extrapolates far too much from the little evidence the Hebrew fragments found at Qumran evince. Furthermore, as I. Epha'al (233) points out, in Josephus, the term "Arabs" had more than one meaning and therefore we cannot be sure to what extent Josephus was the first to make the connection between Ishmael's descendants and the Nabataeans and what he meant by this connection. For a discussion of Millar's thesis and a treatment of the Arab identity of Ishmael in early Islamic sources, see my article, "The Arab Identity of Ishmael in Ancient Judaism and Early Islam," forthcoming and Dagorn, R., *La Geste d'Ismaël.*

77. Josephus, Ant. I, 12, 2 (214), Loeb trans.

78. Ibid., Ant. II, 3, 3 (32).

79. Ibid., Ant. I, 12, 4 (220–21).

80. For a discussion of portrayals of Arabs in the Babylonian Talmud, see R. Kalmin, *Sages, Stories, Authors, and Editors in Rabbinic Babylonia*, 263–72 and J. Retsö, *The Arabs in Antiquity*, chapter 18.

81. Cf. Midrash Tannaim to Deut. 33:2, Mekilta de Rabbi Ishmael, Bahodesh 5, Deut. Rab. Eqeb, Lam. Rab. 3:1, Pesiqta Rabbati 21:2–3, Tanna debe Eliyyahu, hayyeridot 3, and PRE 41.

82. Unlike Sifre Deut. 343, Mekilta Bahodesh 5 answers the question why God offered the Torah to the other nations first. It states, "The nations of the world were asked to receive the Torah in order not to give them a reason to say before the Shekinah, 'Had we been asked to receive the Torah, we would have accepted it upon us.' " The midrash is slightly different in Lamentations Rabbah 3:1. Beginning with an exchange between the people of Israel and God, it reads: "The congregation of Israel said before the Holy One, Blessed be He, 'Thus it was said to me, that no other nation has accepted the Torah but me.' The Holy One, Blessed be He said, 'No, I made all the other nations unfit for your sake.' It said to Him, 'No, they did not accept it. Why did you go to Mount Seir? Was it not to give the Torah to the children of Esau?' " For a discussion of Mekilta Bahodesh 5 and Sifre Deut. 343, see Marc Hirshman, "*Torah le-khol ba'e ha-ʿolam*": *zerem universali be-sifrut ha-Tana'im ve-yahaso le-hokhmat he-ʿamim*, 93ff. Lam. Rab. 3:1 ends with the refusal of the Moabites and the Ammonites to accept the Torah and its acceptance by Israel, "Yes, yes, all that the LORD has spoken we will do and obey" (Exod. 24:7). With the exception of the order in which God offers the Torah and the emphasis on the refusal of the other nations, the midrash is the same. Perhaps there is relevance to the ordering but there is a paucity of evidence to prove this. Cf. Joseph Heinemann, *Aggadot Ve-Toldotehen*, 156, who claims that these redactional changes reflect a different *Sitz im Leben.*

83. We find a similar instance in Mid. Tehillim 81:2, where Balaam mentions Jacob alone because he saw that Abraham produced "refuse—Ishmael and all

the children of Keturah." Similarly, Midrash Tehillim 118:20 reads as follows: "The stone which the builders rejected is the main cornerstone" (Ps. 118:22). [Does the cornerstone refer to] Abraham? Refuse [or base metal]—Ishmael and all the children of Keturah came out of him. Isaac?"

84. Cf. BT. Nedarim 31a and PT. Nedarim 3:8 (38a). See, too, footnote 102, inf.

85. To my knowledge, there is no evidence to suggest that the rabbis were aware of a group that identified itself as the children of Keturah.

86. Cf. Num. Rab. 11:2, Tanḥuma, Naso 17, Yalquṭ Shimʿoni 110, and Jubilees 20:11–13.

87. Cf. BT. Sanhedrin 91a, which includes the following statement by R. Jeremiah b. Abba: "This teaches that he (Abraham) passed on to them the name of uncleanness" (Rashi and the English Soncino translation [ed. I Epstein; London: Soncino Press, 1994] has "the unhallowed arts," i.e., the knowledge of sorcery, demons, etc.). For a discussion of Gen. Rab. 61:7, see Neusner, *Judaism and Its Social Metaphors*, 116ff.

88. The midrash is as follows: Joseph earned merit, etc. [by burying his father] and there was none among his brothers greater than he, as it is said, "Joseph went up to bury his father" (Gen 50:7). [This portion of the Talmud is part of a lengthy discussion of the Mishnah on Sotah 9b.] Why the difference that in the beginning it is written, "So Joseph went up to bury his father; and with him went up all the officials of Pharaoh . . ." followed by "with all of Joseph's household, his brothers, and his father's household" (Gen. 50:7–8), and in the end it is written, "[After burying his father,] Joseph returned to Egypt, he and his brothers" followed by "and all who went up with him to bury his father" (Gen. 50:14)? R. Yohanan said: "In the beginning they saw their glory [of the Israelites], they treated them with respect," as it is written, "And they came to the threshing-floor of Atad [thorns]" (Gen. 50:10). But is there a threshing-floor for thorns? R. Abbahu said: "This teaches that they surrounded Jacob's coffin [or bier] with crowns like a threshing-floor, which is surrounded by thorns because the sons of Esau and of Ishmael and Keturah also came." A tanna taught: "They all came to wage war [against the Israelites]. When they saw Joseph's crown hanging on Jacob's coffin, they all took their crowns and hung them on his coffin." See also earlier discussion of BT. Sotah 9b: "Joseph earned merit by burying his father and there was none among his brothers greater than he, as it is said, 'Joseph went up to bury his father'" (Gen. 50:7).

89. J. Neusner, *Judaism and Its Social Metaphors* (Cambridge: Cambridge University Press, 1989), passim.

90. For a critique of Neusner's thesis, see S. Stern, *Jewish Identity in Early Rabbinic Writings*, xxxi–xxxv.

91. Neusner, 140.

92. Ibid., chapters 7 and 8.

93. Neusner, *From Enemy to Sibling*, 29.

94. Ibid., 14.

95. Ibid.

96. Neusner, *Judaism and Christianity in the Age of Constantine* (Chicago: University of Chicago Press, 1987), 45.

97. He cites no examples of the two struggling. Furthermore, there is only one case in Genesis Rabbah where the two confront one another and, in fact, there is no midrash where Ishmael and Isaac are depicted as "two equal powers."

98. Neusner, *Judaism and Its Social Metaphors*, 139–44.

99. He writes: "The powerful stress of the enduring merit of the patriarchs and matriarchs, the social theory that treated Israel as one large, extended family, the actual children of Abraham, Isaac, and Jacob—these now-familiar metaphors for the fleshy continuity met head on the contrary position framed by Paul and restated by Christian theologians from his time onward," 142.

100. In this regard, Galit Hasan-Rokem's *Tales of the Neighborhood: Jewish Narrative Dialogues in Late Antiquity* (Berkeley: University of California Press, 2003) is one of the finest.

101. The most recent work on the relationship between ancient Judaism and Christianity is the groundbreaking work of D. Boyarin, *Border Lines: The Partition of Judeo-Christianity* (Philadelphia: University of Pennsylvania Press, 2004). See also M. Simon, *Verus Israel: A Study of the Relations between Christians and Jews in the Roman Empire AD 135–425* (London: Littman Library of Jewish Civilizations, 1986; repr. 1996), who argues that the Jewish and Christian communities continued to interact and influence one another. Unlike the recent trend among scholars, Simon's attempt to explore the relationship between Judaism and Christianity as they developed side by side in the Roman Empire assumes that each religion is distinct, despite originary ties that bind all so-called siblings to their forebears. While I do not reject entirely the thesis in its varied iterations, I do call into question the extent to which Christian self-understanding as Israel factored into the development of midrashim that emphasize "unfit" seed of Abraham and Isaac, namely Ishmael and Esau who symbolize Other. See J. Baskin, *Pharoah's Counsellors: Job, Jethro and Balaam in Rabbinic and Patristic Tradition* (Providence: Brown University, 1983), I. Yuval, *Shene goyim be-vitnekh: Yehudim ve-Notsrim, dimuyim hadadiyim [Two Nations in Your Womb: Perceptions of Jews and Christians in the Middle Ages]* (Tel-Aviv: Am Oved, 2000), James Parkes, *The Conflict of the Church and Synagogue: A Study of the Origins of Anti-Semitism* (New York: Hermon, 1974), and Marc Hirshman, *A Rivalry of Genesis: Jewish and Christian Biblical Interpretation*, trans. Batya Stein (Albany: State University of New York Press, 1996). In "Homilies of the Rabbis on the Prophets of the Nations and the Balaam Stories," *Tarbiz* 25 (1955–56): 272–89, Urbach concludes that to a large extent homilies dealing with Balaam are best understood as responses to christological homilies of the Church Fathers. Moreover, E. Mihaly, sup., argues that Sifre Deut. 32:9, Ha'azinu 312 is a response to the tripartite Christian argument as they are referred to in the letter of Barnabas: "The insistence of the author of our Sifre on the choice of Israel having been initiated with Jacob and not Abraham identifies the passage as a polemical one and estab-

lishes the ideational context. The three proof-texts, Deut. 32:9, Deut. 14:2 and Jer. 10:16, immediately suggest a direct and cogent response to the prevailing three part argument for the elect status of the Christians as expounded in the compendia literature (Testimoniallehre) of the time. The three basic points of our passage, as implied in the three proof-texts, and the three parts of the Christian argument as they appear in Barnabas form a perfect whole. It is like finding the missing half of a dialogue, an exact fit" (134). The aforementioned works point to the importance of exploring the ways in which both groups interacted and the way in which such interactions are evinced in exegetical literature. That said, we must not lose sight of internal stimuli as well as rabbinic hermeneutical norms and principles that may have given rise to certain interpretations.

102. Another example worth noting where Esau may indeed symbolize Christianity is PT. Nedarim 3:8 (38a): And is not Esau part of the seed of Isaac? R. Judan b. Shalom said: " 'In Isaac,' but only part of Isaac." R. Huna said, "The use of the *bet* [in Isaac] indicates that the reference is to two, that is, to the son who in the future will inherit both worlds—this world and the world to come [see previous discussion on Gen. Rab. 53:12, sup.]. R. Gershom in the name of R. Aha said, " 'A star shall come out of Jacob' (Numbers 24:17). From whom will a star come out? From the one who is destined to arise from Jacob." R. Aha said in the name of R. Huna, "In the future, Esau the wicked will put on his cloak [*tallit*, or prayer shawl] and sit with the righteous in the Garden of Eden in the world to come and the Holy One, Blessed be He, will drag him and throw him out of there." What is the scriptural basis for this? "Though you nest as high as the eagle and it be among the stars, from there I will pull you down, says the LORD" (Obadiah 1:4). The reference to the eagle in Obadiah immediately calls to mind Rome, its symbol for the supreme god, Jupiter. For Romans, the eagle was a sign of victory. On this passage from PT. Nedarim 3:8, Boyarin, *Dying for God*, 3, comments: "An Esau who wishes to sit with a prayer shawl and study Torah with the righteous in heaven is almost obviously a Christian, not, I think, a Roman 'pagan.' " It is interesting to note the differences among the parallels. Gen. Rab. 53:12, BT. Nedarim 31a and BT. Sanhedrin 59b do not mention Esau the wicked and what will happen in the future. Here, however, we have a reference that seems more likely than not to refer to Christianity, where belief in the two worlds is not the issue, but rather Christian supersessionist claims.

103. Shir ha-Shirim Rabbah draws on many sources such as the Yerushalmi, Genesis Rabbah, Leviticus Rabbah, and Pesiqta de Rab Kahana such that it is difficult to date, although Zunz and Lachs date its final version to the second half of the eighth century. See Strack and Stemberger, 342–43.

104. For an excellent introduction to Jewish apocalyptic literature, J. J. Collins, *The Apocalyptic Imagination*, 2d ed. (Grand Rapids: Eerdmans, 1998). See G. Brooke, "The Kittim in the Qumran Pesharim," and H. Eshel, "The Kittim in the War Scroll and in the Pesharim."

105. Stephen Geller, *Sacred Enigmas: Literary Religion in the Hebrew Bible* (London: Routledge, 1996), 153.

106. Ibid., 154. See the work of M. Taylor, *Anti-Judaism and Early Christian Identity*, M. Niehoff, *Philo on Jewish Identity and Culture*, and R. Schwartz, *The*

Curse of Cain: The Violent Legacy of Monotheism (Chicago: University of Chicago Press, 1997).

Chapter 4. Ishmael in Later Midrashim

1. See the introduction.

2. For a discussion of "a rough parallel" between the rise of Islam and the rise of Christianity, see M. Cohen, *Under Crescent and Cross* (Princeton: Princeton University Press, 1994), 22–29.

3. Since it incorporates earlier material, it is difficult to pinpoint the date of redaction of Midrash Psalms (Midrash Tehilim), also called Shoher Tov. Zunz, for example, locates its redaction in the last centuries of the Geonic period (approx. 690 CE through eleventh century), but Buber proposes an earlier date for the first part, 1–118, and contends that only later editions give the impression of a later date. Albeck, like Zunz, subscribes to the later dating. As Strack and Stemberger note (351), we must assume an extended period of development from the talmudic period to the thirteenth century. Exodus Rabbah (Shemot Rabbah), like Psalms Rabbah, is composed of two parts, the first an exegetical midrash on Exod. 1–10, the second a homiletic midrash on Exod. 12–40. Zunz dates the entire work to the eleventh or twelfth century, whereas Herr considers the first part later than the second, thus dating it no earlier than the tenth century. Shinan maintains that the origin of Exod. Rab. I is tenth century (Strack and Stemberger, 335–37). Tanḥuma or Yelamdenu midrashim, according to Strack and Stemberger, "are a group of homiletic midrashim on the Pentateuch which are transmitted in many versions," and include not only the two editions of Tanḥuma, the Ordinary Edition and the Buber, but also "various handwritten recensions, . . . ExodR II, NumR II, DeutR, parts of PesR and other midrashim" (331). The commonly held date of this literature is the early ninth century. See also A. Kensky, *Midrash Tanhuma Shemot*, introduction. For a discussion on the question of whether or not there was ever one edition of Tanḥuma, see E. Urbach, "*Sridei Tanhuma Yelammedenu*," *Kobez al Yad* 6 (16), part I (Jerusalem, 1966), 1–54, esp. 3. Given the complex textual transmission of Deuteronomy Rabbah, it is difficult to date it with certainty, but based on its language and reference to Palestinian rabbis and locations, it more likely than not originated prior to the Babylonian Talmud. Nonetheless its textual history makes it impossible to date as early as the fifth century. Zunz dates it to the tenth century, although Lieberman disagrees with this late dating. To be sure, further work in the field of dating rabbinic texts is sorely needed, but until then I assume these texts were redacted in the postamoraic period, after the rise of Islam in the mid-seventh century.

4. As examined in the previous chapter, Shir Ha-Shirim Rabbah 7,3,3, a midrash dealing implicitly with Christianity, exemplifies this phenomenon of addressing the then contemporary situation in the context of the future.

5. Translated from Lieberman, *Midrash Devarim Rabbah*, 3d edition (Jerusalem: Shalem, 1974), 83.

6. Lieberman, 39.

7. Cf. Tanḥuma, Va-'Etḥanan 6 and Yalkkut Shimʿoni, Va-'Etḥanan 820 (vol. 4, 68).

8. See discussion in previous chapter and footnote 59, sup.

9. Cf. Deut. Rab. 4:5 where an astrologer represents Sarah in the *mashal.*

10. So, too, in Exod. Rab. 1:1.

11. The day he sold his birthright. Cf. BT. Baba Batra 16b.

12. Cf. Gen. Rab. 67:8, discussed on page 61 of previous chapter.

13. S. Buber, ed., *Midrash Tehillim* (New York: OM, 1947).

14. Cf. Midrash Tehillim 1:5, which retains an earlier version.

15. See pages 77–76.

16. Tan. Toledot 5 (Buber) reads as follows: "Another interpretation of 'Behold, the eye of the Lord [is on those who fear Him]' (Ps. 33:18). This is Isaac: 'On those who wait'—since he was waiting for the Holy One, Blessed be He, 'To deliver their soul from death'—when Ishmael sought to kill him, as stated, 'Then Sarah saw the son of Hagar the Egyptian playing' (Gen. 21:9). Now 'playing' can only mean 'killing,' as it is said, 'Let now the young men arise and play before us' (2 Sam. 2:14)." While this is the general tendency to denigrate Ishmael in later rabbinic portrayals of him, in Tan. Ḥayye Sarah 3 (Buber), another midrash pertaining to Gen. 21:9, there is less indication that Ishmael represents Islam or that there is a strong hostility toward him: " 'She is good to him and not bad [all the days of her life]' (Prov. 31:12). This is Sarah, as it is said, 'And because of her [Sarah] it went well with Abraham' (Gen. 12:16). 'She looks for wool and flax' (Prov. 31:13): [in choosing] between Ishmael [flaxen] and Isaac [pure wool], as it is stated, 'Then Sarah saw the son of Hagar the Egyptian . . . and said to Abraham, 'Cast out this slave woman [and her son]' (Gen. 21:9ff)." While this midrash does not impute infamous behavior to Ishmael, it nonetheless reiterates his lower, oppositional status vis-à-vis Isaac.

17. For a discussion on the nature of the Tanḥuma and its relationship to Yelamdenu, whether the two names are interchangeable or designate two different works, or a genre of midrash, see Strack and Stemberger, 330–33.

18. This is not found in the Buber edition.

19. Cf. BT. Sanhedrin 89b and PRE 31. BT. Sanherdrin 89b includes the following exhortation: "[God said to him] I have tested you with many trials and you withstood them all. Now, for My sake, stand in this trial so others will not say, 'There is no reality in the first one [trials].' " Later in the chapter, I will discuss the version found in PRE 31.

20. Translated from Rivka Ulmer, *Pesiqta Rabbati: A Synoptic Edition of Pesiqta Rabbati Based upon All Extant Manuscripts and the Editio Princeps*, vol. 1 (Atlanta: Scholars Press, 1997), 165.

21. In the Parma manuscript, he is like the moon.

22. Cf. Num. Rab. 2:13: "The stars, however, will not be ashamed . . . because all of them are righteous, [as it is said,] 'every part of you is fair, my love, [there is no blemish in you]'" (Song of Songs 4:7).

23. Num. Rab. 2:13, (see note above) another version of this midrash, makes this even more explicit. There are only three other parallels to this type of midrash in later midrashic corpora. See Tan. Balaq 12 (Buber and Warsaw editions), Num. Rab. 20:14, and Yalquṭ Shimʿoni, Balaq 765.

24. The rabbis play on the word *yiśtargû*, "lashed tight," which they render, *śerigût* "intermittently."

25. David Ben Judah Luria (1798–1855) of Lithuania was a notable rabbinic commentator who is best known for his commentaries to *Pirkei de Rabbi Eliezer* (1852), as well as for his notes to the Talmud and glosses to the Midrash Rabbah.

26. On the dating of Lamentations Rabbah, see Buber's introduction, 9–10, and especially P. Mandel, *Midrash Lamentations Rabbati: Prologemonon and a Critical Edition to the Third Parasha*, vol. 2 (Hebrew University Doctoral Dissertation, 1997), 13–23, where he discusses the views of previous scholars such as Zunz, Weiss, Margoliouth, J. Abrahams, and A. Winkler. For a discussion of the use of Ishmael to represent Islam in *piyyutim*, see Yosef Yahalom, "The Transition of Kingdoms in Eretz Israel (Palestine) as Conceived by Poets and Homilists," *Shalem* 6 (1992): 1–22 (Hebrew).

27. According to the Qur'an, Abraham is the prototypical *ḥanīf*, pure monotheist, one whose exceptional morality enables him to have a special relationship with God. Mentioned explicitly in twenty-five chapters (more than one hundred times) in the Qur'an, Abraham is hailed the first believer and the exemplary Muslim. As stated in Sura 3:67, "Abraham was not a Jew or a Christian but was an upright person who submitted and was not one of those who associate." For other references to Abraham's righteousness and devotion only to the one true God, see for example surahs 3:95, 4:125, 6:161, and 16:123.

28. Sozomen, *The Ecclesiastical History of Sozomen*, book 6, chapter 38, trans. E. Walford (London: Bohn, 1855), 309–10.

29. On the issue of pre-Islamic Arab monotheism, P. Crone, *Meccan Trade and the Rise of Islam* (Princeton: Princeton University Press, 1987), 190, observes: "What Sozomen's information adds up to is that by the fifth century the Arabs themselves had become familiar with the idea that they were Abrahamic monotheists by origin, at least in the Gaza area . . . and that some of them reacted by becoming what the Islamic tradition describes as *hanīfs*." See, U. Rubin, "Hanīfiyya and Kaʿba: An Inquiry into the Arabian Pre-Islamic Background of din Ibrahim," *Jerusalem Studies in Arabic and Islam* 13 (1990): 107, who writes: "Generally speaking, the pre-Islamic Arabs seem to have been well aware of their genealogical descent from Abraham and Ishmael, and, in fact, the authority of Quraysh among the rest of the Arab tribes was based on this descent." Cp. R. Dagorn, *La Geste d'Ismaël.*

30. For a general introduction to PRE, see Zunz, *Ha-Drashot be-Yisrael*, 134–40, 417–24; Gerald Friedlander, trans., *Midrash Pirke de Rabbi Eliezer* (London,

1916; repr. New York: Sepher-Hermon, 1981), xiii–lvii; and Stack and Stemberger, 332–33. On the use of narrative in PRE, see Ofra Meir, "Hasipur Hadarshani Bemidrash Qadum Ume'uchar," *Sinai* 86 (1980): 246–66; Jacob Elbaum, "On the Character of the Late Midrashic Literature" (Hebrew), *Proceedings of the Ninth World Congress of Jewish Studies* 3 (4 vols.; Jerusalem: World Congress of Jewish Studies, 1986), 57–62; id., "Rhetoric Motif and Subject-Matter—Toward an Analysis of Narrative Technique in Pirke de-Rabbi Eliezer" (Hebrew), *Jerusalem Studies in Jewish Folklore* 13/14 (1991–92): 99–126; id., "From Sermon to Story: The Transformation of the Aqedah," *Prooftexts* 6 (1986): 97–117. The status of PRE in the rabbinic corpus is problematic. Its narrative structure as biblical expansion is similar to that of the book of Jubilees (second century BCE) and its style significantly differs from that of earlier midrashic corpora, which are redacted compilations of interpretations of biblical verses.

Even though the author used several sources, PRE's structure indicates that it is ostensibly the work of one author, probably a Palestinian. As J. Rubenstein, "From Mythic Motifs to Sustained Myth: The Revision of Rabbinic Traditions in Medieval Midrashim," *Harvard Theological Review* 89:2 (1996): 131–59, notes, the style of PRE, as well as that of Tanḥuma, represents a transition, "a step between the mythic perspective of the rabbinic period and the pervasive mythic thinking of kabbalah" (158). Cf. Joseph Dan, *Hasipur Haʿivri Bimei Habeinayim* (Jerusalem: Keter, 1974), esp. 21, 135–36. See, too, Anna Urowitz-Freudenstein, "Pseudepigraphical Support of Pseudepigraphal Sources: The Case of PRE," in J. C. Reeves, ed., *Tracing the Threads: Studies in the Vitality of Jewish Pseudepigrapha*, (Atlanta: Scholars Press, 1994), 35–54. And see especially, Avigdor Shinan, *Aggadatam shel Meturgammim* (Jerusalem: Makor, 1979), 162–65. On the folkloristic aspects of *Pirke de Rabbi Eliʿezer*, see Dina Stein, *Memrah, Magyah, Mitos: Pirke de-Rabi Eliʿezer le-or meḥḳar ha-sifrut ha-ʿamamit* (Jerusalem: Magnes Press, 2004).

31. As noted above, unlike most rabbinic texts, PRE, despite its composite nature, seems to have been written by one author. See Friedlander, xiiiff.

32. In translating all chapters of PRE, I have used the folio edition of Rabbi David Luria (Radal), Vilna, 1837, as the base text and have consulted the following manuscripts and editions: the Constantinople edition of 1514, which is the first printed edition, the Venice edition of 1544, the critical edition of C. M. Horowitz, *Pirke de-Rabbi Eliezer: A Critical Edition, Codex C. M. Horowitz* (Jerusalem: Makor, 1972), and Michael Higger, "Pirke Rabbi Eliezer," *Horeb* 8 (1946): 82–119; vol. 9 (1947): 94–166; vol. 10 (1948): 185–294, Lewis Barth, ed., HUC MS. 75 and MS. 2043, *www.usc.edu/dept/huc-la/pre-project/graphics/index-01.html*. I have also referred to Friedlander's translation, which is based on "a valuable unedited MS. belonging to Abraham Epstein of Vienna" (xiv). Noteworthy manuscript variants are found in the following notes.

33. The name Ishma*el* means "God [*El*] will hear."

34. As discussed in the previous chapter, PT. Berakot 1:6 (4a), Mekhilta, Pisḥa 16, and Gen. Rab. 45:8 include four names: Isaac, Ishmael, Solomon, and Josiah. In Mekilta De-Rabbi Ishmael, one finds: "And there are three who were called from

the mouth of the Holy One, Blessed be He: Isaac, Solomon, and Josiah. . . . There are some who say that also Ishmael among the Gentiles."

35. In this section I will discuss all references to Ishmael, with the exception of chapter 30 of PRE, which relates the story of Abraham's visits to Ishmael.

36. Shem was born circumcised. See Schechter *Aboth de Rabbi Natan*, 2.

37. Leviticus 19:24–25 reads as follows: "In the fourth year all its fruit shall be set aside for jubilation before the LORD; and only in the fifth year may you use its fruit—that its yield to you may be increased: I the LORD am your God." Thus, although the children of Keturah were born to Abraham after his circumcision, they are not of the first fruits set aside to the LORD, so to speak. I thank Joel Kaminsky for bringing this to my attention.

38. In chapter 38 we read: "Esau said to Jacob, 'Divide into two parts all that our father left for us and I will choose since I am the firstborn.' " Jacob said [to himself], "This wicked man has not satisfied his eye with wealth," as it is said, "Neither are his eyes satisfied with wealth" (Eccles. 4:8). What did Jacob do? He divided it into two parts—all that his father left was one part, and the land of Israel the other. What did Esau do? He went to Ishmael in the desert to consult with him, as it is said, "And Esau went to Ishmael" (Gen. 28:9). Ishmael said to Esau, "The Amorite and the Canaanite are in the land and Jacob trusts that he will inherit the land. Take what your father left you and Jacob will have nothing." In this midrash Esau and Ishmael are pitted against Jacob, the sole inheritor of the land of Israel and heir of the covenant with God. The midrash alters the biblical context but retains the significance of Esau going to Ishmael, of separating the bypassed firstborn sons from the chosen. The attitude toward Ishmael is not as conspicuously unfavorable as it is toward Esau. The midrash refers to Esau, as "this wicked man," and describes his voracious appetite. Nothing is said about Ishmael, although the advice he offers is intended to help Esau and harm Jacob.

39. This is despite the views of such scholars as A. Schussman and Bernard Heller. See a summary of their work on this subject, inf.

40. Cf. Gen. Rab. 55:7, Tan. Vayyera 42 and BT. San 89b. See the brief discussion on page 93.

41. This image is found at the end of the story of Abraham's visit to Ishmael in Sefer ha-Yashar.

42. Cf. Lev. Rab. 20:2 and Eccles. Rab. 9:6. Cp. Gen. Rab. 56:2, Pesiqta de Rab Kahana, Tan. Wayyera 46, and Midrash Ha-Gadol where the names are not mentioned. Cf. also Seder Eliyyahu Rabbah 25 (Ish Shalom, ed., 138–39).

43. Heinemann, *Aggadot Ve-Toldotehen*, 186ff. Heinemann, however, disagrees with Heller's reading of the midrash. Heller is of the opinion that this is an attempt to scorn Ishmael. That is, he claims the author of PRE takes a position on the controversy found in Qur'anic commentaries as to which of Abraham's sons is nearly sacrificed. The Qur'anic version of the Aqedah omits Isaac's name. Ishmael's name, however, is also not mentioned, thus the identity is ambiguous. Heinemann agrees

with Heller that this midrash, not found in earlier midrashim, is polemical. Yet, it is unconcerned with Ishmael's role in the Aqedah. For a discussion on the sacrifice of Abraham's son in Islam, see N. Calder, "From Midrash to Scripture: The Sacrifice of Abraham in Early Islamic Tradition," *Le Museon* 101 (1988): 375–402, S. Bashear, "Abraham's Sacrifice of His Son and Related Issues," *Islam* 67 (1990): 243–77, R. Firestone, "Merit, Mimesis, and Martyrdom: Aspects of Shiʿite Metahistorical Exegesis on Abraham's Sacrifice in Light of Jewish, Christian, and Sunni Muslim Tradition," *JAAR* 66 (1998): 93–116.

44. Heinemann, *Aggadot Ve-Toldotehen*, 189 (trans.).

45. B. Visotzky, "Jerusalem in Geonic Era Aggadah," in Lee Levine, ed., *Jerusalem: Its Sanctity and Centrality to Judaism, Christianity, and Islam* (New York: Continuum, 1999), 443, draws our attention to chapter 38 of PRE where the Samaritans are treated derisively.

46. See the previous chapter for an analysis of Gen. Rab. 55:4.

47. Heinemann, *Aggadot Ve-Toldotehen*, 122ff.

48. "Abraham said to Isaac, 'My Son, do you see what I see?' Isaac answered, 'Yes.' Abraham then turned to his two servants and said, 'Do you see what I see?' 'No,' they replied. Since you do not see it, 'Stay here with the ass' (Gen. 22:5), for you are like the ass. . . . R. Isaac said, 'Everything happened as a reward for worshipping. Abraham returned from Mount Moriah only as a reward for worshipping': 'And the people believed . . . then they bowed their heads and worshipped' (Exod. 4:31). The Torah was given only as a reward for worshipping: 'And worship from afar' (Exod. 24:1)" (Gen. Rab. 56:2).

49. As noted above, cf. Lev. Rab. 20:2, Tan. Wayyera 46, Pisiqta de Rav Kahana 26:3, and Eccles. Rab. 9:1.

50. Heinemann refers to Philo of Alexandria who writes, "Israel—one who sees God" (123). He also discusses the notion of "seeing" as it is found in the story of Joseph and Potiphar's wife (124ff.).

51. See pages 56–57 of previous chapter and note 48, above.

52. For a provisional synoptic edition of Vayyiqra Rabbah, see *http://www.biu.ac.il/JS/midrash/VR.*

53. M. Grünbaum, *Neue Beiträge zur Semitischen Sagenkunde* (Leiden: Brill, 1893), 99; S. Krauss, *Studien zur byzantinisch-jüdischen Geschichte* (Leipzig: G. Fock 1914), 145; B. Heller, "Muhammedanisches und Antimuhammedanisches in den Pirke Rabbi Eliezer," *MGWJ* 33 (1925): 47–54; J. Heinemann, *Aggadot Ve-Toldotehen*, 181–99; H. Schwartzbaum, *Mi-meqor Yisrael ve-Yishmael: Yahadut ve-Islam be-Aspaqlariyat ha-Folqlor* (Tel Aviv: Don, 1975), 220–25; Aviva Schussman, "Abraham's Visits to Ishmael—The Jewish Origin and Orientation" (Hebrew), *Tarbiz* 49 (1980): 325–45. See also R. Firestone, *Journeys in Holy Lands: The Evolution of the Abraham-Ishmael Legends in Islamic Exegesis* (Albany: State University of New York Press, 1990), 76–79, who deals with the significance of the story in the Islamic Abraham-Ishmael cycle and illustrates the parallels between the Islamic and

"Biblicist" sources, and, more recently, G. Newby, "Text and Territory: Jewish-Muslim Relations 632–750 CE," in Benjamin H. Hary, John Hayes, and Fred Astren, eds., *Judaism and Islam: Boundaries, Communications and Interactions* (Leiden: Brill, 2000), 83–95.

54. The sources are known as hadith, which literally means "narrative," "talk." *al-Hadith* is an account of what the Prophet Muhammad said and did, a tradition which came to be considered second to the Qur'an in authority after the death of the Prophet in 632. Hadith reports are recorded in the sources as small units of information that were passed on orally. Each small tradition within a larger compilation has two essential features: the *isnad*, chain of authorities tracing the tradition back to the original source, and the *matn*, the text. Terms of orality such as *haddathani*, "so-and-so reported to me," and *akhbarana*, "so-and-so related to us" are used in the *isnad* in order to link together the transmitters of the tradition. For a thorough analysis of hadith literature, its transmission and process of standardization, see G. H. A. Juynboll, *Muslim Tradition: Studies in Chronology, Provenance and Authorship of Early Hadith* (Cambridge: Cambridge University Press, 1983).

55. In *Demonizing the Queen of Sheba: Boundaries of Gender and Culture in Post-biblical Judaism and Medieval Islam* (Chicago: University of Chicago Press, 1993), Jacob Lassner has located in Islamic sources discernible traces of Jewish lore in the story of the Queen of Sheba's visit to Solomon's court. See especially chapter 6, "The Transfer and Absorption of Cultural Artifact," 120ff., for an engaging discussion of scholarly forays into the murky process of literary transmission and a careful treatment of intercommunal literary relations between Muslims and Jews in the medieval period.

56. I am not using the terms "social" and "cultural" interchangeably. "Society" implies a set of interrelationships among people and institutional structures, whereas "culture" includes all those institutions but also implies a set of traditions about those very institutions. Culture is socially transmitted knowledge and behavior patterns shared by a group of people. It is the set of ideas, rituals, beliefs, and attitudes that underlie the various relationships that make up society. I thank Ellen Oxfeld for helping me clarify the relationship between these terms.

57. H. Lazarus-Yafeh, *Intertwined Worlds* (Princeton: Princeton University Press, 1992), 4. See also S. Rosenblatt, "Rabbinic Legends in Hadith," *Muslim World* 35 (1947): 237–52, and S. D. Goitein, "The Intermediate Civilization/The Hellenic Heritage in Islam," in *Studies in Islamic History and Institutions* (Leiden: Brill, 1966), 54–70. On the role of Christianity and Judaism, in particular, in the origins and development of Islam, see M. Cook and P. Crone, *Hagarism: The Making of the Islamic World* (Cambridge: Cambridge University Press, 1977), and M. Cook, *Muhammad* (New York: Oxford University Press, 1983; reissued 1996), 77–89, G. R. Hawting, *Idea of Idolatry and the Emergence of Islam: From Polemic to History* (Cambridge; New York: Cambridge University Press, 1999), Robert Hoyland, *Seeing Islam as Others Saw It: A Survey and Evaluation of Christian, Jewish and Zoroastrian Writings on Early Islam* (Princeton: Darwin Press, 1997), B. Harry, J. Hayes and F. Astren, eds., *Judaism and Islam: Boundaries, Communications and Interactions: Essays in Honor of William M. Brinner* (Leiden: Brill, 2000), Uri Rubin,

Between Bible and Qur'an: The Children of Israel and the Islamic Self-Image (Princeton: The Darwin Press, 1999), and John Wansbrough, *The Sectarian Milieu: Content and Composition of Islamic Salvation History* (Oxford; New York: Oxford University Press, 1978).

58. The story is found in later midrashic compilations, in Midrash ha-Gadol and Yalquṭ Shimʿoni, Wayyera 95, both dated to the thirteenth century. See critical editions of M. Margalioth, *Midrash Ha-Gadol al Hameshah Humshe Torah*, vol. 1 (Jerusalem: Mossad Harav Kook, 1947), 339–42, and D. Hyman, D. N. Lerrer, and I. Shiloni, eds., *Yalkut Shimʿoni al ha-Torah le Rabbenu Shimoʿon ha-Darshan*, vol. 1 (Jerusalem: Mossad Harav Kook, 1973), 424–25. The story is also found in Sefer ha-Yashar, dated to the beginning of the sixteenth century. See J. Dan, *ha-Sipur ha-ʿIvri biyeme ha-Benayim: ʿIyunim betoldotav* (Jerusalem: Keter, 1974), 137–38, who claims that the work is a product of the Jewish Renaissance in Italy.

59. Moshe Perlman, "The Medieval Polemics between Islam and Judaism," in S. D. Goiten, ed., *Religion in a Religious Age* (Cambridge: Association for Jewish Studies, 1974), 103–38, offers a nuanced definition of polemics: "Polemics is controversy, discussion with an opponent. Polemics may be direct, frank and frontal, or veiled, indirect and, of course, may vary from gentle to suave to vehement and violent. When society includes widely differing factions with varying positions, attitudes and views, the relations between them will be pervaded with polemics, of greater or lesser intensity, degree, and varying level of domain" (103).

60. In rabbinic tradition, God gave Abraham ten trials, the last of which is the Aqedah, the binding of Isaac. Other trials include migration from his father's home and taking Sarah to Pharaoh to be his wife. See Jubilees 16:15–18 and S. Schechter, *Aboth de Rabbi Natan: Edited from Manuscripts with Introduction, Notes and Appendices* (Vienna: Lippe, 1887), chapter 33 in version A, chapter 36 in version B. See also Lewis Barth's publication of Cambridge Add. 1497, ff. 54r–61v as well as Oxford MS. Opp. Add. 4. 79, which contains not only a complete version of the legend, but also material differing from that in PRE. Unlike PRE's version, this text is a homily. According to Barth, "Closer examination indicates that our text is an original composition containing a number of unique readings of the Abraham legend. It may well represent a version of the ten trials which is earlier than PRE" (1). Lewis Barth, "Lection for the Second Day of Rosh Hashanah: A Homily Containing the Legend of the Ten Trials of Abraham" (Hebrew), *HUCA* lviii (1987): 1–48.

61. The rabbis play on *nitrabâh*, "to grow up," and *rōbeh*, "archer," which have the same root: *resh*, *bet*, *heh* (*rbh*).

62. His name is missing in the printed editions, in Midrash Ha-Gadol and in the Yalquṭ.

63. "From this world and from the world to come" is found in the Venice manuscript.

64. Found in the Venice manuscript.

65. The Venice edition reads *dardûr*, "water bottle," and Radal explains this to mean leather bottle, *nod*. Cf. Gen. Rab. 53:13, Sifre Num. 115 and Yalquṭ, Num.

750 which also read "water-barrel." Epstein's manuscript and the first edition read *radid*, "a (female's) wrap of fine texture, veil" (Jastrow, *A Dictionary of the Targumim, the Talmud Babli and the Yerushalmi, and the Midrashic Literature*, 1453. See also J. Levy, *Wörterbuch über Die Talmudim und Midraschim*, vol. 2 (Berlin: Benjamin Harz, 1924), and Alexander Kohut, ed., *ʿArukh Ha-Shalem*, vol. 3 (Vienna: Menorah, 1926).

66. Evidently, the water bottle would drag and leave an impression in the sand.

67. Found in the Venice manuscript.

68. Some editions read "twenty-four" or "twenty-seven."

69. Some editions read "thirteen."

70. "To err" and "to wander" are the same word.

71. According to an aggadic tradition, the well is one of the ten things God created on the eve of the first Sabbath in the week of Creation. Chapter 19 of PRE begins as follows: "Ten things were created on the eve of Sabbath during twilight and they are: the mouth of the earth, the mouth of the well, the mouth of the ass, the rainbow, manna, the staff of Moses, the Shamir [worm created in order to cut the stones of the Temple; see BT. Giṭṭin 68a, BT. Sotah 48b, and PT. Sotah 13, 24b], the alphabet, writing, and the tablets [given to Moses on Mount Sinai]." Cf. M. 'Abot 5:9, BT. Pesaḥim 54a, Sifre Deut. 355, Pal. Targum, Num. 22:28.

72. The first editions read "ford" instead of "daughters."

73. This is the name found in the Venice manuscript. In later editions "ʿEssah" and "ʿEphah" are found. ʿEphah is found in 1 Chronicles 2:46: "And ʿEphah, Caleb's concubine, bore Haran and Moza and Gazez; and Haran fathered Gazez."

74. The version in Yalkut reads: "Exchange the threshold of the house for it is not good and it is not fit for you."

75. Friedlander notes, 221, that the reference may be to the Muslim possession of Baghdad in Babylon.

76. The following section on the fifteen things that the children of Ishmael will do in the future, which concludes the chapter, is not found in the Luria edition but is found in most manuscripts and in the early editions such as the Venice, Prague, and Amsterdam. It is quite reasonable to conclude that Luria's edition, printed in Warsaw, lacks this section due to censorship.

77. S. Baron, *A Social and Religious History of the Jews*, vol. 3 (Philadelphia: JPS, 1957), 163, suggests that this is a reference to the land measurement, an innovation of the Islamic administration that took place particularly during the reign of Muʿawiyya, the founder of the Umayyad dynasty of caliphs, who ruled from 661–80.

78. Visotzky, 446 n.31, proposes that this is a reference "to the valley before the Golden Gate, between the Mount of Olives and the Temple Mount, where today lies a Muslim cemetery, which is often enough the site of grazing flocks of sheep."

79. See Visotzky, 446 n.32.

80. Probably of rubble.

81. Samuel Krauss, 145, states that the building is a reference to the Mosque of ʿUmar, the foundation of which was laid by the Caliph ʿUmar after his conquest of Jerusalem in 636 CE.

82. See discussion later in the chapter.

83. There are seventeen accounts of the story, eleven of which are attributed to Ibn ʿAbbās. My use of one rather than the others does not affect my thesis. Though I am using al-Ṭabarī's (d. 923) version, *Ta'rīkh al-Rusul wal-Mulūk*, ed M. J. De Goeje, as *Annales*, vol. 1 (Leiden: Brill, 1964), whose authority is Ibn ʿAbbās, the essential details are found in the accounts of al-Azraqī (d. 858), *Kitāb Akhbār Mecca*, ed. F. Wustenfeld, as *Chroniken der Stadt Mecca* (Leipzig, 1858); repr. ed.; *Akhbār Makka al-Musharrifa*, vol. 1 (Beirut, n.d.); al-Bukharī (d. 869) *al-Jamiʿ al-Ṣaḥiḥ* (Lahore, 1979); al-Ṭabarsī (d. 1153), *Jamiʿ al-Bayan 'an Ta'wīl Āy al-Quran* (Beirut: Dar al-Maktaba, n.d.); and Ibn Kathir (d. 1373), *Qiṣaṣ al-Anbiyāʾ* (Beirut, 1982). Six anonymous authorities are found in al-Yaʿqūbī (d. 897), *Ta'rīkh*, M. T. Houtsma, ed., and titled *Historia* (Leiden: Brill, 1969); al-Masʿūdī (d. 956), *Muruj al-Dhahab wa-Maʿadin al-Jawahir* (Beirut: Dar al-Andalus, 1965); al-Thaʿlabī (d. 1045), *ʿArā'is al-Majalis* (Cairo: Mustafa al-Babi al-Halabi, 1954); al-Kisā'ī (twelfth century), *Qiṣaṣ -al-Anbiyāʾ*, Isaac Eisenberg, ed., and titled, *Vita Prophetarum* (Leiden: Brill, 1922); Ibn al-Athīr (d. 1232), *al-Kāmil fī al-Ta'rīkh*, vol. 1 (Beirut: Dar Ṣadir lil-tibaʿati wal-nashir, 1965); and Mujīr al-Dīn (d. 1520–21), *al-Uns al-Jalīl Bita'rīkh al-Quds wal-Khalīl* (Amman: Maktabat al Muḥtasab, 1973). Cf. Firestone, *Journeys in Holy Lands*, chapter 10. I would like to thank Shahab Ahmed for assisting me in locating some of these sources. I call attention to noteworthy variants when necessary.

84. The verb also means "to go down." See discussion, inf.

85. The sacred precinct of Mecca.

86. In most versions she is inhospitable, in other versions she complains, and in one she lacks intelligence. In all versions neither she nor the second wife inquires as to the stranger's identity.

87. In al-Tabarī's version, there is no mention that the second wife is a Jurhumite. In nine of the seventeen versions, however, he marries another Jurhumite.

88. In fourteen of the seventeen versions, Abraham asks her what they eat and in nine of them, she responds "meat and water." In five her response is "milk and meat."

89. The meaning of this statement is uncertain. It may mean that even though she only brought out two items, her offer was generous.

90. Literally, "standing place." Today it means "shrine" or "place of martyrdom."

91. Ishmael's wife washes his head in six versions (she anoints his head in one) while he stands on a stone, called the Maqām, or on a jug. In these versions, there

is a discrepancy in details. In four of them, he stands on a block of stone, whereas in two of them he stands on a jug. In either case Abraham leaves his footprint. This added information about where Abraham stood offers an explanation for Maqām Ibrāhīm, the stone bearing Abraham's footprint found in the Kaʿba, the cubelike sanctuary located at the center of the Grand Mosque in Mecca (cf. Firestone, *Journeys in Holy Lands*, 210). In pre-Islamic Arabia, the Kaʿba served as the central shrine in Mecca that housed the 360 idols of tribal patron deities. It was also the site of the annual fair and pilgrimage that brought Mecca significant revenue. According to Muslim tradition, it was first built by Abraham and Ishmael and the sacred black stone embedded in the Kaʿba was given to Abraham by Gabriel as a symbol of God's covenant with Ishmael. Tradition also relates that when Muhammad returned victoriously to Mecca, he immediately cleansed the Kaʿba of idols and restored it to the rightful worship of one God. Today the Kaʿba is the focus of the Hajj, the obligatory trip to Mecca during the twelfth month, Dhu al-Hijja. See *Encyclopedia of Islam* (new edition), vol. 6, for a discussion of the various traditions on Maqām Ibrāhīm. In addition to this tradition associating Maqām Ibrāhīm with Abraham's visit, another tradition says that Abraham's footprints were imprinted on the stone while he was building the Kaʿba with Ishmael.

92. I thank Michael Fishbein for reading and commenting on my translation.

93. See also M. Grünbaum, 124–31. Cf. Shinan, 163–64, who rejects the suggestion that there is an anti-Islamic polemic in PRE.

94. For a comparison of Sefer ha-Yashar and PRE, see Heinemann, *Aggadot Ve-Toldotehen*, 181–82.

95. The rabbis associated characteristics such as vulgarity, love of war, idolatry, and harlotry with horse riding. Moreover, they did not look favorably upon hunting. See the *Encyclopedia ha-ʿIvrit*, vol. 25 (534) and vol. 28 (589–88).

96. In rabbinic literature, shepherds of small animals were considered thieves but this did not apply to shepherds of camels. On raising small animals, see BT. Baba Qamma 80a. Also in BT. Sanhedrin 25b, shepherds of small cattle cannot give testimony.

97. Cf. Job 22:7, Prov. 25:21, 2 Kings 6:22. Deut. 23:4–5 reads as follows: "An Ammonite or a Moabite shall not enter into the assembly of the LORD; even to the tenth generation shall none of them enter into the assembly of the LORD forever because they did not meet you with bread and water in the way when you came out of Egypt."

98. For example, see S. Schechter, *Aboth de Rabbi Nathan*, chapter 7, 33–35, and BT. Sanhedrin 103b.

99. Most of the Islamic sources do not mention the names of Ishmael's wives and there is no consensus among those that do. Names that do not have significance in Islamic history are used. For example, the name of the second wife in al-Yaʿqūbī is al-Chayfa bint Madād, al-Sayyida bint Madād in al-Thaʿlabī, and Halah

bint Amran in al-Kisāʿī. al-Masʿūdī mentions the names of the wives, Eljada bint Saʿad, and Sama bint Muhalhal respectively.

100. ʿAyeshah was the daughter of Abu Bakr, companion of the Prophet and first caliph. She was the favored wife of Muhammad and lived fifty years after he died. She left more hadiths (reports) about the Prophet than anyone else and she was said to have had a codex of the Qur'an.

101. ʿAyeshah is not found in later manuscripts of PRE, nor are the names mentioned in either Sefer ha-Yashar or Midrash Ha-Gadol. The names ʿAyeshah and Fatima, however, are found in the Yalkut and in Ps-Jonathan, which leads Shinan, in *Targum ve-Aggadah bo*, 176–85, and others to believe that Ps-Jonathan borrowed from PRE. See also A. Shinan, *Aggadatam shel Meturgamim* (Jerusalem: Makor, 1979), 162–65. For a detailed discussion of the relationship between Ps-Jonathan and PRE, see Moshe Ohana, "La Polémique judéo-islamique et l'image d'Ismaël dans Targum Pseudo-Jonathan et dans Pirqe de Rabbi Eliezer," *Augustinianum* 15 (1975): 367–87. Ohana argues that the mention of ʿAyeshah and Fatima is evidence of Ps-Jonathan's use of PRE and not vice versa. That is, Ps-Jonathan presupposes the history of the two wives, otherwise the terse reference would have no meaning. That Ps-Jonathan presupposes this familiarity does not necessarily lead to the conclusion that one source borrowed from the other, especially if the conclusion is based on this one example. For a critique of Ohana and Shinan, see Robert Hayward, "The Date of Targum Pseudo-Jonathan: Some Comments," *JJS* 40 (1989): 7–30, "Targum Pseudo-Jonathan and Anti-Islamic Polemic," *JSS* 34 (1989): 77–93, and "Pirque de Rabbi Eliezer and Targum Pseudo-Jonathan," *JJS* 42 (1991): 215–46. As Shinan, however, demonstrates in "The Relationship between Targum Psuedo-Jonathan and Midrash Pirqe De-Rabbi Eliezer" (Hebrew), *Teudah* 11 (1996), in many instances knowledge of the midrash in PRE adds to one's understanding of the targum. The targum to Gen. 18:21 is a case in point.

102. The dynasty was created in North Africa and Egypt. It seized power in 909 and in 969 conquered Eygpt, where it built a new capital. The dynasty's rule came to an abrupt end when Salāh al-Dīn conquered and restored Sunni rule in 1171. The Fatimids were notably more tolerant toward Jews and Christians than Sunnis. On a related note, Gordon Newby maintains that the use of Fatima is significant for understanding the sociopolitical context of PRE. Fatima, not only the beloved daughter of Muhammad, but also the wife of Ali, is a prominent Shiʿite figure since she is the mother of the line of imams. In depicting her favorably, according to Newby, the author of PRE is "aligning himself with the position taken among the ʿIsawiya and the Ghulat," a proto-shiʿite with whom the author of PRE seems to identify. Regarding these Muslim groups, Newby writes: "They not only shared political ambitions to rid themselves of the Umayyads, but they shared a similar outlook about Messianism. We see, then, that the mission of the author of Pirqe Rabbi Eliezer was to reassert the validity of the Jewish claim to Abraham, while at the same time, aligning himself with the position taken among the ʿIsawiya and the Ghulat" ("Text and Territory: Jewish-Muslim Relations 632–750 CE," 94). Newby's contention, albeit intriguing, requires further elaboration.

103. M. Cohen, *Under Crescent and Cross* (Princeton: Princeton University Press, 1994), 195. In "Persecution, Response, and Collective Memory: The Jews of Islam in the Classical Period," 145–64, in Daniel Frank, ed., *The Jews of Medieval Islam: Community, Society and Identity* (Leiden: Brill, 1995), Cohen comments: ". . . the dearth of literary sources devoted to persecution of Jews in the Islamic world during the classical centuries reflects a milieu in which there was simply much less of the kind of violent persecution of Jews *as Jews* than that which gave rise to the doleful literature and other memorializing traditions of Christian lands." See also, B. Lewis, *The Jews of Islam* (Princeton: Princeton University Press, 1984). Cf. S. D. Goitein, *A Mediterranean Society*, vol. 1 (Berkeley: University of California Press, 1967), and M. Schwartz, "The Position of Jews in Arab Lands," *Muslim World* 60 (1970): 6–24, for an exceptionally positive depiction of Jewish-Muslim relations in the medieval period.

104. Steven Wasserstrom, *Between Muslim and Jew: The Problem of Symbiosis under Early Islam* (Princeton: Princeton University Press, 1995). Focusing on the period from the eighth through the tenth centuries, Wasserstrom explores the concept of creative symbiosis by looking at the Judeo-Isma'ili interchange and the ways in which Jews and Muslims shared the imaginative world of apocalypse, as well as the intellectual world of philosophy. In the same vein as Hava Lazarus-Yafeh, Wasserstrom notes, "I would emphasize that the debtor-creditor model of influence and borrowing must be abandoned in favor of the dialectical analysis of intercivilizational and interreligious process" (11).

105. See Stith Thompson, *Motif-Index of Folk Literature*, vols. 1 and 3 (Bloomington: Indiana University Press, 1956, 1966), C521 and F378.1.

106. The verb used, *nāzal*, has a double meaning—literally, to reside and to go down. Quite possibly, the Hebrew version translated the Arabic as *laredet*, to go down.

107. Heinemann, *Aggadot Ve-Toldotehen*, 191.

108. In Sefer Ha-Yashar, the first wife is the Egyptian wife whom his mother chooses; he chooses the second wife, a Canaanite. In Midrash ha-Gadol and in Yalkut, however, Ishmael chooses the first wife, a Moabite.

109. Schussman, 327.

110. Margalioth edition, 339–42.

111. See the previous discussion of these names.

112. Schussman, 342.

113. Before entering the land of Canaan, the Israelites camped on the plains of Moab where they began to have sexual relations with the Moabite women (Num. 25). It is true that Moab is the product of incest, but it is also true that Ruth descended from Moab. Also see Deut. 23 and Gen. 19.

114. For a discussion of the Abraham stories in the Qur'an, see W. Bijlefeld, "Controversies around the Qur'anic Ibrahim Narrative and Its 'Orientalist' Interpretations," *Muslim World* 62 (1982): 81–94.

115. See R. Firestone, *Journeys in Holy Lands*, 76–79. The Arabization of Ishmael in Islamic sources is a topic worthy of study in its own right and would doubtless shed light on various aspects of the emergence of Islam in the medieval period as a dominant sociopolitical, religious presence in non-Arab regions of the world.

116. Acknowledging the inadequacy of the term "Judeo-Christian," the term "Biblicist" is used to denote the shared scriptural environment of Jews and Christians. Firestone, x.

117. Firestone, 79.

118. On the development of this genealogical system, see also Werner Caskel, *Gamharat an-Nasab, Das genealogische Werk des Hisam ibn Muhammad al-Kalbī*, vols. 1 and 2 (Leiden: Brill, 1966), 19, 39–40 J. Obermann, "Early Islam," in Robert C. Dentan, ed., *The Idea of History in the Ancient Near East* (New Haven: Yale University Press, 1955; repr. 1967), and I. Goldhizer, *Muslim Studies*, trans. and ed., *Geste* C. R. Barber and S. M. Stern (London: George Allen and Unwin, 1967), 98–198. See R. Dagorn, *La Geste d'Ismaël* who argues that the Abraham and Ishmael tradition was non-existent among Arabs of the pre-Islamic period.

119. W. Montgomery Watt in *Encyclopedia of Islam*, vol. 2, 603–604. On the genealogy of Ishmael in Arabic sources, see Werner Caskel, *Encyclopedia of Islam*, 2d ed., vol. 1 (Leiden: Brill, 1960), 544. According to a tradition attributed to Ibn ʿAbbas, the Jurhumite taught Ishmael Arabic. See, for example, al-Ṭabarī, *Taʾrīkh al-Rusūl Wal-Mulūk*, 270, 274–309, 351f., 11 12–23 and al-Yaʿqūbī, *Taʾrīkh*, 22–6, 252f.

120. F. Donner, "From Believers to Muslims: Confessional Self-Identity in the Early Islamic Community," *Al-Abhath* 50–51 (2003): 16.

121. Firestone, *Journeys in Holy Lands*, 72.

122. Ephʿal, 235. According to Ephʿal, these systems were combined several generations before Muhammad, whereas J. Obermann, "Early Islam," 237–309, esp. 290–305, dates the combination to several decades after the death of Muhammad. Muhammad's victories, Obermann argues, made him a hero of "a new kind of 'nobility' " and gave his descent "a new kind of 'glory.' "

123. As F. Rosenthal, "Nasab" in *Encyclopedia of Islam*, vol. 7, 966–97, writes: "Genealogy provides the historical validation of kinship and all that it involves. Kinship always dominated group life in human society and to a large extent still does today. . . . [K]inship continued to remain a most important factor in Muslim society, for reasons such as the enduring determination of "nobility" with its attending privileges on the basis of tribal descent (and descent from the Prophet and ʿAli) and, for instance, the survival of pre-Islamic social custom, the strong trend toward heredity in the bureaucracy and in the crafts and trades, or the eventual domination of the scholarly establishment at certain periods by family relationships. . . . With the 3rd/9th century, the preoccupation with genealogy was firmly entrenched as part of the literary and historiographical heritage."[123]

124. R. Hoyland, *Arabia and the Arabs: From the Bronze Age to the Coming of Islam* (London; New York: Routledge, 2001), 243.

125. For the purposes of comparison, the story of Abraham's visits should be examined in other Jewish sources such as in Midrash Ha-Gadol, Yalquṭ Shimʿoni, and Sefer ha-Yashar. Unlike in PRE where verses from Gen. 21 are used as prooftexts, in Midrash Ha-Gadol the biblical verses provide the organizing framework for the story. For the most part, the story of Abraham's visits is the same. Ishmael takes a wife from Moab who treats Abraham as persona non grata; he divorces her and marries a gracious woman whom his mother chooses for him from Egypt. Except for places where the Yalkut adds midrashim from elsewhere, the story in the Yalkut is practically identical to that found in PRE. For example, in the Yalkut we read that Abraham wrapped a veil around Hagar's waist because he wanted to see the road that Ishmael took. (It is understood that, like the water bottle, the veil would drag and mark the traveled path, or it might be the case that the veil was of a bright color easily identified from afar.) The Yalquṭ also retains the names of Ishmael's wives, ʿAyeshah and Fatima.

126. G. Friedlander, 215. Actually *qaššāt* means Sagittarius, a pun on *qeššet.*

127. Radal's commentary on chapter 30, 66b.

128. See chapter 3, sup.

129. Heinemann, *Aggadot Ve-Toldotehen*, 189–91.

130. See "Hagar: The Desolation of Rejection" (esp. 20–22), chapter 1 of Phylis Trible's *Texts of Terror* (Philadelphia: Fortress, 1984).

131. Cf. The previous discussion of Gen. Rab. 53:14, 36, 69, 151n.18.

132. Islam is perceived as a mighty nation: "Of the seventy languages the Holy One, Blessed be He created in His world, He did not put His name on one of them except for Isra*el*. Since He made the name of Ishmael similar to Israel, woe to him who shall live in his days, as it is said, 'Woe to the one who shall live when God establishes him' " (Num. 24:23) (PRE 30). It is the nation that will wage three wars, the last of which is a weighty war against Rome.

133. See S. Baron, *A Social and Religious History of the Jews*, 163, and n.77, sup.

134. H. Graetz, *Geschichte der Juden*, vol.5 (Leipzig, 1861), 197; Z. Fraenkel, *MGWJ*, 8 (1859): 112.c. See also Friedlander, 221 n.7, who cites both scholars.

135. A. Grossman, "Yahaso shel ha-Halifa al-Maʿmum el ha-Yehudim," *Zion* 44 (1979): 94–110. He draws his evidence from Jewish sources such as Rav Sherira Gaon and R. Samuel b. Eli, as well as from Arab authors such as Ghazi ibn al-Wasiti, Ibn Kayyim al-Jauziyah, and Ibn al-Naqash. See also Moshe Gil, "The Exilarchate," in Daniel Frank, ed., *The Jews of Medieval Islam: Community, Society and Identity* (Leiden: Brill, 1995), 33–65, who writes, ". . . al-Ma'mun's decree afforded legitimacy to the external organization and re-grouping of religious dissidents. We may assume, in fact, that the decree encouraged the spread of religious dissent among Jews, a phenomenon familiar to us from our knowledge of early Karaism" (59–60).

136. See Heinemann, *Aggadot Ve-Toldotehen*, 156, who sets out to demonstrate that the Palestinian targums preserve the earliest exegetical version of the midrash as it is found in the Mekhilta and Sifre. The original intent of the midrash, he contends, was to elucidate Deut. 33:2, "The LORD came from Sinai, and he rose upon them from Seir and he appeared from Mount Paran and he came from holy multitudes." Later versions include the Ammonites and Moabites whereas the Palestinian targums mention only Esau and Ishmael. Heinemann argues that new motifs were combined with the original exegetical story and as a result the story developed into a polemical tale reflecting a new and different period. While there is much merit in the general thrust of his assertion, it nonetheless rests on a specious supposition. His argument assumes a chronological progression from the shortest to the longest version and does not take into account that the redactors of the targums may have had access to a version closely related to that of PRE in which the Moabites and Ammonites are not mentioned.

137. After he was sent out of his father's house, Ishmael dwelt in Paran (Gen. 21:21).

138. Heinemann supports his argument that originally the exegetical midrash referred only to Esau and Ishmael by observing the addition of the Ammonites and Moabites after Esau and Ishmael. This is not the case, however, in the Mekhilta or in Sifre Deuteronomy where they are mentioned before the Ishmaelites.

139. The Ishmaelites brought Joseph to Egypt.

140. The fact that Tanna debe Eliyyahu is dated earlier than PRE does not mean PRE borrowed from the former. The case may be that the version found in PRE was influenced by the version found in Tanna debe Eliyyahu or vice versa. For the dating of Tanna debe Eliyyahu, see Strack and Stemberger (369ff.), who date the composition after the redaction of the Babylonian Talmud and before the ninth century. The problems involved in dating these midrashic compilations makes it impossible to claim with certainty that one borrowed from another. What we can say with some confidence is that these later works contain reworked midrashim that reflect changes in rabbinic thought.

141. Heinemann states that "the other nations of the world" are mentioned *only* in PRE and attributes this deliberate change to the author of PRE.

142. Tanna debe Eliyyahu, Pirke Hayyaridot, 3: They said to him, "We are unable to abandon the thing that our fathers did for they stole Joseph and brought him down to Egypt, for it is written, 'For indeed I was stolen from the land of the Hebrews' (Gen. 40:15). And from there he sent [messengers] to all the nations of the world and said to them, "Do you accept for yourselves the Torah?" They said to him, "What is written in it?" "You shall have no other gods before me" (Exod. 20:3). They said to Him, "We are unable to abandon the law of our fathers who served idols. We have no delight in the Torah but give your Torah to your people, as it is said, 'The LORD will give strength to His people, the LORD will bless his people with peace'" (Ps. 29:11).

143. See S. Schwartz's discussion of Josephus and the Greco-Roman attitude toward the preservation of ancestral forms of piety. *Josephus and Judaean Politics* (Leiden: Brill, 1990), 192ff.

144. Heinemann, *Aggadot Ve-Toldotehen*, 195.

145. The one exception is found in chapter 41 where God offers the Torah to the nations of the world.

146. H. A. Wolfson, *The Philosophy of the Church Fathers*, vol. 1 (Cambridge: Harvard University Press, 1956), 27.

147. See Jacob Elbaum, "Messianism in Pirke de-Rabbi Eliezer: Apocalypse and Midrash," *Teudah* 11 (1996): 245–66, where he demonstrates, inter alia, the ways in which the author of PRE tailors Gen. Rab. 44:17, which mentions four kingdoms—Babylonian, Persian, Greek, and Roman—in order to include a fifth kingdom, Islam.

148. See Gen. 15:9ff.

149. Other editions read "escape."

150. Elbaum, 249ff.

151. See also Mekilta, Bahodesh 9 (236 of Horowitz, 268 of Lauterbach), and Lev. Rab. 13:5.

152. As in chapter 28, the children of Ishmael are depicted as a nation that the Son of David will destroy in the future because the other nations "intermixed" with them. Thus, we read in chapter 44: "R. Yose said: When Sennacharib came to the land of Israel all the nations around the land of Israel saw the camp of Sennacharib and they were very frightened and every man fled from his place, as it is said, 'I have erased the borders of peoples and I have robbed their treasures' (Isa. 10:13). They entered the wilderness and intermixed with the children of Ishmael and all of them were ten nations, as it is said, 'The tents of Edom and the Ishmaelites, Moab and the Hagarites, Gebal and Ammon and Amalek, Philistia with the inhabitants of Tyre, Asshur also is joined with them' (Ps. 83:6–8). All of them in the future will fall by the hand of the Son of David, as it is said, 'O my God, make them like the whirling dust'" (Ps. 83:14).

153. See the following: Jacob Mann, "Proceedings of the Society at Cincinatti," *Journal of the American Oriental Society* 47 (1927): 364; B. Lewis, "An Apocalyptic Vision of Islamic History," *Bulletin of the School of Oriental and African Studies* 13/2 (1950): 308–38; M. Cook and P. Crone, *Hagarism* 5ff.; R. Hoyland, *Seeing Islam as Others Saw It*, 307ff.; Steven Wasserstrom, *Between Muslim and Jew: The Problem of Symbiosis under Early Islam* (Princeton: Princeton University Press, 1995); and Uri Rubin, *Between Bible and Qur'an*, 32ff.

154. See Friedlander's introduction for a discussion of PRE's use of earlier sources such as the book of Jubilees.

155. A study, which I will not undertake at this juncture, into the development of Ishmael's symbolic significance will demonstrate that in time, the name Ishmael,

for example in *piyyutim*, was synonymous with the world of Islam. For a list of payyetanic epithets for Israel's enemies, which includes Christians, Arabs, and Muslims, see Appendix 16 of L. Zunz, *Die Synagogale Poesie des Mittelalters* (Berlin: 1855), 437–55. For work on piyyutim, see, for example, E. Fleischer, *Tefilah u-minhage tefilah Erets-Yiśre'eliyim bi-Tekufat ha-Genizah* (Jerusalem: Magnes, 1988), ibid.; *Shirat ha-Kodesh ha-ʿIvrit bi-Yeme ha-Benayim* (Jerusalem: Keter, 1975); Y. Yahalom, *Sefat ha-Śhir shel ha-Piyuṭ ha-Erets-Yisraeli ha-Kadum* (Jerusalem: Magnes, 1985), ibid.; M. Sokoloff, *Shirat Benei Ma'arava* (Jerusalem: Israeli National Academy of Sciences and Humanities, 1999); Shulamit Elizur, *The Piyyutim of Rabbi El'azar Birabbi Qillar* (Hebrew) (Jerusalem: Magness, 1988).

Conclusions

1. See, for example, TS Arabic Box 53.2 in M. Gil, *Eretz Yisrael be-Tequfa ha-Muslimit ha-Rishonah (634–1099)*, vol. 2 (Tel Aviv: Tel Aviv University, 1983), 3–7, line 4, where in a guide for pilgrims dated to the eleventh century, we find the following description of the Temple Mount: ". . . the mosque where Ishmael prays." It is interesting to note that M. Gil's work on the period of the Geonim is titled *In the Reign of Ishmael: The Period of the Geonim* (Hebrew).

2. Carl E. Schorske, *Fin-a-siècle Vienna: Politics and Culture* (New York: Knopf, 1979), xxii.

Bibliography

Primary Jewish Sources

Barth, Louis, ed., HUC MS 75 and MS 2043, *www.usc.edu/dept/huc-la/pre-project/graphics/index-01.html.*

Buber, S., ed., *Midrash Tehillim.* New York: OM, 1947.

———, ed. *Midrash Tanhuma.* Jerusalem: s.n., 1964.

Dan, Joseph, ed. *Sefer ha-Yashar.* Jerusalem: Bialik Institute, 1986.

Finkelstein, Louis. *Sifre al Sefer Devarim.* New York: JTS, 1993.

Higger, M. "Pirke Rabbi Eliezer." *Horeb* 8–10 (1946–48).

Hoffman, David. *Midrash Tannaim al Sefer Devarim.* Tel Aviv: s.n., 1962.

Horowitz, M. *Pirke de-Rabbi Eliezer: A Critical Edition, Codex C.* Jerusalem: Makor, 1972.

Hyman, D, D. N. Lerrer, and I. Shiloni, eds. *Yalkut Shimʿoni al ha-Torah le Rabbenu Shimoʿon ha-Darshan,* vol. 1. Jerusalem: Mossad Harav Kook, 1973.

Kensky, Allan. *Midrash Tanhuma Shemot: A Critical Edition of "Midrash Tanhuma Shemot" (Standard Edition) through Beshallah.* PhD. diss. JTS, 1990.

Lauterbach, Jacob Z. *Mekhilta de-Rabbi Ishmael.* 3 vols. Philadelphia: JPS, 1933–35.

Liebermann, Saul. *Midrash Devarim Rabbah,* 3d ed. Jerusalem: Shalem, 1974.

Rabbi Luria, David (Radal). *Pirke Rabbi Eliezer.* Vilna, 1837.

Mandel, Paul. *Midrash Lamentations Rabbati: Prologemonon and a Critical Edition to the Third Parasha, vol. II.* PhD diss. Hebrew University, 1997.

Margalioth, M. *Midrash Ha-Gadol al Hameshah Humshe Torah,* vol. 1. Jerusalem: Mossad Harav Kook, 1947.

Schechter, Solomon. *Aboth de Rabbi Nathan: Edited from Manuscripts with an Introduction, Notes and Appendices.* Vienna: Lippe, 1887.

Shinan, Avigdor. *Midrash Shemot Rabbah, Chapters I–XIV: A Critical Edition Based on a Jerusalem Manuscript, with Variants, Commentary and Introduction.* Tel Aviv: Dvir, 1984.

Theodor, J., and Ch. Albeck. *Midrash Bereshit Rabba: Critical Edition with Notes and Commentary.* 3 vols. Berlin 1912–36, with corrections; repr., Jerusalem, 1965, with corrections.

Ulmer, Rivka. *Pesiqta Rabbati: A Synoptic Edition of Pesiqta Rabbati Based upon All Extant Manuscripts and the Editio Princeps*, vol. 1. Atlanta: Scholars Press, 1997.

Primary Arabic Sources

al-Azraqī, Abū-Walīd Muḥammad b. ʿAbdallāh b. Aḥmad. *Akhbār Makka.* 2 vols. Ed. F. Wusenfeld as *Chroniken der Stadt Mecca.* Leipzig, 1858. Repr. ed., *Akhbār Makka al-Musharrifa.* Beirut, n.d., vol. 1.

al-Bukhārī, Abu ʿAbdallāh Muḥammad b. Ismāʿīl b. Ibrāhīm b. al-Mughīra b. Bardizbah Abū ʿAbdallāh al-Juʿfī. *al-Jamiʿ al Ṣaḥiḥ.* Lahore, 1979.

Ibn al-Athīr, ʿIzz al-Dīn Abū al-Ḥassan ʿAlī. *al-Kāmil fī al-Taʾrīkh*, 5 vols. Beirut: Dar-Ṣadir lil-tibāʿati wal-nashir, 1385/1965.

Ibn Kathīr, ʿImād al-Dīn Ismāʿīl b. ʿUmar. *Tafsīr al-Qurʾān al-ʿAẓīm*, 4 vols. Cairo: ʿIsa al-Bābī al-Ḥalabī, n.d.

———. *Qisas al Anbiyaʾ.* Beirut: 1402/1982.

al-Kisāʾī, Muḥammad b. ʿAbdallāh. *Qiṣaṣ al-Anbiyāʾ.* Ed. Isaac Eisenberg and titled, *Vita Prophetarum.* Leiden: Brill, 1922.

al-Masʿūdī, Abū al-Ḥasan ʿAlī b. al-Ḥusayn. *Murūj al-Dhahab wa-Maʿādin al-Jawāhir.* 4 vols. Beirut: Dār al-Andalūs, 1385/1965.

Mujīr al-Dīn, ʿAbd al-Raḥmān b. Muḥammad Abū al-Yaman al-Ḥanbalī. *al-Uns al-Jalīl Bitaʾrīkh al-Quds wal-Khalīl.* 2 vols. Amman: Maktabat al-Muḥtasab, 1973.

al-Ṭabarī, Abu Jaʿfar Muḥammad b. Jarīr. *Jāmiʿ al-Bayān ʿan Taʾwīl Āy al-Qurʾān.* 30 volumes in 15. Beirut: Dār al-fikr, 1405/1984.

———. *Taʾrīkh al-Rusul wal-Mulūk*, vol. 1. Ed. M. J. De Goeje as *Annales.* Leiden: Brill, 1964.

al-Ṭabarsī, Radī al-Dīn Abū ʿAlī al-Fadl b. al-Ḥasan Amīn al-Dīn. *Majmaʿ al-Bayān fī ʿUlūm al-Qurʾān.* 30 parts in 6 volumes. Beirut: Dār al-Maktaba, n.d.

al-Tahʿlabī, Abū Ishāq Aḥmad b. Muḥammad b. Ibrāhīm al-Nīsābūrī. *ʿArāʾis al-Majālis.* Cairo: Muṣṭafā al-Bābī al Ḥalabī, 1374/1954.

al-Yaʿqūbī, Aḥmad b. Abī Yaʿqūb b. Wāḍiḥ. *Taʾrīkh.* Ed. M. T. Houstma as *Historiae.* Leiden: Brill, 1969.

Secondary Sources

Aberbach, Moses, and B. Grossfeld. *Targum Onkelos to Genesis: A Critical Analysis Together with an English Translation of the Text.* New York: Ktav, 1982.

Alexander, Philip S., and Alexander Samely, eds. *Bulletin of the John Rylands University Library of Manchester* 75:3 (1993) [Theme Issue, Artefact and Text: The Recreation of Jewish Literature in Medieval Hebrew Manuscripts].

Alon, Gedaliah. "Jewish Christians: The Parting of the Ways." In *The Jews in Their Land in the Talmudic Age (70–640 C.E.)*. 2 vols., ed. and trans. Gershon Leve. Jerusalem: Magnes, 1984.

Alter, Robert. *The Art of Biblical Narrative*. New York: Basic, 1981.

———. *Genesis: Translation and Commentary*. New York: Norton, 1996.

Aminoff, Irit. *The Figures of Esau and the Kingdom of Edom in Palestinian Midrashic—Talmudic Literature in the Tannaitic and Amoraic Periods*. PhD. Diss. Melbourne University, 1981.

Bamberger, Bernard. *Fallen Angels*. Philadelphia: Jewish Publication Society, 1952.

Baron, S. *A Social and Religious History of the Jews*, vol. 3. Philadelphia: Jewish Publication Society, 1957.

Barth, Fredrik, ed. *Ethnic Groups and Boundaries*. Boston: Little, Brown, 1969.

Barth, Lewis. "Lection for the Second Day of Rosh Hashanah: A Homily Containing the Legend of the Ten Trials of Abraham" (Hebrew). *HUCA* lviii (1987): 1–48.

Bashear, S. "Abraham's Sacrifice of His Son and Related Issues." *Islam* 67 (1990): 243–77.

Baskin, Judith R. *Pharoah's Counsellors: Job, Jethro and Balaam in Rabbinic and Patristic Tradition*. Providence: Brown University, 1983.

———. *Midrashic Women: Formations of the Feminine in Rabbinic Literature*. Hanover: University Press of New England, 2002.

Beal, Timothy. *The Book of Hiding: Gender, Ethnicity, Annihilation and Esther*. London: Routledge, 1997.

Beer, Moshe. "The Attitude of the Sages toward Riding Horses" (Hebrew). *Cathedra* 60 (1991): 17–35.

Bijlefeld, W. "Controversies around the Qur'anic Ibrahim Narrative and Its 'Orientalist' Interpretations." *Muslim World* 62 (1982): 81–94.

Boyarin, D. *Intertextuality and the Reading of Midrash*. Bloomington: Indiana University Press, 1990.

———. *Carnal Israel*. Berkeley: University of California Press, 1993.

———. *Border Lines: The Partition of Judeo-Christianity*. Philadelphia: University of Pennsylvania Press, 2004.

———. "De/Re Constructing Midrash." In *Current Trends and the Study of Midrash*, ed. Carol Bakhos. Leiden: Brill, 2006.

Brett, Mark G. *Genesis: Procreation and the Politics of Identity*. London: Routledge, 2000.

Brooke, George. "The Kittim in the Qumran Pesharim." *In Images of Empire*, ed. Alexander Loveday. JSOT Supp. Series 122. Sheffield: JSOT Press, 1991.

Bruns, Gerald L. *Hermeneutics Ancient and Modern*. New Haven: Yale University Press, 1992.

Calder, Norman. "From Midrash to Scripture: The Sacrifice of Abraham in Early Islamic Tradition." *Le Museon* 101 (1988): 375–402.

Caskel, Werner. *Gamharat an-Nasab, Das genealogische Werk des Hisam ibn Muḥammad al-Kalbī*, vols. 1 and 2. Leiden: Brill, 1966.

Charlesworth, James, trans. *The Old Testament Pseudepigrapha 2*. Garden City: Doubleday, 1985.

Chase, Emily Parke. "Promises, Blessings, and Curses: Hagar and the Wild Ass." *The Bible Translator* 50 (1999): 215–19.

Clifford, J., ed. *Writing Culture: The Poetics and Politics of Ethnography*. Berkeley: University of California Press, 1986.

Coats, G. W. "Strife without Reconciliation: A Narrative Theme in the Jacob Traditions." In *Werden und Wirken des Alten Testaments*, ed. R. Albertz et al. Göttingen: Vandenhoeck and Ruprecht, 1980.

Cohen, Gershon. "Esau as Symbol in Early Medieval Thought." In *Studies in the Variety of Rabbinic Cultures*. Philadelphia: Jewish Publication Society, 1991.

Cohen, Mark. *Under Crescent and Cross*. Princeton: Princeton University Press, 1994.

Cohen, Shaye J. D. *The Beginnings of Jewishness: Boundaries, Varieties, Uncertainties*. Hellenistic Culture and Society 31. Berkeley: University of California Press, 1998.

———, ed. *The Synoptic Problem in Rabbinic Literature*. Brown Judaic Series. Providence: Brown University, 2000.

Collins, John J. *The Apocalyptic Imagination: An Introduction to Jewish Apocalyptic Literature*. 2d ed. Grand Rapids: Eerdmans, 1998.

Cook, Michael. *Muhammad*. New York: Oxford University Press, 1983; reissued 1996.

———, and Patricia Crone. *Hagarism: The Making of the Islamic World*. Cambridge: Cambridge University Press, 1977.

Cooper, Alan. "Hagar In and Out of Context." *Union Seminary Quarterly Review* 55 (2002): 35–46.

Crone, Patricia. *Meccan Trade and the Rise of Islam*. Princeton: Princeton University Press, 1987.

Cushman, P. *Constructing the Self, Constructing America: A Cultural History of Psychotherapy*. New York: Addison Wesley, 1995.

Dagorn, René. *La Geste D'Ishmaël: d'après l'onomastique et la tradition arabes*. Genève: Librairie Droz, 1981.

Dan, Joseph. *ha-Sipur ha-ʿIvri biyeme ha-benayim: ʿIyunim betoldotav*. Jerusalem: Keter, 1974.

———. "Matai nithaber 'Sefer Ha-Yashar'?" (Hebrew). In *Sefer Dov Sadan*, ed. S. Werses et al. Tel Aviv: Hakibbutz Hameuchad, 1977.

Davidson, Arnold I. *The Emergence of Sexuality: Historical Epistemology and the Formation of Concepts*. Cambridge: Harvard University Press, 2001.

de Lange, N. R. M. "Jewish Attitudes to the Roman Empire." In *Imperialism in the Ancient World*, ed. P. D. A. Garnsey and C. R. Whittaker. Cambridge: Cambridge University Press, 1978.

de Vaux, Roland. *Ancient Israel*. New York: McGraw Hill, 1961.

Diamond, Eliezer. *Holy Men and Hunger Artists: Fasting and Asceticism in Rabbinic Culture*. New York: Oxford University Press, 2004.

Donner, Fred McGraw. *The Early Islamic Conquests*. Princeton: Princeton University, 1981.

———. *Narratives of the Islamic Origins: The Beginnings of Islamic Historical Writing*. Princeton: Darwin, 1998.

———. "From Believers to Muslims: Confessional Self-Identity in the Early Islamic Community." *Al-Abhath* 50–51 (2003): 9–53.

Donner, H. "Adoption Oder Legitimation? Erwangungen Zur Adoption Im Alten Testament Auf Dem Hintergrund Der Altorientalischen Rechte." *Oriens Antiquus* 8 (1969): 87–119.

Dunn, James D. G. *The Parting of the Ways: between Christianity and Judaism and Their Significance for the Character of Christianity*. London: SCM; Philadelphia: Trinity, 1991.

Elbaum, Jacob. "On the Character of the Late Midrashic Literature" (Hebrew). *Proceedings of the Ninth World Congress of Jewish Studies* 3 (1986): 57–62.

———. "From Sermon to Story: The Transformation of the Aqedah." *Prooftext* 6 (1986): 97–117.

———. "Rhetoric Motif and Subject-Matter—Toward an Analysis of Narrative Technique in Pirke Rabbi Eliezer" (Hebrew). *Jerusalem Studies in Jewish Folklore* 13/14 (1991–92): 99–126.

———. "Messianism in Pirke de-Rabbi Eliezer: Apocalypse and Midrash" (Hebrew). *Teudah* 11 (1996): 245-66.

Elizur, Shulamit. *The Piyyutim of Rabbi Elʿazar Birabbi Qillar*. Jerusalem: Magnes Press, 1988.

Eph'al, Israel. "'Ishmael' and 'Arab(s)': A Transformation of Ethnological Terms." *JNES* 35 (1976): 225–35.

———. *The Ancient Arabs: Nomads on the Borders of the Fertile Crescent, Ninth to Fifth Centuries BC* (Hebrew). Jerusalem: Magnes, 1984.

Epstein, J. N. *Introduction to the Literature of the Tannaim* (Hebrew). Jerusalem: Magnes/Dvir, 1957.

Eshel, Hanan. "The Kittim in the War Scroll and in the Pesharim." *Historical Perspectives: From the Hasmoneans to Bar Kokhba in Light of the Dead Sea Scrolls.* Proceedings of the Fourth International Symposium of the Orion Center for the Study of the Dead Sea Scrolls and Associated Literature, 1999, ed. David Goodblatt, Avital Pinnick, and Daniel Schwartz. Leiden: Brill, 2001.

Esposito, John. *Islam: The Straight Path.* New York: Oxford University Press, 1988.

Firestone, Reuven. "Abraham's Son as the Intended Sacrifice (Al-Dhabih, Qur'an 37:99–113): Issues in Qur'anic Exegesis." *JSS* 34 (1989): 95–131.

———. "Merit, Mimesis, and Martyrdom: Aspects of Shi'ite Meta-historical Exegesis on Abraham's Sacrifice in Light of Jewish, Christian, and Sunni Muslim Tradition." *JAAR* 66 (1998): 93–116.

———. *Journeys in Holy Lands: The Evolution of the Abraham-Ishmael Legends in Islamic Exegesis.* Albany: State University of New York Press, 1990.

Fishbane, Michael. *Biblical Myth and Rabbinic Mythmaking.* Oxford, N.Y.: Oxford University Press, 2003.

Fisch, Menahem. *Rational Rabbis.* Bloomington: Indiana University Press, 1997.

Fleischer, Ezra. *Tefilah u-minhage tefilah Erets-Yiśre'eliyim bi-teḳufat ha-Genizah.* Jerusalem: Magnes, 1988.

———. *Shirat ha-Ḳodesh ha-'Ivrit bi-Yeme ha-Benayim.* Jerusalem: Keter, 1975.

Fonrobert, Charlotte. *Menstrual Purity: Rabbinic and Christian Reconstructions of Biblical Gender.* Stanford: Stanford University Press, 2000.

Foucault, Michel, and Lawrence D. Kritzman. *Politics, Philosophy, Culture Interviews and Other Writings, 1977–1984*, ed. and trans. Lawrence D. Kritzman. New York: Routledge, 1988.

Fraade, Stephen D. "Interpreting Midrash 1: Midrash and the History of Judaism." *Prooftexts* 7 (1987): 179–94.

———. *From Tradition to Commentary: Torah and Its Interpretation in the Midrash Sifre to Deuteronomy.* Albany: State University of New York Press, 1991.

Fraenkel, J. "Hermeneutic Problems in the Study of the Aggadic Narrative." *Tarbiz* 47 (1978): 139–72 (Hebrew).

———. "Chiasmus in Talmudic-Aggadic Narrative." In *Chiasmus in Antiquity: Structures, Analyses, Exegesis*, ed. John W. Welch. Hildesheim: Gerstenberg, 1981.

———. *Darkhei ha'aggada vehamidrash*. Masada: Yad Letalmud, 1991.

Frank, Daniel, *Jews of Medieval Islam: Community, Society and Identity*. Proceedings of an International Conference held by the Institute of Jewish Studies, University College London, 1992. Leiden; New York: Brill, 1995.

Freedman, David, ed. *Anchor Bible Dictionary*. New York: Doubleday, 1992.

Friedlander, Gerald, trans. *Midrash Pirke de Rabbi Eliezer.* London, 1916; repr. New York: Sepher-Hermon, 1981.

Fuchs, Esther. *Sexual Politics in the Biblical Narrative: Reading the Hebrew Bible as a Woman*. Journal for the Study of the Old Testament Supplement Series 310. Sheffield, Eng.: Sheffield Academic Press, 2000.

Gafni, Isaiah. *Land, Center and Diaspora Jewish Constructs in Late Antiquity*. Journal for the Study of the Pseudepigrapha. Supplement series. Sheffield, Eng.: Sheffield Academic Press, 1997.

Gallagher, Catherine, and Stephen Greenblatt. *Practicing New Historicism*. Chicago: University of Chicago Press, 2000.

Geertz, Clifford. *The Interpretation of Cultures: Selected Essays*. New York: Basic, 1974.

Geller, Stephen. *Sacred Enigmas: Literary Religion in the Hebrew Bible*. London: Routledge, 1996.

Gil, Moshe. *Eretz Yisrael be-Tequfa ha-Muslimit ha-Rishonah (634–1099)*, vol. 2. Tel Aviv: Tel Aviv University, 1983.

———. "The Exilarchate." In *The Jews of Medieval Islam: Community, Society and Identity*, ed. Daniel Frank. Leiden: Brill, 1995.

Goitein, S. D. "The Intermediate Civilization/The Hellenistic Heritage in Islam." In *Studies in Islamic History and Institutions*. Leiden: Brill, 1966.

———. *A Mediterranean Society*, vol. 1. Berkeley: University of California Press, 1967.

Goldenberg, Robert. *The Nations That Know Thee Not: Ancient Jewish Attitudes toward Other Religions*. New York: New York University Press, 1998.

Goldhizer, Ignaz. *Muslim Studies*, trans. and ed. C. R. Barber and S. M. Stern. London: George Allen and Unwin, 1967.

Goldin, Judah. *Studies in Midrash and Related Literature*, ed. Barry Eichler and J. Tigay. Philadelphia: Jewish Publication Society, 1988.

Goshen-Gottstein, Alon. *The Sinner and the Amnesiac: The Rabbinic Invention of Elisha Ben Abuya and Eleazar Ben Arach*. Stanford: Stanford University Press, 2000.

Graetz, H. *Geschichte der Juden*, vol. 5. Leipzig, 1861.

Greenspahn, Frederick. *When Brothers Dwell Together: The Preeminence of Younger Siblings in the Hebrew Bible*. New York: Oxford University Press, 1994.

Grossman, A. "Yahaso shel ha-Halifa al-Ma'mun el ha-Yehudim." *Zion* 44 (1979): 94–110.

Grünbaum, M. *Neue Beiträge zur Semitischen Sagenkunde.* Leiden: Brill, 1893.

Hackett, J. A. "Rehabilitating Hagar: Fragments of an Epic Pattern." In *Gender and Difference in Ancient Israel*, ed. Peggy Day. Minneapolis: Fortress, 1989.

Halbertal, Moshe. *People of the Book: Canon, Meaning, and Authority.* Cambridge: Harvard University Press, 1997.

Hall, Edith. *Inventing the Barbarian: Greek Self-definition through Tragedy.* New York: Oxford University Press, 1989.

Hall, Jonathan M. *Ethnic Identity in Greek Antiquity.* Cambridge, Eng.: Cambridge University Press, 1997.

———. *Hellenicity between Ethnicity and Culture.* Chicago: University of Chicago Press, 2002.

Halperin, Raphael. *Atlas Eytz Chayim: Tannaim wa-Amoraim*, 2 parts. Tel Aviv: Hakodesh Ruah Ya'acov, 1980.

Harry, B., John Hayes, and Fred Astren, eds. *Judaism and Islam: Boundaries, Communications and Interactions: Essays in Honor of William M. Brinner.* Leiden: Brill, 2000.

Hasan-Rokem, Galit. *Web of Life: Folklore and Midrash in Rabbinic Literature*, trans. Batya Stein. Stanford: Stanford University Press, 2000.

———. *Tales of the Neighborhood: Jewish Narrative Dialogues in Late Antiquity.* Berkeley: University of California Press, 2003.

Hawting, G. R. *Idea of Idolatry and the Emergence of Islam: From Polemic to History.* Cambridge; New York: Cambridge University Press, 1999.

———. *First Dynasty: The Umayyad Caliphate AD 661–750.* London; New York: Routledge, 2000.

Hayes, Christine. *Between the Babylonian and Palestinian Talmuds.* New York: Oxford University Press, 1997.

———. *Gentile Impurities and Jewish Identities: Intermarriage and Conversion from the Bible to the Talmud.* Oxford: Oxford University Press, 2002.

Hayward, Robert. "Targum Pseudo-Jonathan and Anti-Islamic Polemic." *JSS* 34 (1989): 77–93.

———. "The Date of Targum Pseudo-Jonathan: Some Comments." *JJS* 40 (1989): 7–30.

———. "Pirque de Rabbi Eliezer and Targum Pseudo-Jonathan." *JJS* 42 (1991): 215–46.

———. "Inconsistencies and Contradictions in Targum Pseudo-Jonathan: The Case of Eliezer and Nimrod." *JSS* 37(1992): 31–55.

Heinemann, Joseph. *Derashot be-tsibur bi-tekufat ha-Talmud.* Jerusalem: Mosad Byalik, 1970.

———. *Aggadot Ve-Toldotehen.* Jerusalem: Keter, 1974.

———. "The Nature of Aggadah." In *Midrash and Literature*, ed. G. Hartman and S. Budick. New Haven: Yale University Press, 1986.

Heinemann, Yizhaq. *Darkhei ha'aggadah*. Jerusalem: Magnes, 1970.

Heller, Bernard. "Muhammedanisches und Antimuhammedanisches in den Pirke Rabbi Eliezer." *MGWJ* 33 (1925).

Herr, Moshe David. "Midrash." In *Encyclopedia Judaica*, vol. 11. Jerusalem: Keter, 1972.

Hirshman, Marc. "The Greek Fathers and the Aggada on Ecclesiastes: Formats of Exegesis in Late Antiquity." *HUCA* 59 (1988): 137–65.

———. *Ha-Mikra u-Midrasho: ben Hazal le-avot ha-Kenesiyah*. Tel Aviv: Hakibbutz Hameuchad, 1992.

———. *A Rivalry of Genesis: Jewish and Christian Biblical Interpretation*, trans. Batya Stein. Albany: State University of New York Press, 1996.

———. *"Torah le-khol ba'e ha-ʿolam": zerem universali be-sifrut ha-Tana'im ve-yahaso le-hokhmat he-ʿamim*. Tel Aviv: Hakibbutz Hameuchad, 1999.

———. "Theology and Exegesis in Midrashic Literature." In *Interpretation and Allegory: Antiquity and the Modern Period*, ed. Jon Whitman. Leiden: Brill, 2000.

———. "Rabbinic Universalism in the Second and Third Centuries." *HTR* 93, 2 (2000): 101–15.

Hoy, David Couzens. *The Critical Circle*. Berkeley: University of California Press, 1982.

Hoyland, Robert G. *Seeing Islam as Others Saw It: A Survey and Evaluation of Christian, Jewish and Zoroastrian Writings on Early Islam*. Princeton: Darwin, 1997.

———. *Arabia and the Arabs: From the Bronze Age to the Coming of Islam*. London; New York: Routledge, 2001.

Hyman, Aaron. *Sefer Toldot Tannaim ve-Amoraim*, 3 vols. London 1910; repr., Jerusalem: Kiryah Ne'emanah, 1964.

Jansen, W. Hugh. "The Esoteric-Exoteric Factor in Folklore." In *The Study of Folklore*, ed. Alan Dundes. Englewood Cliffs: Prentice Hall, 1965.

Jastrow, Marcus. *A Dictionary of the Targumim, the Talmud Babli and the Yerushalmi, and the Midrashic Literature*. New York: Judaica Press, 1996.

Juynboll, G. H. A. *Muslim Tradition: Studies in Chronology, Provenance and Authorship of Early Hadith*. Cambridge: Cambridge University Press, 1983.

Kalmin, Richard. *Sages, Stories, Authors and Editors in Rabbinic Babylonia*. Atlanta: Scholars Press, 1994.

———. "Patterns and Developments in Rabbinic Midrash of Late Antiquity." In *Hebrew Bible/Old Testament: The History of Interpretation*, vol 1, ed. Magne Saebø. Göttingen: Vandenhoeck and Ruprecht, 1996.

———. *The Sage of Jewish Society of Late Antiquity*. London: Routledge, 1999.

———. "Rabbinic Portrayals of Biblical and Postbiblical Heroes." In *The Synoptic Problem in Rabbinic Literature*, ed. Shaye Cohen. Providence: Brown University, 2000.

Kaminsky, Joel S. "Humor and the Theology of Hope: Isaac as a Humorous Figure." *Interpretation* 54 (2000): 363–75.

Klawans, Jonathan. *Impurity and Sin in Ancient Judaism*. Oxford: Oxford University Press, 2000.

Kohut, Alexander, ed. *ʿArukh Ha-Shalem*, vol. 3. Vienna: Menorah, 1926.

Kraemer, David. "On the Reliability of Attributions in the Babylonian Talmud." *HUCA* 60 (1989): 175–90.

Krauss, Samuel. *Studien zur byzantinisch-jüdischen Geschichte*. Leipzig: G. Fock, 1914.

Kugel, James. "Two Introductions to Midrash." In *Midrash and Literature*, ed. G. Hartman and S. Budick. New Haven: Yale University Press, 1986.

———. *In Potiphar's House: The Interpretive Life of Biblical Texts*. New York: Harper Collins, 1990.

———. *The Bible as It Was*. Cambridge: Belknap Press of Harvard University Press, 1997.

———. *Traditions of the Bible: A Guide to the Bible as It Was at the Start of the Common Era*. Cambridge: Harvard University Press, 1998.

Kunin, Seth Daniel. *The Logic of Incest: A Structuralist Analysis of Hebrew Mythology*. Journal for the Study of the Old Testament Supplement Series 185. Sheffield, Eng.: Sheffield Academic Press, 1995.

Lassner, Jacob. "The Origins of Muslim Attitudes towards the Jews and Judaism." *Judaism* 39 (1990): 494–507.

———. *Demonizing the Queen of Sheba: Boundaries of Gender and Culture in Postbiblical Judaism and Medieval Islam*. Chicago: University of Chicago Press, 1993.

Lazarus-Yafeh, Hava. *Intertwined Worlds*. Princeton: Princeton University Press, 1992.

Le Deaut, R. "A propos d'une définition du midrash." *Biblica* 50 (1969): 395–413.

Levenson, Jon D. *The Death and Resurrection of the Beloved Son: The Transformation of Child Sacrifice in Judaism and Christianity*. New Haven: Yale University Press, 1993.

———. "The Universal Horizon of Biblical Particularism." In *Ethnicity and the Bible*, ed. Mark G. Brett. Leiden: Brill, 1996.

Leviant, Curt. "Parallel Lives: The Trials and Traumas of Isaac and Ishmael." *Bible Review* 15 (1999): 20–25.

Levine, Lee I. *The Galilee in Late Antiquity*. New York: Jewish Theological Seminary of America, 1992.

Levy, Jacob. *Wörterbuch über Die Talmudim und Midraschim*, vol. 2. Berlin: Benjamin Harz, 1924.

Lewis, Bernard. "An Apocalyptic Vision of Islamic History." *Bulletin of the School of Oriental and African Studies* 13/2 (1950): 308–38; repr. in idem.

———. *Studies in Classical and Ottoman Islam (Seventh to Sixteenth Centuries)*. Variorum CS 54; London: Variorum Reprints, 1976.

———. *The Jews of Islam*. Princeton: Princeton University Press, 1984.

Lyke, Larry. "Where Does the Boy Belong? Compositional Strategy in Genesis 21:14." *CBQ* 56 (1994): 637–48.

Maher, Michael. *Targum Pseudo-Jonathan: Genesis, Translation with Introduction and Notes*. The Aramaic Bible, vol. 1B. Collegeville: Liturgical Press, 1992.

Mandelbaum, Irving J. "Tannaitic Exegesis of the Golden Calf Episode." In *A Tribute to Geza Vermes: Essays on Jewish and Christian Literature and History*, ed. Philip R. Davies and Richard T. White. Sheffield, Eng.: JSOT Press, 1990.

Margalioth, M., ed. *Encyclopedia of Talmudic and Geonic Literature: Being a Biographical Dictionary of the Tannaim, Amoraim and Geonim*, 2 vols. (Hebrew). Tel Aviv: Yavneh, 1995.

Meir, Ofra. "Hasipur Hadarshani Bemidrash Qadum Ume'uchar." *Sinai* 86 (1980): 246–66.

———. *The Darshanic Story in Genesis Rabba* (Hebrew). Tel Aviv: Hakibbutz Hameuhad, 1987.

———. *The Poetics of Rabbinic Stories* (Hebrew). Tel Aviv: Sifriyat Poʿalim, 1993.

Mendels, Doron. *The Land of Israel as a Political Concept in Hasmonean Literature*. Texte und Studien zum Antiken Judentum 15. Tübingen: Mohr Siebeck, 1987.

Mihaly, Eugene. "A Rabbinic Defense of the Election of Israel." *HUCA* 35 (1964): 103–43.

Milikowsky, C. "The *Status Quaestionis* of Research in Rabbinic Literature." *JJS* 39 (1988): 201–11.

Millar, Fergus. "Hagar, Ishmael, Josephus and the Origins of Islam." *JJS* 44 (1993): 23–45.

Montgomery, James A. *Arabia and the Bible*. New York: Ktav, 1969.

Neufeld, E. *Ancient Hebrew Marriage Laws, with Special Reference to Special Semitic Laws and Customs*. London: Longmans, Green, 1944.

Neusner, Jacob. *Ancient Israel after Castastrophe: The Religious Worldview of the Mishnah*. Charlottesville: University Press of Virginia, 1983.

———, and Ernest Frerichs, eds. *To See Ourselves as Others See Us: Christians, Jews and "Others" in Late Antiquity*. Chico: Scholars Press, 1985.

———. *Reading and Believing: Ancient Judaism and Contemporary Gullibility*. Atlanta: Scholars Press, 1986.

———. *From Enemy to Sibling: Rome and Israel in the First Century of Western Civilization*. The Ben Zion Bokser Memorial Lecture. New York: Queens College, 1986.

———. *Midrash as Literature*. Lanham: University Press of America, 1987.

———. *Midrash in Context*. Atlanta: Scholars Press, 1988.

———. *From Literature to Theology in Formative Judaism: Three Preliminary Studies*. Atlanta: Scholars Press, 1989.

———. *Judaism and Its Social Metaphors*. Cambridge: Cambridge University Press, 1989.

———. *Canonical History of Ideas: The So-Called Tannaite Midrashim*. Atlanta: Scholars Press, 1990.

———. "Judaism and Christianity in the First Century: How Shall We Perceive Their Relationship?" In *A Tribute to Geza Vermes: Essays on Jewish and Christian Literature and History*, ed. Philip R. Davies and Richard T. White. Sheffield, Eng.: JSOT Press, 1990.

———. *Rabbinic Judaism: Structure and System*. Minneapolis: Fortress, 1995.

Newby, Gordon. "Text and Territory: Jewish-Muslim Relations 632–750 CE." In *Judaism and Islam: Boundaries, Communications and Interactions*, ed. Benjamin H. Hary, John Hayes, and Fred Astren. Leiden: Brill, 2000.

Niehoff, Maren. *Philo on Jewish Identity and Culture*. Texts and Studies in Ancient Judaism 86. Tübingen: Mohr Siebeck, 2001.

Novak, David. *The Image of the Non-Jew in Judaism: A Historical and Constructive Study of the Noachide Laws*. New York and Toronto: Mellen, 1983.

Obermann, Julius. "Early Islam." In *The Idea of History in the Ancient Near East*, ed. Robert C. Dentan. New Haven: Yale University Press, 1955; repr., 1967.

Ohana, Moshe. "La Polémique judéo-islamique et l'image d'Ismaël dans Targum Pseudo-Jonathan et dans Pirke de Rabbi Eliezer." *Augustinianum* 15 (1975): 367–87.

Oppenheimer, Aharon. "The Attitude of the Sages towards the Arabs." In *Jewish Studies in a New Europe: Proceedings of the Fifth Congress of Jewish Studies in*

Copenhagen 1994, ed. Ulf Haxen, et al. Copenhagen: C. A. Reitzel A/S International Publishers, Det Kongelige Bibliotek, 1998.

Ormiston, Gayle L., and Alan D. Schrift, eds. *The Hermeneutic Tradition: From Ast to Ricoeur*. New York: State University of New York Press, 1990.

Parkes, James. *The Conflict of the Church and Synagogue: A Study of the Origins of Anti-Semitism*. New York: Hermon, 1974.

Perlman, Moshe. "The Medieval Polemics between Islam and Judaism." In *Religion in a Religious Age*, ed. S. D. Goiten. Cambridge: Association for Jewish Studies, 1974.

Peskowitz, Miriam. *Spinning Fantasies: Rabbis, Gender and History*. Berkeley: University of California Press, 1997.

Porton, Gary. "Defining Midrash." In *The Study of Ancient Judaism*, ed. J. Neusner. New York: Ktav, 1981.

———. "Forbidden Transactions: Prohibited Commerce with Gentiles in Earliest Rabbinism." In *To See Ourselves as Others See Us*, ed. J. Neusner and Ernest Frerichs. Chico, CA: Scholars Press, 1985.

———. *Goyim: Gentiles and Israelites in Mishnah-Tosefta*. Atlanta: Scholars Press, 1988.

Pritchard, James B., ed. *The Ancient Near East: An Anthology of Texts and Pictures*. Princeton: Princeton University Press, 1958.

Rajak, Tessa. "The Jewish Community and Its Boundaries." In *The Jews among Pagans and Christians in the Roman Empire*, ed. Judith Lieu, John North, and Tessa Rajak. London: Routledge, 1994.

Redfield, Robert. *The Primitive World and Its Transformations*. Ithaca: Cornell University Press, 1953.

Retsö, Jan. *The Arabs in Antiquity: Their History from the Assyrians to the Umayyads*. London; New York: RoutledgeCurzon, 2003.

Reuther, Rosemary Radford. *Faith and Fratricide: The Theological Roots of Anti-Semitisim*. New York: WIPF and Stock, 1997.

Ricoeur, Paul. *The Rule of Metaphor: Multidisciplinary Studies of the Creation of Meaning in Language*, trans. Robert Czerny. Toronto: University of Toronto Press, 1977.

Rogerson, J. W. *Myth in Old Testament Interpretation*. Berlin: De Gruyter, 1974.

Rosenberg, Joel. *King and Kin: Political Allegory in the Hebrew Bible*. Bloomington: Indiana University Press, 1986.

Rosenblatt, S. "Rabbinic Legends in Hadith." *Muslim World* 35 (1947): 237–52.

Rubenstein, J. "From Mythic Motifs to Sustained Myth: The Revision of Rabbinic Traditions in Medieval Midrashim." *HTR* 89 (1996): 131–59.

———. *Talmudic Stories: Narrative Art, Composition, and Culture*. Baltimore: Johns Hopkins University Press, 1999.

———. *The Culture of the Babylonian Talmud*. Baltimore: Johns Hopkins University Press, 2003.

Rubin, Uri. "Hanīfiyya and Kaʿba: An Inquiry into the Arabian Pre-Islamic Background of din-Ibrahim." *Jerusalem Studies in Arabic and Islam* 13 (1990): 85–112.

———. *The Eye of the Beholder: The Life of Muhammad as Viewed by the Early Muslims*. Princeton: Darwin, 1995.

———. *Between Bible and Qur'an: The Children of Israel and the Islamic Self-Image*. Princeton: Darwin, 1999.

Said, Edward. *Orientalism*. New York: Vintage, 1978.

Sanders, E. P. *Jewish and Christian Self-Definition*. Philadelphia: Fortress, 1980.

Sarna, Nahum. *Understanding Genesis*. New York: McGraw Hill, 1966.

———. *Genesis*. Jewish Publication Society Torah Commentary. Philadelphia: Jewish Publication Society, 1989.

Schäfer, P. "Research into Rabbinic Literature: An Attempt to Define the *Status Quaestionis*." *JJS* 37 (1986): 139–52.

———. "Once Again the *Status Quaestionis* of Research in Rabbinic Literature: An Answer to Chaim Milikowsky." *JJS* 40 (1989): 89–94.

Schremer, A. "Eschatology, Violence, and Suicide: An Early Rabbinic Theme and Its Influence in the Middle Ages." In *Apocalypse and Violence*, ed. A. Ammanat and J. J. Collins. New Haven: Yale Center for Environmental Studies, 2004.

Schussman, Aviva. "Abraham's Visits to Ishmael—The Jewish Origin and Orientation" (Hebrew). *Tarbiẓ* 49 (1980): 325–45.

Schwartz, Joshua. "A Child's Wagon" (Hebrew). *Tarbiẓ* 63 (1993): 375–92.

———. "Ishmael at Play: On Exegesis and Jewish Society." *HUCA* 66 (1995): 203–21.

Schwartz, Regina, ed. *The Book and the Text: The Bible and Literary Theory*. Cambridge: Basil Blackwell, 1990.

———. *The Curse of Cain: The Violent Legacy of Monotheism*. Chicago: University of Chicago Press, 1997.

Schwartz, Seth. *Josephus and Judaean Politics*. Leiden: Brill, 1990.

———. *Imperialism and Jewish Society, 200 B.C.E. to 640 C.E.* Princeton: Princeton University Press, 2001.

Schorske, Carl E. *Fin-a-siècle Vienna: Politics and Culture*. New York: Knopf, 1979.

Schwartzbaum, H. *Mi-meqor Yisrael ve-Yishmael: Yahadut ve-Islam be Aspaqlariyat ha-Folqlor*. Tel Aviv: Don, 1975.

Shahîd, Irfan. *Rome and the Arabs: A Prologomenon to the Study of Byzantium and the Arabs*. Washington, D.C.: Dumbarton Oaks, 1984.

———. *Byzantium and the Arabs in the Fourth Century*. Washington, D.C.: Dumbarton Oaks, 1984.

Shapira, Amnon. "Traces of an Anti-Moslem Polemic in Targum Yerushalmi A to the Story of the Aqueda" (Hebrew). *Tarbiẓ* 54 (1984/85): 293–96 .

Shinan, Avigdor. *Aggadatam shel Meturgamim*. Jerusalem: Makor, 1979.

———. *Mikra Ehad Ve-Targumim Harbeh*. Jerusalem: Hakibbutz Hameuchad, 1993.

———, and Y. Zakovitch. "Midrash on Scripture and Midrash within Scripture." *Scripta Hierosolymitana* 31 (1986): 259–77.

———. "Dating Targum Pseudo-Jonathan: Some More Comments." *JJS* 41 (1990): 57–61.

Silberman, L. H. "Listening to the Text." *JBL* 102 (1983): 3–26.

Simon, Marcel. *Verus Israel: A Study of the Relations between Christians and Jews in the Roman Empire AD 135–425*. London: Littman Library of Jewish Civilizations, 1986; repr., 1996.

Smith-Christopher, Daniel L. "Between Ezra and Isaiah." In *Ethnicity and the Bible*, ed. Mark G. Brett. Leiden: Brill, 1996.

Sozomen. *The Ecclesiastical History of Sozomen*, trans. E. Walford. London: Bohn, 1855.

Speiser, E. A. "Background and Function of the Biblical Nasi." *CBQ* 25 (1963): 111–17.

———. *The Anchor Bible*: *Genesis*. Garden City: Doubleday, 1964.

Stein, Dina. *Memrah, Magyah, Mitos: Pirke de-Rabi Eli'ezer le-or meḥḳar ha-sifrut ha-'amamit*. Jerusalem: Magnes Press, 2004.

Steinberg, Naomi. "The Genealogical Framework of the Family Stories in Genesis." *Semeia* 46 (1989): 41–50.

———. *Kinship and Marriage in Genesis: A Household Economics Perspective*. Minneapolis: Augsburg, 1993.

Steinmetz, Devorah. *From Father to Son: Kinship, Conflict and Continuity in Genesis*. Louisville: Westminster, 1991.

Stern, David. "Rhetoric and Midrash: The Case of the Mashal." *Prooftexts* 1 (1981): 261–91.

———. *Parables in Midrash*. Cambridge: Harvard University Press, 1991.

———. *Midrash and Theory: Ancient Jewish Exegesis and Contemporary Literary Studies*. Evanston: Northwestern University Press, 1996.

Stern, Sacha. "Attribution and Authorship in the Babylonian Talmud." *JJS* 45 (1994): 28–51.

———. *Jewish Identity in Early Rabbinic Writings*. Leiden: Brill, 1994.

Strack, Herman, and Gunter Stemberger, eds. *Introduction to the Talmud and Midrash*. Minneapolis: Fortress, 1992.

Swartz, Merlin. "The Position of Jews in Arab Lands Following the Rise of Islam." *Muslim World* 60 (1970): 6–24.

Syren, Roger. *The Forsaken First-Born: A Study of a Recurrent Motif in the Patriarchal Narratives*. Sheffield, Eng.: JSOT, 1993.

———. "Ishmael and Esau in the Book of Jubilees and Targum Pseudo-Jonathan." In *The Aramaic Bible: Targums in Their Historical Context*, ed. D. R. G. Beattie and M. J. McNamara. Sheffield: JSOT, 1994.

Taylor, Miriam. *Anti-Judaism and Early Christian Identity: A Critique of the Scholarly Consensus*. Leiden: Brill, 1995.

Teubal, Savina. "Sarah and Hagar." In *A Feminist Companion to Genesis*, ed. Athalya Brenner. Sheffield: Sheffield Academic Press, 1997.

Thompson, Stith. *Motif-Index of Folk Literature*, vols. 1 and 3. Bloomington: Indiana University Press, 1956, 1966.

Thompson, T. *The Historicity of the Patriarchal Narratives: The Quest for the Historical Abraham*. Berlin: Walter de Gruyter, 1974.

Trible, Phyllis. *Texts of Terror*. Philadelphia: Fortress, 1984.

Urbach, Ephraim. "Homilies of the Rabbis on the Prophets of the Nations and the Balaam Stories" (Hebrew). *Tarbiẓ* 25 (1955–56): 272–89.

———. "*Sridei Tanhuma Yelammedenu*" (Hebrew). *Kobez al yad* 6 (1966): 1–54.

Urowitz-Freudenstein, Anna. "Pseudepigraphical Support of Pseudepigraphal Sources: The Case of PRE." In *Tracing the Threads: Studies in the Vitality of Jewish Pseudepigrapha*, ed. J. C. Reeves. Atlanta: Scholars Press, 1994.

———. *An Investigation of Exegetical Methods in the Tannaitic Midrashim: A Study of Texts That Mention Individual Women*. PhD. diss. JTS, 1997.

Vanderkam, J. C., trans. and ed. *The Book of Jubilees: A Critical Text*. Lovanii: Peeters, 1989.

———. *The Book of Jubilees*. Sheffield, Eng.: Sheffield Academic Press, 2001.

Van Seters, J. *Abraham in History*. New Haven: Yale University Press, 1975.

Vawter, Bruce. *On Genesis: A New Reading*. Garden City: Doubleday, 1977.

Visotzky, Burton. "Two Types of Midrash Study." *Conservative Judaism* 41 (1989): 65–71.

———. *The Midrash on Proverbs*. New Haven: Yale University Press, 1992.

———. *Fathers of the World: Essays in Rabbinic and Patristic Literatures*. Tübingen: Mohr, 1995.

———. "Jerusalem in Geonic Era Aggadah." In *Jerusalem: Its Sanctity and Centrality to Judaism, Christianity and Islam*, ed. Lee Levine. New York: Continuum, 1999.

———. *Golden Bells and Pomegranates: Studies in Midrash Rabbah*, Texts and Studies in Ancient Judaism, 94. Tübingen: Mohr Siebeck, 2003.

von Rad, G. *Genesis: A Commentary*, trans. John H. Marks. London: SCM, 1972.

Wansbrough, John. *Quranic Studies: Sources and Methods of Scriptural Interpretation*. Oxford: Oxford University Press, 1977.

———. *The Sectarian Milieu: Content and Composition of Islamic Salvation History*. Oxford; New York: Oxford University Press, 1978.

Weinfeld, M. "The Universalist Trend and the Isolationist Trend in the Period of the Restoration to Zion" (Hebrew). *Tarbiẓ* 23 (1964): 228–42.

Wenham, Gordon J. *Word Biblical Commentary*, 2. Dallas: Word Books, 1994.

Westermann, C. *Genesis 12–36: A Commentary*, trans. John J. Scullion S.J. Minneapolis: Augsburg, 1981.

Winnett, F. V. "The Arabian Genealogies in the Book of Genesis." In *Translating and Understanding the Old Testament: Essays in Honor of Herbert Gordon May*, ed. H. T. Frank and W. I. Reed. Nashville: Abingdon, 1970.

Wolfson, Harry A. *The Philosophy of the Church Fathers*. Cambridge: Harvard University Press, 1956.

Wright, Addison. *A Literary Genre: Midrash*. Staten Island: Alba House, 1967.

Yadin, Azzan. *Scripture as Logos: Rabbi Ishmael and the Origins of Midrash*. Philadelphia: University of Pennsylvania Press, 2004.

Yahalom, Yosef. "The Transition of Kingdoms in Eretz Israel (Palestine) as Conceived by Poets and Homilists" (Hebrew). *Shalem* 6 (1992): 1–22.

———. *Sefat ha-shir shel ha-piyuṭ ha-Erets-Yisraeli ha-ḳadum*. Jerusalem: Magnes, 1985.

———, and M. Sokoloff. *Shirat Benei Maʿarava*. Jerusalem: Israeli National Academy of Sciences and Humanities, 1999.

Yuval, Israel. *Shene goyim be-vitnekh: Yehudim ve-Notsrim, dimuyim hadadiyim* (*Two Nations in Your Womb: Perceptions of Jews and Christians in the Middle Ages*). Tel-Aviv: Am Oved, 2000.

Zunz, Leopold. *Die Synagogale Poesie des Mittlealters*. Berlin: 1855.

———. *Ha-drashot be-Yisrael*, ed. H. Albeck. Jerusalem: Mossad Bialik, 1954.

Index